Andreas Holzinger

with assistance from G. Searle

Multimedia Basics Volume 1: Technology

Dedicated to
my wife Angela and
my daughters Katharina and Barbara
most cordially.

Dr. Andreas Holzinger, PhD, MSc, MPh, BEng, CEng, DipEd
with assistance from G. Searle, BSc

Multimedia Basics
Volume 1: Technology

Technological Basics of
Multimedial Information Systems

Translation of the original German Second Edition

FIREWALL MEDIA
(An Imprint of Laxmi Publications Pvt. Ltd.)
22, Golden House, Daryaganj,
New Delhi 110002 India
Ph : 011-23 25 25 74 *Fax* : 011-23 25 25 72
E-mail : colaxmi@hotmail.com

Andreas Holzinger, married, two children, born 1963 in Graz, Austria. Radio- and Television Technician, Experiences in the Information Technology Industry (BOSCH), Foreman for Industrial Electronics & Instructor. College of Further Education Bournemouth, England, 1985/1986 with Hon. in Computer Science. College of Technology. 1987 to 1991 Assistant Lecturer for Electronics. Award of engineering degree (CEng) for Communications engineering, 1991. Diploma as Lecturer for Adult Education (DipEd). Studies of Communication engineering (BEng), Physics and Psychology (MSc) as well as Media Sciences and Sociology (MPh) at Graz University of Technology and Graz University. Scientific work on computer aided mathematics instruction. Computer Science and Information Processing (EDP) consultant at the University. Doctoral promotion with „summa cum laude" in Cognitive Science (PhD). Lecturer at the Institute for Information processing and computer supported new Media (IICM) at Graz University of Technology (Head: Professor Hermann Maurer) since 1998. Directorate assistant at the Institute of Medical Informatics, Statistics and Documentation (IMI) at Graz University Hospital (Head: Professor Günther Gell) since 1999. Consultant of the Austrian Government. Austrian expert in the European Commission in Educational Multimedia Software (eLearning). Numerous Publications, Talks and Lectures at home and abroad. Leader of several projects. Organizer of national and international Conferences (e.g. Hospital Information Systems 1999, From PACS to Internet, Information-Systems, Multimedia and Telemedicine 2000). Member and Scientific Adviser in numerous Programme Committees. Memberships include the Association of Computing Machinery (ACM, USA), the IEEE Computer Society (USA), the American Association for the Advancement of Computers in Education (AACE, USA), the German Society for Informatics (GI) the German Society for Psychology (DGP), the German Society for Media in Science (GMW). Board Member of the Austrian Computer Society (OCG, President: Professor A Min Tjoa). Head of the Austrian Computer Society office Graz. Andreas works, teaches and researches currently in Information-Systems – Multimedia – Human-Computer Interaction (HCI) – Usability – Internet/Intranet.
eMail: andreas.holzinger@uni-graz.at

Gig Searle, born 1953 in Negombo, Sri Lanka, grew up in England. After giving up accountancy work, she went back to university to learn about computers. She is currently employed at the Institute of Medical Informatics, Statistics and Documentation (Graz University), and working on her thesis for a Master of Science degree in computers. She is a member of the British Computer Society.
eMail: gig.searle@uni-graz.at

Homepage (English and German): **http://www.basiswissen-multimedia.at**

ISBN : 81-7008-243-9
Price : Rs 195
1st English Edition of the original German Second Edition

Layout: Camera Ready Files of the author

„Adults worry a lot these days. Especially, they worry about how to make other people learn more about computers. They want to make us all "computer-literate". Literacy means both reading and writing, but most books and courses about computers only tell you about writing programs."

MARVIN MINSKY, *1984, Media Lab, Massachusetts Institute of Technology*

Marvin Minsky, born 1927, international computing pioneer at the Media Lab and founder (with John McCarthy) of the AI Lab at the MIT (Massachusetts Institute of Technology), President of the American Association for Artificial Intelligence

Foreword

Multimedia and Internet, Hypertext and Hypermedia – thrilling terms on the threshold to the next millennium. Just as 2500 years ago, as the age of writing began, we stand today at the beginning of an age of new information and communication technologies which will have a lasting influence on our culture.

Currently Multimedia includes the combination of audio, video and interaction. But behind these terms it often conceals more than it shows: It is not only a question of text, language, music, pictures and video-clips, but also of other forms of representation such as diagrams, technical drawings, cartographic materials and graphic formulas; from such different fields as mathematics to chemistry, of three-dimensional models and environments, of the visualization of high-dimensional events and something fundamentally new: working with abstract pictures and films, that – although still hardly visible today – a new quality of the archiving of information and emotion is shown. Techniques for the processing of smell, taste and touch-information are also under development. Conclusively, Multimedia contains all media that can be registered by the human senses.

Multimedia has a special significance as a subarea of the field of information systems within computer science: On the one hand through its importance in the practical use, on the other hand through the extremely high interdisciplinary character. In this field it is not only possible, but necessary, to summarize anything which can enhance the productivity and the content of human work and human knowledge concerning the communication between human and computer.

Once more the importance of computer science as a basis for a modern information society becomes obvious. Rapid developments lead to increasingly simpler and faster access to information. Small mobile devices which make information constantly available everywhere are already on the market. However, that is only the top of the iceberg. The mobile-phone (in Germany called „Handy"), that is actually a genuine computer, a video telephone, a camera, a payment-device, a travel guide and a lot more is, or soon will be an integral part of our lives and life without it inconceivable.

Occasionally crucial voices arise against the introduction of these „New media". Some of the arguments are convincing: There is no evolution without at least potential disadvantages. The fact is, however, that we are already surrounded by these media and still much more approaches.

However, with the engagement of these New media new chances arise, new professions, new branches of industry, essentially – new growth!

Thus the education of the following generations must be fundamentally broad and correspondingly interdisciplinary.

In Europe we often talk about an information society of „lifelong learning". For Dr. Holzinger „lifelong learning" is not a catchword. Starting in 1978 as a television technician apprentice (trainee) with information technology, he currently works, researches and teaches at Graz University with success. In his Europe-wide activity as an expert on the subject of multimedia, as a member of international societies and through his diverse participation in international congresses – he looks over his own horizons.

When building a house, one usually begins with the foundation. The firmer and stronger this foundation is, the larger and higher one can build the house. Dr. Holzinger is always occupied with the latest developments in the field of multimedia and „New media", without, however, neglecting the foundation the „basic principles" – as we can see in this book.

With clear learning objectives, didactically carefully processed material and examination questions and answers in every module, the book is not only suitable as a support for instruction units, courses and lectures, but also for private study and as a reference.

The book is aimed at everyone involved with the „New media". We hope for a large circulation – in the interest of an interdisciplinary computer science – and congratulate Dr. Holzinger on this further milestone on his noteworthy career.

Professor DDr. Hermann Maurer, PhD, Head, Institute for Information Processing and Computer Supported New Media (IICM), Graz University of Technology,

Professor Dr. Günther Gell, PhD, Head, Institute for Medical Informatics, Statistics and Documentation (IMI)), Graz University,

Professor Dr. A Min Tjoa, PhD, MEng, President, Austrian Computer Society (OCG), Head, Institute for Software Technology (IFS), Vienna University of Technology.

„Within computer science, in the last 30 years particularly the machine stood in the foreground of scientific investigation. The human being had to adapt to the technical factors. In future this will move, however, increasingly more to the human being that works with this machine. Thus, computer science will develop increasingly interdisziplinary."

PROFESSOR HEINZ ZEMANEK,
During his speech in the festival room of the academy of the sciences in Vienna, on the occasion of his eightieth birthday.

Heinz Zemanek, born in 1920, Austrian computer pioneer, founder of the Austrian Computer Society (OCG), IBM-Fellow, former president of the International Federation for Information processing (IFIP)

Preface

„Multimedia" as a subarea of information systems includes fascinating qualities that have impressed me since 1978 – the beginning of my professional activity in information technology (IT). In Europe people are of the monophonic opinion that we stand at the beginning of an „information society". Multimedia and Internet – the New media – will become increasingly more influential in all fields.

Particularly in the elementary education an interdisciplinary training becomes increasingly more important, in order to prepare Europe's youth for the upcoming "digital age" in the best possible way . The English speak legitimately of "computer literacy". Attempts of this kind are enormously important in order to make a communal Europe strong, competent and prepared for competition. For instance, a defined goal of the initiative "eEurope" is that, by the year 2003 all pupils and students leaving school should be "digitally literate". Additionally, every university and every college should be a „Multimedia learning-centre". Many countries in Europe have already started attempts to reach these ambitious aims. For example in Austria the activities of the Federal Ministry for education, science and culture (bm:bwk) and the Federal Ministry for economy and work (bm:wa) with the initiative multimedia business Austria (www.mba.at) or in Germany the „initiative information society Germany" (www.iid.de) of the Federal Ministry for education and research (bmb+f) and the action programme (www.bmwi.de/multimedia.html) of the Federal Ministry for economy and technology (bmwi). Such initiatives are principally to be supported because with the subject „Multimedia" – however hackneyed this word may seem – the possibility exists to combine, under this title, basic knowledge in an interdisciplinary manner for the future "information Society".

eEurope: http://europa.eu.int/comm/information_society/eeurope

This book emerged from an interdisciplinary lecture at Graz University. Its modular construction makes an individual use in various teaching courses possible, in different educational facilities – for all professions having something to do with „New media". A preface is also a good opportunity to pronounce thanks. I am grateful to many people: The professors Guenther Gell and A Min Tjoa. Particularly to professor Hermann Maurer, not only for enabling the realisation of my new lecture and for the confidence placed in me, but particularly for his thorough scientific support. With pleasure I think of the first time Hermann Maurer sent me to the „international ring" at my first conference. Moreover my thanks are meant for my close colleagues, the colleagues at other institutes and of course all my students. In particular I thank the many people in different countries who supported me in some way. Be it productive discussions, crucial reviews, careful check of manuscript sections (for example Hedwig Lang, Siegfried Holzinger ...), helpful references, more active eMail alternations or simply thrilling conversations, in which the importance and the future of this subject became manifest. Finally I thank the Vogel-book publisher in Würzburg for their pleasant cooperation. I also found the comments of „non-information scientists" interesting, that showed the didactic problems of learning for non-technical people. An individual enumeration would explode the frame of a preface. My most sincere thanks are meant for you all. The greatest thanks are meant for my wife Angela and my small daughters Katharina and Barbara, who have supported me, coped without me while I was working and pulled me out from between computers and meter high stacks of books.

What ever is done, the laying down of time resistant basic principles should never be forgotten. Which is what this book aims to do!

Preface to the Second German Edition

In the second edition - in addition to supplements and improvements in all modules - I followed current trends and thus particularly the module "Video" was strongly expanded. The design of the Internet links in the module appendix was completely changed: All links on the accompanying web pages "www.basiswissen-multimedia.at" are now "live" and "clickable" and particularly editorially, rapidly changeable and extendable. A Glossary in every module now helps to acquire the necessary vocabulary. Exercises and themes for debates were also added to the examination questions. I would like to thank most cordially many people for valuable notes, supplements and correction-proposals again. Among others: Professor Heinz Zemanek, Thomas Kleinberger, Natascha Andrae, Professor Andreas Graesser and Berndt Sevcik. Very special thanks again to my wife Angela and my two small assistants Katharina and Barbara.

Graz, Austria — Andreas Holzinger

Table of Contents

Module 0: Introduction to Multimedia Basics

Module 1: Information and Communication

Module 2: Signals and Coding

Module 3: Audio Technology

Modul 4: Graphics Technology

Module 5: Video Technology

Module 6: Multimedia via Internet

Module 0: Introduction to Multimedia Basics

„It's a PC. It's a TV. It's Multimedia!"

Business Week, October 9, 1989

Dear reader! The first of the three volumes students textbooks „Multimedia Basics" lies in front of you.
The following introduction is intended to give a short outline of the logical structure and the didactic background.
Volume 1 deals primarily with the „Computer", Volume 2 with the „Human" and Volume 3 with the Interaction „Human–Computer".
First of all, we will answer some questions: What is multimedia, who needs „knowledge" about multimedia, what is multimedia for and why "multimedia over the Internet?"

1: Computer –
2: Human –
3: Human–Computer

What?
Who?
What for?

1 What is Multimedia?

At the threshold of the 21st century one word is in all mouths: Multimedia. But what is actually concealed behind this word?

Old wine in a new bottle? As early as the fifties the term „multimedia" became very popular to designate slide-shows using original new technics to mix several projections and blend in accompanying sound. In 1995 this word was elected "word of the year" in Germany by the Society for german language ([2], [W1]). The word practically permeated into all areas of life – although with completely different meanings.

Fig. 0.1 The magic word multimedia ... [W1]

And therein lies a problem, multimedia has become one of the most frequently misused catchwords.

The literal meaning derives from the roman multus = „a lot, multiple, many" ... and medium = „device for the exchange of information" (which actually is a information system).

Although the word „Multimedia" is now scorned due to the overuse, and misuse, of this term and even, occasionally, causes tired gestures of dismissal, an incredible amount of basic knowledge lies hidden behind this designation; fundamental and important for all areas of education dealing with the "New media" – and the Internet.

Multimedia Basics are fundamental for many new jobs

Multimedia becomes really fascinating through the employment of efficient computers at reasonable cost. The view of the computer as a digital calculating machine has changed permanently. For example, today, by using extremely economical multimedia software, the living room can be turned into an interactive learning centre.

Worldwide, CD-ROMs with new software continuously emerge on the market (a discernible amount is teaching software). An estimated 100 million DM, approx. 35 million pounds sterling, worth had already been sold in 1993 (and that was already in the IT stone-age).

Multimedia – an enormous growing market

Sales turnover in the multimedia branch in Germany was reliably estimated at 270 billion DM (!) for the year 1998 – and the corresponding belief that this is actually an area of marked expansion:

„The market which connects itself to the magic word "multimedia" grows exponentially and will keep on growing. A management consultancy predicted the emergence of 2 millions new jobs by the year 2000 in Germany alone. Whether one shares their optimism to this extent or not: it is certain that many occupations will, one day, be concerned with multimedia ([1])."

Multimedia includes the application of audio (Language, sound, music ...), video (Text, graphics, still frames, animations, films ...) and user interactivity (over keyboard, mouse, touchpad, screentouch ...).

Fig. 0.2 Different possibilities for using media supply

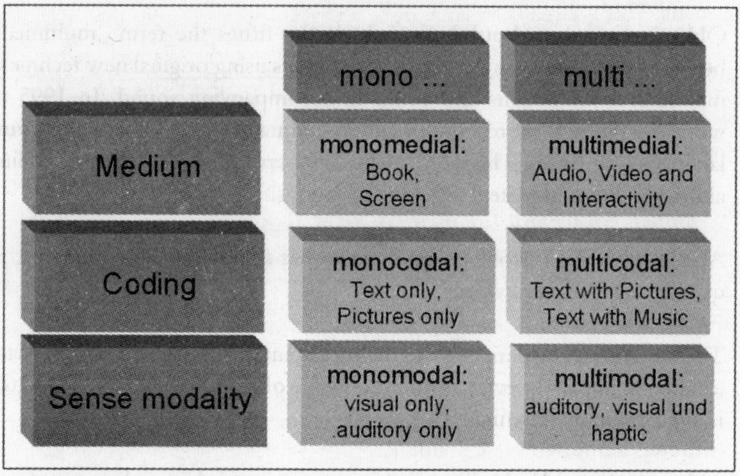

Multimedia: Chance for comprehensive work

Multimedia is probably so exciting, because it opens the chance per se for Interdisciplinarity and subject comprehensive cooperation.

In computer science, for example, the question of didactics, pedagogy and learning psychology rarely stood in the centre of the interest.

At scientific congresses one meets dynamic computer science professors who develop computer based tutorials, but actually relinquish the question of the didactic pedagogic psychological basis of their work, with a shrug, to pedagogues, psychologists and sociologists ([2]).

However, psychologists and pedagogues frequently do not have access to the technological basis – or do not want to.

Interdisciplinarity: Combination of Computer Science and Cognitive Science

---

Research and studies on the field "Multimedia" must therefore be interdisziplinary.

---

2 Who needs „Knowledge" about Multimedia? Why?

The education of computer scientists, telematics (in the eighties the study of telematics were established as a combination of computer science, telecommunications and electronics, thanks to an initiative of the professors Hermann Maurer and Hans Leopold at Graz University of Technology) and software engineers at colleges and technical universities are essentially excellent – but chiefly concentrate on „technological contents". This is an inescapable fact. But all software – not just learning software – is for use by humans. This is equally a fact.

Technicians and engineers should also have rudimentary knowledge on the subject of man-machine interaction, in particular a basic understanding of human beings; e.g. how their memory works, how they organization knowledge, their learning behaviour and the most suitable implications for the utilization of the computer as a learning and working medium.

HCI – Human Computer Interaction

However, this fundamental knowledge must first be made available.

This book series arose from as interdisciplinary (modular structured) lecture (2 + 1 hours a week) at the IICM (Institute for Information Processing and Computer Supported New Media)[W2].

modular structure enables individual use in different lectures

Multimedia is therefore divided in three parts:

1) Multimedia **Technology** (computer)

2) Multimedia **Learning** (human)

3) Multimedia **Design** (human-computer interaction)

This set of books exactly follows the logical structure below (figure 0.3):

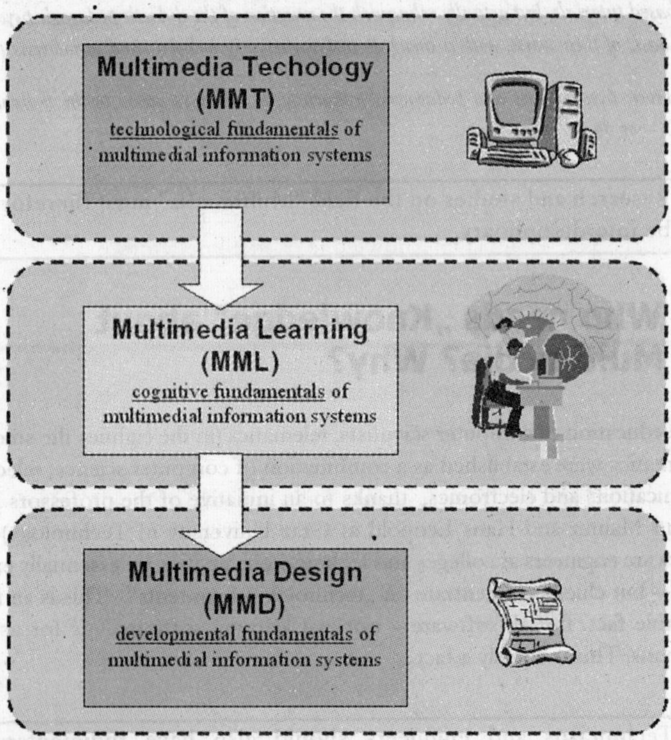

Fig. 0.3 Structure of the three books „Multimedia Basics“

Computer

Multimedia technology (MMT) deals with the technological basics of multimedial information systems. The topics comprise basics of information and communication (IaC), signals, audio, picture and video techniques (under special consideration of the psychophysics of the senses) and technological bases of multimedia via Internet.

Human

Multimedia learning (MML) deals with cognitive basics of multimedial information systems. Basics of the information organization in the human memory, knowledge organization, theories of learning, historical development of the computer assisted learning, media didactics and the working with learning software (Influences such as motivation, attention and Arousal (stimulation)) are some of the topics.

Human-Computer

Multimedia design (MMD) deals with development technical basics of multimedial information systems. The topics includes principles of software engineering and project management, basics of design (human-machine interaction, typography, picture design, audio design, communication) and finally the enormously important field of the software evaluation.

The division of these topics into concrete lectures (with MML as a kernel) emerges with a ratio of approximately 20:60:20 because the greatest educational deficit is to be found in the area of multimedia learning. On the other hand the high interdisciplinary character of the subject makes it impossible to leave out the concrete topics of technology and software engineering..

For a basic education MMT, MML und MMD should be scheduled for 2+1 weekly hours each

The procurement of maximally time consistent basic principles and the avoidance of – interesting indeed, but sometimes short-lived – specialist knowledge is extremely important.

In Europe people are of the monophonic opinion that the area of „multimedia" will become increasingly more important for our information society – we are still at the beginning of this development! New jobs require a new educational basis – new basic knowledge.

eEurope - eLearning

The modular setup of this textbook makes a maximum of flexibility possible in order to provide optimum support for students and teachers.

Every module can be utilized separately and as required. The great advantage however, is the high interdisciplinarity. Within these three volumes practically the entire fundamental knowledge about multimedia is covered, information which would otherwise have to be gleaned from a number of books and articles.

If required, specific information can be found via the full references and the accompanying pages in the Internet.

Multimedia Basics should constitute the **basis** of education for all occupations which deal with the „New Media" .

3 What is Multimedia for?

A widespread assumption is:

„Multimedia evokes a response from several senses simultaneously ... which is why information retention is improved."

More than one human sense responds to multimedia – which improves memory retention.

The following picture shows the most popular representation of the field of media-pedagogy and instruction psychology. Many publications and lectures are based on this unconsidered and naive assumption:

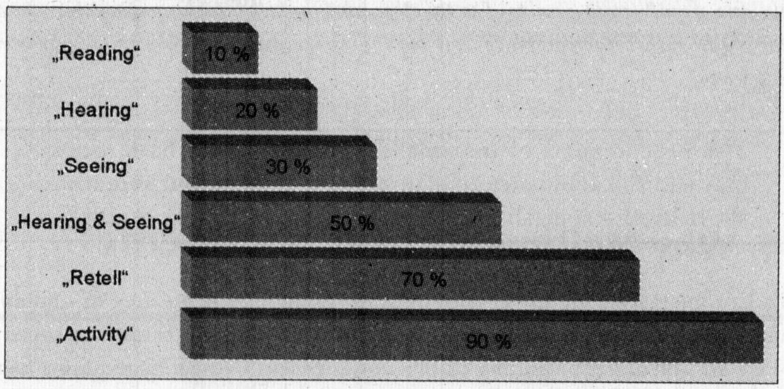

Fig. 0.4 The naive assumption is often offered as "proof" for the effectiveness of Multimedia

Nevertheless, such a representation **is problematic.** Probably this is also why no scientific sources can be found for this diagram. In figure 0.4 sense modality and encoding have been confused: Seeing and Hearing are **modality specific activities,** but Reading and Recital are **code specific activities** [3].

Summary Theory Realism Theory

This assumption is based on a naive theory of sense accumulation, which in turn is based on a simple historical realism theory. In this theory it is taken for granted that *"real" (substantial)* objects have a higher value than their symbolic representation.

In Volume 2 „Multimedia Basics“ these phenomena are *fundamentally* dealt with.

Fact: the numerical data in figure 4.0 must be put into perspective.

We must critically examine what exactly is meant by „Reading“, „Seeing“, and so forth – very different *perception* situations scarcely produce comparable values.

The flow of communication becomes more complicated with the application of Multimedia since the users must process a higher communication competence.

Nuremberg Funnel is not realizable, even with the use of Multimedia.

Concerning the field of mulitmedial learning it must be stated at the outset that multimedia cannot *directly* improve „learning success“ .

The long sought Nuremberg funnel can not be found in multimedia

Chances through Motivation, Attention and Arousal

However, through increased motivation, improved attention and higher arousal (stimulation) the application of multimedia can provoke a more intense *concentration on the subject matter* and – in this way – achieve direct results in learning and retention.[5].

Additionally, procedures can be made visible through screen simulations - for example in mathematics – that could not easily be displayed on a traditional blackboard. [4].

4 Why Multimedia over the Internet?

The most exciting approach at the moment – and particularly in the future – is multimedia via the Internet, the presentation of text, graphics, audio, video and interaction (!) in a hypermedia application within a standard browser (figure 0.5).

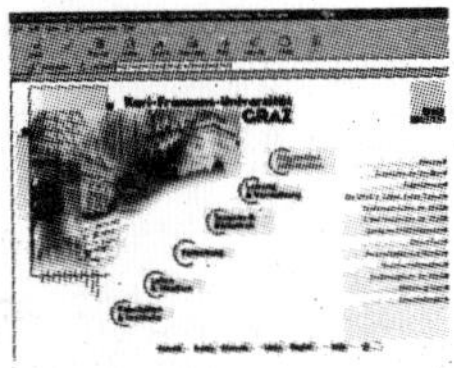

Fig. 0.5 A Browser enables the work with Multimedia data

> The WWW (World Wide Web) is probably the *most successful networked information system* in the history of mankind. The usability of the Interface is definitely one of its main advantages.

Through the introduction of WWW browsers „clicking“ became a familiar concept of Hypermedia information systems among almost all computer users worldwide .

The concepts appear to be new and unique. However, we should not forget that such systems as MEMEX (memory expander), augment, Xanadu, Zog, Owl, MUPID and other WWW hypertext systems have contributed a great deal to the investigation and development of today's hypermedia and multimedia systems.

Due to the importance of the Internet, the demand for new technologies in **telecommunication** has increased.

The Future of Multimedia will be determined by use of broadband networks

For example with modern ADSL technology (Asymmetric Digital Subscriber Line) it is possible to use conventional two wire telephone lines for high speed multimedia application.

In the same way the use of available cable TV networks becomes conceivable as a broadband medium for multimedia applications. ATM (Asynchronous transfer mode) presents completely new approaches for the implementation of universal broadband networks.

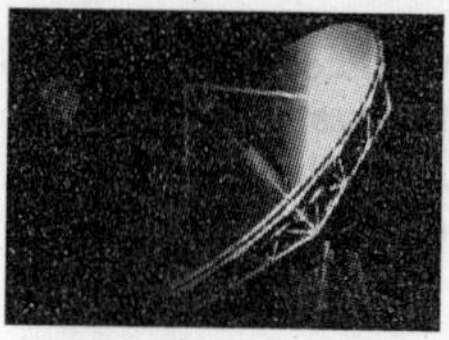

Fig. 0.6 The significance of satellite communication increases

Due to the rapid growth of the Internet, the importance of communication satellites is increasing. In the future multimedia will be distributed efficiently via satellites. This is of particular importance to such areas as tele-medicine, tele-education and video conferences, because the data *transfer* rate on extra terrestrial message paths is higher than currently on the congested conventional lines.

Quoted and maintaining literature to this Introduction:

[1] LEHNER, FRANZ; BRAUNGART, GEORG; HITZENBERGER, LUDWIG, ED. (1999): *Multimedia in Lehre und Forschung: Systeme - Erfahrungen - Perspektiven (Gabler Edition Wissenschaft: Information-Engineering und IV-Controlling).* Wiesbaden: Gabler. 108f.

[2] OBERLE, THOMAS; WESSNER, MARTIN (1998): *Der Nürnberger Trichter: Computer machen lernen leicht!? (Forum Beruf und Bildung; Bd. 10).* Alsbach: LTV-Verlag Leuchtturm.

[3] ISSING, LUDWIG J.; KLIMSA, PAUL (1997): *Information und Lernen mit Multimedia.* 2. Auflage. Weinheim: Psychologie Verlags Union. 68f.

[4] HOLZINGER, ANDREAS (1997): Computer Aided Mathematics Instruction with Mathematica 3.0. *Mathematica in Education and Research, Vol.6, No.4,* 37-40. Santa Clara (CA): Telos-Springer.

[5] HOLZINGER, ANDREAS (1999): Multimedia - eine interdisziplinäre Disziplin innerhalb des Faches Informationssysteme. *GMW FORUM, Zeitschrift der Gesellschaft für Medien in der Wissenschaft,* 4/99, 18-20. Siegen: Gesellschaft für Medien in der Wissenschaft GMW e.V., Universiät Siegen.

Internet-Links to this Introduction:

[W1] http://www.geist.de/gfds/verlag-D.html (Homepage of the „Gesellschaft für deutsche Sprache“ , Wiesbaden, D)

[W2] http://www-ang.kfunigraz.ac.at/~holzinge/mml (Homepage of the lecture „Multimedial Learning“ at Graz University of Technology, Graz, A)

[W3] http://www.basiswissen-multimedia.at (Homepage of this book, with updated literature and links for each module, Graz University, A)

Module 1: Information and Communication

„The word information, in this theory,
is used in a special sense that must not be confused
with its ordinary usage.
In particular,
information must not be confused with meaning."

Claude E. Shannon on page 8 in his „Mathematical Theory of Communication"

Learning objectives

Multimedia Systems are **Information Systems** (IS) in which *all* kinds of auditory and visual information are offered. In order to understand various types of information and information processing, a thorough understanding of the basic principles involved is necessary. This knowledge is presented in the following **Information and Communication Theory**.

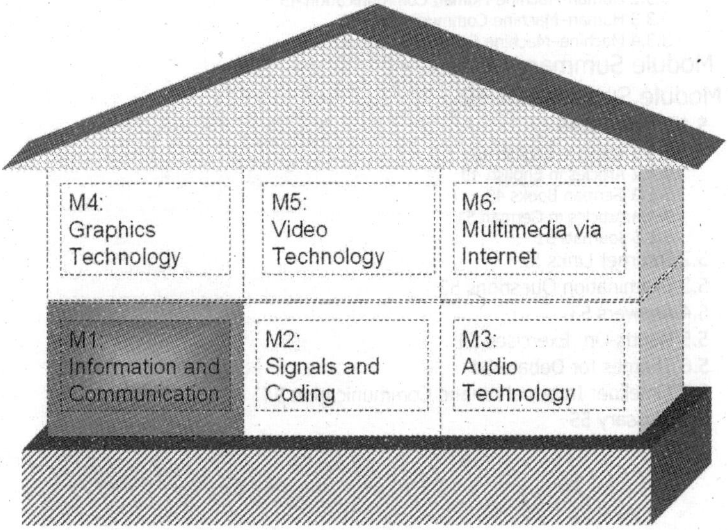

Information and Communication is not only important in computer science, but is also of central importance to the existence of (civilised) life in our world, only consider the transmission of hereditary information (genetic blueprints) or the inter-communication of living beings.

In each case the information transmitted, and the systems used for these interchanges, become increasingly complicated and abstract.

Fig. 1.1 Computer Science and Information Technology (IT) are the basis of the modern information society

With the entrance into the **digital world** of information processing with multimedia – distributable over world-wide networks – a completely *new media* is made available. The society in which we live is becoming increasingly more dependant on **information**. Due to satellite technology, optical fibre technology and millions of cross-linked computers worldwide, the technical possibilities of information and communication (IaC) have increased an inconceivable amount. All these elements set the foundation for a world wide **Society of Knowledge.**

Computer Science and Information Technology are continually breaking down currently putative boundaries. With data transfer rates exceeding 10 Gigabits per second, the post-modern information society becomes reality. The Internet penetrates our everyday life with a nearly infinite abundance of information. Information obtains an increasingly important position.

In the industry 75% of employees no longer work with material, but with information. Up to 50% of product costs and more than 50% of indirect costs are information expenditure.

However, just at a time in which (almost) everyone has the possibility of accessing an practically unlimited amount of information, it is necessary to provide a permanent and basic knowledge of signals, data, information, knowledge and communication.

Signals in the next Module; Knowledge in Volume 2

1 Information

The Human as an Information Processing System

People can be viewed as information processing systems (IPS). Every IPS consists of

- Input channels (Receivers and sensors),
- Processing elements (Processors and memories) as well as
- Output channels (Effectors and actuators).

People are, however, more than mere data processing systems: They are information interpreters, ambiguity solvers and problem analysts.

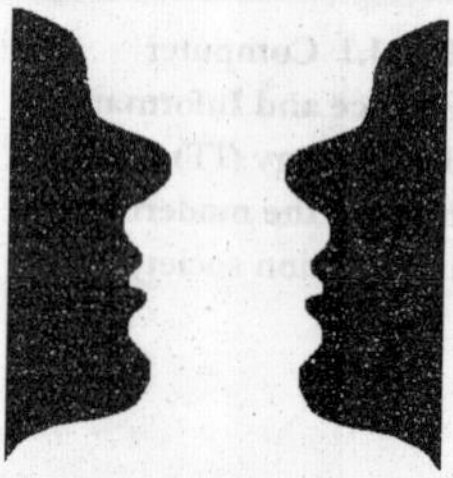

Fig. 1.2 The „Rubin cup", so named after the Danish psychologist Edgar Rubin, it illustrates that the figures in the picture can only be recognised individually - not both simultaneously

For example, what does the „shadow figure" represent in the picture 1.2: Two faces or a vase? Which of the figures was recognised first?

The **interpretation** of information – in the example of *visual information* - is always dependent on the person who absorbs and evaluates this information subjectively.

Multimedia-systems are **interactive information systems.** The fundamentals of **information processing** are valid.

However, before occupying ourselves with information processing some central questions must be answered: What are signals? What is data? What actually is meant by information? What is knowledge?

The fundamentals of „Signals" are dealt with in Module 2 of this volume and the topic „Knowledge" in Module 2 of Volume 2 „Multimedia Basics: Learning".

1.1 Terms and Definitions

The use of such terms as *signal, data, information* and *knowledge* are in everyday use. We „send signals", „pass on data", „obtain information" and „acquire knowledge". However, in connection with Information Systems we need to have these terms clearly defined.

1.1.1 Signals

Signals as physical information carriers

According to the DIN i44 300 standard (DIN = Deutsche Industrie Norm, German Industrial Standard), Signals represent the **physical carriers** for data which act as carriers of information in turn. As shown in module 2, we distinguish between two essentially different kinds of signals:

- **analog signals,** consisting of **continuous functions,** and
- **digital signals,** consisting of **discrete (single) characters.**

Signals are *functions* or *characters* which, via auditory, visual or other physical-technical means, can be used to transmit data.

Example: In a multimedia-production the speakers' words are the information intended for the listeners. A microphone changes the sound signals into electric signals. These are digitised and stored, for example on CD-ROM. With a digital analog converter, amplifier and loudspeaker the information „Speech" is reconstructed (see module 3).

1.1.2 Data

Data are facts. To quote the DIN 44 300 again – „This term represents signs or continuous functions, on the basis of known or assumed arrangements, for the purpose of transmitting information".

In computer science data are coded information stored in computer systems. The information can be represented by character strings **(digital data)** or continuous mathematical functions **(analog data)** and processed by machines.

Data are coded Information

Since the book series „Basics Multimedia" is not limited to technical basics, we must further classify data as follows:

Quantitative data are information to which defined **numerical values** can be ascribed (for example 1, 2, 3 ...).

Qualitative data are information in the form of **non-numeric attributes** which can be divided into different classes (for example „feminine", „masculine" or „neuter").

Qualitative data can be partially converted (coded) into quantitative data (for example „feminine = 1", „masculine = 2").

A quick way to differentiate between data, information, and knowledge is by utilizing a practical day-to-day application. Consider the word „Multimedia", which consists of the alphanumeric characters m-u-l-t-i-m-e-d-i-a. Each alphanumeric character can be represented by ASCII code (see Module 2). This ASCII code is stored in the computer's memory and is called data. This data (ASCII a = 01100001) is fairly meaningless by itself; only the forming of words (and sentences) is the beginning of having information.

1.1.3 Information

The term information (lat. informatio = „idea", „instruction", „training") is employed in the various disciplines of science and technology differently:

In nature, for example, information is defined as „every difference that makes a difference" (BATESON), or to be more specific: „Information is the alteration process, that leads to an increase in knowledge (SCHUCAN)" or a further specification: „Information is a usable answer to a given question" (ZEHNDER).

In telecommunication the information theory as defined by SHANNON & WEAVER is used (see chapter 2).

Basically information is only statements or news which bring something new. Therefore information must have an information content – a meaning (Chapter 2.2). Simply expressed, frequent monotonous events do not offer anything new and cannot be classed as information in this sense.

The „news content" not the „weight of content" defines information

New, surprising or *rare* occurrences are (information-technical) informative. The information lies in the signals *change.*

Experiment: A voice producing a uniformly monotonous and repetitive tone, for example the sound „aaaaaa......" over a longer period of time, then modulated by vocal information, for example by reading this text out loud.

Fig. 1.3 Norbert Wiener established Information as the third basic component – next to matter and Energy [W7]

Information is a sequence of physical signals, fluctuating (changing) in time or space and consisting of a material **carrier** and the **information content.**

NORBERT WIENER„ founder of cybernetics (Theory of communication and regulation systems in living organisms, social organizations and technical systems), even establishes information as the **third basic component** in his system environment.

KUHLEN (1999) gives an interesting definition: „Information is a subset of knowledge which is necessary in actual action situations and is not available before the information is processed. Accordingly, information is significantly dependent on the context factors of the users and the utilization".

The dependence on the **context** becomes particularly obvious in the theory and practice of communication (see chapter 3).

1.1.4 Knowledge

Knowledge is applied Information

Knowledge (German: Wissen; Latin: scientia; Greek: episteme) is the result – the aim of (human) information processing.

> Knowledge and thinking are inseparably in connection to the human brain: Knowledge is (in the human memory) organized, available and applicable information.

Fig. 1.4 Heinz Zemanek (born 1920), the computer pioneer, during his address on his eightieth birthday [W6]

According to HEINZ ZEMANEK, stored information certainly appertains to knowledge, but this first becomes knowledge when the context, supplied by the unique combination of our sense organs – and exactly this is achieved by multimedia technology – is processed by human intelligence.

Neither a telephone directory nor a database are knowledge – however, with knowledge one can extract considerable sense from both (Heinz Zemanek).

Fig. 1.5 Heinz von Foerster (born in 1911 in Vienna) was one of the „architects" of cybernetics, together with Warren McCulloch, Norbert Wiener, John von Neumann and others [W10]

HEINZ VON FOERSTER (1998) asserts – conform with the Constructivism (see Volume 2), – that knowledge *can not be imparted:* It can not be treated as an object, a thing that one can transfer from A to B – like sugar or coffee – to accord a specific effect in an organism.

Knowledge is „forward looking" and probabilistic: that means that the value of any knowledge is only high if the predictions are correct with reference to the (relevant) transmission channel.

This is in contrast to information, which is possibilistic, since the most improbable signs contain the most information content (see chapter 2.1).

More about that in the module „Knowledge" in the volume 2.

Signals	physical carriers
Data	encoded information
Information	signal alteration
Knowledge	applied information

Fig. 1.6 Summary of the terms used

2 Information Theory

Fig. 1.7 Claude E. shannon (born 1918 in Michigan) established his information theory in 1948. He died on 24th February 2001 [W2]

The information theory arose from the work of CLAUDE ELWOOD SHANNON and represents a fundamental **basis for computer science.**

The information theory is used for mathematical description of information systems and is closely influenced by telecommunications.

With the aid of a homogeneous theory, it is possible to compare different methods of information transmission and to optimize the individual components of a transmission system.

An information system is subject to the laws of telecommunications and can be represented by the communication model from SHANNON & WEAVER as shown in Fig. 1.8.

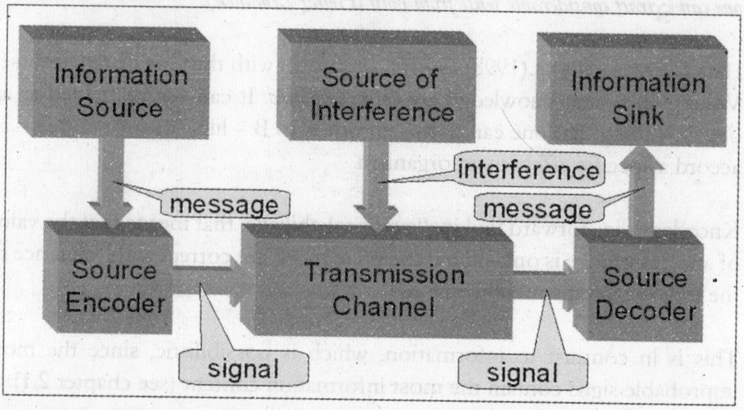

Fig. 1.8 The communication model from Shannon & Weaver describes the flow of information between sender and receiver

The information theory is also an important component of psychophysics (see module 3) and is necessary for the psychological analysis of communication (see chapter 3).

2.1 Information content

In the information theory according to SHANNON & WEAVER the information content of a message is defined from a purely mathematical viewpoint and the importance of the information is completely ignored.

With reference to our definition of the term information, based on telecommunications engineering usage (Chapter 1.1.3), the information content of a message must possess the following characteristics:

- The information content I_x of an information x must be greater the smaller the probability p_x of the occurrence (the bigger the „surprise value“).
- An information with the probability $p_x = 1$ must have the information content $I_x = 0$.
- The information content of independent messages should be additive.

However, when speaking of information content, it must be distinguished between first of all, whether discrete characters with the same occurrence probability or discrete characters with different occurrence probability are employed.

2.1.1 Information content of discrete characters with equal probability of occurrence

The information content I results from the entire character set s. If, for example, we take the whole numbers from 0 to 15 we get a character set of $s = 16$. Putting these numbers into binary we get:

$$15 = 1 \cdot 2^3 + 1 \cdot 2^2 + 1 \cdot 2^1 + 1 \cdot 2^0 = 1111$$

$$14 = 1 \cdot 2^3 + 1 \cdot 2^2 + 1 \cdot 2^1 + 0 \cdot 2^0 = 1110$$

through to

$$0 = 0 \cdot 2^3 + 0 \cdot 2^2 + 0 \cdot 2^1 + 0 \cdot 2^0 = 0000$$

lb = binary logarithm to the base of 2, also referred to as ld (logarithm dualis) i.e. $\log_2$

In order to represent our character set of $s = 16$ in digital form, we therefore need a four-digit (4 bit) binary number, thus 4 = lb (16). Therefore it follows that the information content:

$$I = lb(s)$$

I Information content in bit
s Quantity of different characters (number set)
lb binary logarithm (= base 2)

The use of the logarithm to the base 2 is only a question of scale. The basis 2 was chosen because, for the simplest case of a symmetrical binary information with $p_x = 0{,}5$ the information content of a character becomes $I_x = 1$ bit.

The unit for information capacity is the **bit.**

---

binary digit – the unit of information

The term **bit** („binary digit“) used to have two different meanings:

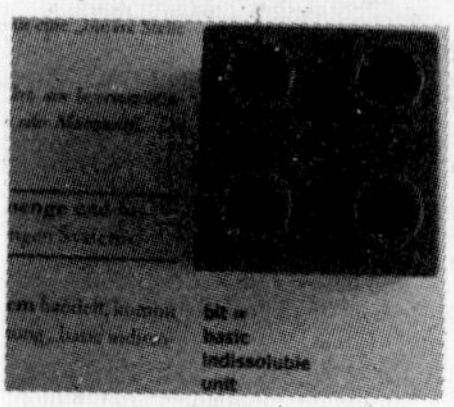

Fig. 1.9 A binary cell is, so to speak, the „smallest brick"

- A binary digit, 0 or 1. This is usually displayed as an integer. These „bits" are the individual and basic pieces of data in computers.
- A measure of uncertainty, H, or information R. This can be any real number because it is an average. This is the measure that SHANNON originally used to discuss communication systems and is known properly as „the Shannon".

In principle something contains the information content of one bit when it includes two possibilities (e.g.: A light switch on/off or the toss of a coin heads/tails). The binary elements„0" and „1" are used as the basic components.

In digital Multimedia a bit is **the smallest binary information** capacity and describes the logical state of a two-value system.

---

bit = basic indissoluble unit

The fact that it is a matter of a minimum system is expressed by the term „basic indissoluble unit", initially introduced by SHANNON.

An different example from „informational routine": How large is the information content of a seven-digit safe code (1234567)?

s = 10 (for the digits of 0 ... 9) from this:
I = 7 lb(10) bit = 7 x 3,32 bit = 23,26 bit

To the declaration: lb 10 = ^{2}lg10

$$2^x = 10 \Rightarrow x\log(2) = \log(10)$$

$$x = \frac{\log(10)}{\log(2)} = \frac{1}{0,30103} = 3,3219281$$

2.1.2 Information content of discrete characters with unequal occurrence probability

In our previous examples, it is assumed that the probability p_x of occurrence is equal for all characters (numbers).

The p_x of a character given s possible characters is then

$$p_x = \frac{1}{s}$$

Laplace Probability

whereby this expression – known from the Probability Theory – represents the number of favourable results divided by the number of possible results.

Therefore the following is valid for the information content:

$$I_x = lb(s) = lb\left(\frac{1}{p_x}\right)$$

If every character has an individual probability p_{xi} the equation reads:

$$I_{xi} = lb\left(\frac{1}{p_{xi}}\right)$$

These facts can be graphically illustrated as follows:

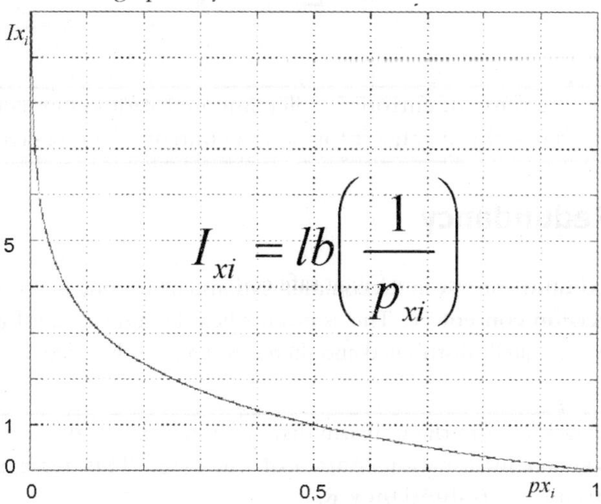

Fig. 1.10 Information content (with varying character probability)

The information content should be independent of the code form and depend exclusively on the probability with which the receiver expects the information.

Fig. 1.11 Absolutely homogenous order of 12 „Lego-Bricks“

Fig. 1.12 Absolutely disorder

Messages that are expected with high probability, have a low information content, whereas those expected with small probability have a correspondingly high information content. Examples with Lego bricks (Figures 1.11 until 1.13) help to clarify these facts and to illustrate the following question: Which order contains the maximal informational content?

Figure 1.11 shows a completely uniform arrangement of 12 Lego bricks: The information content is small. In picture 1.12 the 12 Lego bricks are in absolute disorder: The occurrence of a specific order is accidental and extremely improbable and is therefore the arrangement with the highest information content. Generally the „average“ is the rule: A defined arrangement, for example the „house“ in picture 1.13.

Fig. 1.13 A defined order with a distinct „construction plan“

2.2 Entropy

Entropy is the degree of disorder within a system

The term entropy is borrowed from Thermodynamics (Calorific Theory), where entropy is a measure of statistical disorder (uncertainty) in a thermodynamic system.

For the **average information content** of a message, we can take the arithmetic mean value as the sum of all p_{xi} multiplied individual information content I_i:

A higher Entropy value H means a greater uncertainty about the meaning of the message

$$H = \bar{I_x} = \sum_{i=1}^{s} p_{xi} lb\left(\frac{1}{p_{xi}}\right)$$

H – in the sense of entropy in telecommunications engineering – designates the average information content of a message.

2.3 Redundancy

The **maximum** entropy in telecommunications engineering is also referred to as **decision content** H_0. This is given when the individual information elements are equally distributed and therefore statistically independent.

A deviation from the uniform distribution causes a decrease in the average information content of a message. This decrease is referred to as **redundancy** R.

Assertion:

$$R = H_0 - H$$

and

$$r = \frac{H_0 - H}{H_0}$$

R redundancy
H_0 decision content (mean entropy)
r relative redundancy

Example: Assuming the occurrence probability of all alphabetic characters in a language ($s = 26$) to be equal ($p_x = 1/26$) and also assuming the letters to be independent of each other, the information content of one letter (and also the mean value) would be $H_0 = I_x = \text{lb}(26) = 4{,}7$ bit.

However, in actual fact the letter „e“ occurs far more frequently in the English language than the letter „z“. Taking this frequency in account, the true entropy is $H = 4{,}1$ bit/Symbol.

It must be also be taken into consideration that certain combinations of letters occur more frequently than others. For example, the probability is higher that the letter "a" will be followed by "n" rather the "o". Taking these conditional probabilities into consideration one arrives at: $H = 3$ bit/Symbol.

If still the dependencies of the conditional probability on all longer alphabetic orders and also the impossibility of the occurrence of specific alphabetic orders are considered besides, a value of $H =$ shows to 1,3 bit/Symbol.

With that, following values can be applied for the English language:

Information-theoretical numbers of the English language

$H = 1{,}3$ bit/Symbol
$R = 3{,}4$ bit/Symbol
$r = 0{,}5$

Compare: 73 % of the German language are redundant

---

50 % of the English language are redundant („superfluous“), and 50% are information supporting.

This redundancy of the language is **not** unwanted. Although these indeed the actual information increases and slow down the flow of information, an error recognition and error correction with faulty news are allowed by that.

Information without redundancy is absolutely worthless, because it has no reliability

2.4 Flow of Information

The data transfer rate of any information becomes increasingly important. This rate is called information flow and defined as follows:

$$F = \frac{H}{t_m}$$

whereby:

$$t_m = \sum p_x t_x$$

F Flow of Information in bit/s
t_m average period for the transfer of one character in s/Symbol

2.5 Channel capacity

For distributed information systems (for example: net based multimedia systems) it is especially important to know the upper limit of capacity of the transmission channels employed.

With the term "Channel", we mean an arbitrary path which the information can take from the sender to the receiver.

The channel capacity is the maximum information flow which can be transmitted via a communication channel without error.

The flow of information is dependent on the information source and on the transmission channel.

The channel capacity is an important quality criterion for Information Systems

Whereas the channel capacity is independent of the information source capabilities and depends only on the type of transmission channel.

It is a question of the absolute upper limit of performance; it can be computed as follows:

$$C = F_{max} = \left(\frac{H}{t_m}\right)_{max}$$

C channel capacity in bit/s

For a transmission channel disturbed by interference i.e. noise (interference is also, although in this case unwanted, information) with a bandwidth B the following formula is valid:

$$C = B lb\left(1 + \frac{P_S}{P_N}\right)$$

B Bandwidth in Hz (hertz, 1/s, see glossary)
P_S Signal Power Output in W (watts, S = Signal)
P_N Noise Power Output in W (N = Noise)

In actual usage the information flow in a transmission channel remains far below the channel capacity. Taking into consideration:

$$lb(x) = \frac{lg(x)}{lg(2)}$$

we proceed to a base 10 Logarithm and obtain with lg(2)~0,3::

$$C \approx \frac{B}{3} 10\,lg\left(1 + \frac{P_S}{P_N}\right)$$

whereby

$$10\,lg\left(1 + \frac{P_S}{P_N}\right) = \rho$$

This ρ represents the signal-interference ratio (in dB), and is generally known as the signal-to-noise ratio **SNR** (in dB).

dB = Dezi-Bel, see Module 3, chapter 2.3.2

In most cases the signal is very much higher than the interference, then applies:

$$P_S \gg P_N$$

$$\rho \approx 10\,lg\left(\frac{P_S}{P_N}\right)$$

The channel capacities of transmission channels are very different:

Transmission channel	B	r	C
Telegraphy	25 Hz	15 dB	75 bit/s
Analogue Telephone	3,1 kHz	40 dB	50 kbit/s
FM-Radio	15 kHz	60 dB	300 kbit/s
Television	5 MHz	45 dB	75 Mbit/s
ISDN	64 kHz	60 dB	64 kbit/s
Broadband (ATM)	10 MHz	45 dB	155 Mbit/s
Comparison: Eye	285 THz	-	10 Mbit/s

Fig. 1.14 Channel capacities of some typical channels
B = Bandwidth
r = Signal-to-Noise ratio
C = Channel capacity

The problematic of Bandwidth will be discussed in Module 6 „Multimedia via Internet"

A rising demand for channel capacity, with a continuously increasing rate of data to user interfaces, has arisen from the increase in the number of Internet-users and the growing supply in the multimedia-field. Nowadays, data at rates in the Gbit/s and Tbit/s range are only transmitted over wide areas via optical transmission channels (glass fibre). The glass fibre comes closer to the user (FTTH-Fibre To The Home).

FTTH = „fiber to the home"

2.6 Information Cuboid

The portable information capacity (the "information volume") can be vividly pictured as cuboids and are occasionally also referred to as "information cuboids" (Figure 1.15).

The lengths of the ashlar's sides (the parameters) depend on the

- available bandwidth *B*,
- noise margin ρ and
- available transmission time t_m.

An information cuboid can be represented graphically:

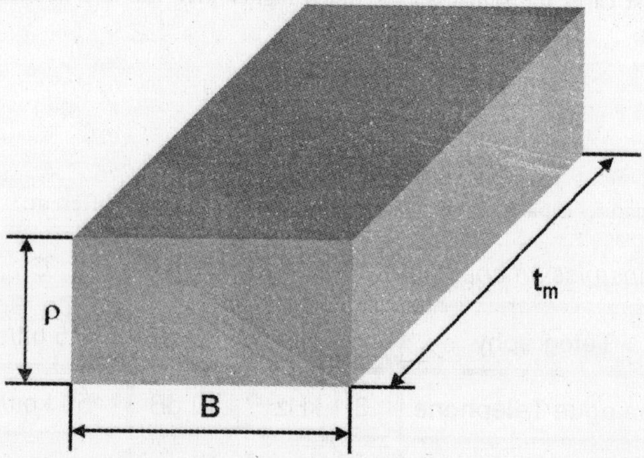

Fig. 1.15 Information cuboid, with Bandwidth *B*, Signal-to-Noise ratio ρ and transmission time slot t_m

The correct dimensioning of these three parameters is necessary for an optimal information transfer.

Example: For an Internet-Service-Provider (ISP) both bandwidth and transmission time are important values for measuring the accessibility (Channel capacity) of his customers to the external net (Internet).

According to SHANNON the volume of the information ashlar is equal to the theoretical limit of the maximum portable information capacity.

---

3 Communication

The development of a Mathematical Theory of Communication by SHANNON & WEAVER – following on the preparatory work of NYQUIST, HARTLEY and KÜPFMÜLLER – covers the subject of discrete signals in detail.

Meaning

The concept of information according to SHANNON & WEAVER only concentrates on technical-mathematical communication. The **meaning** of the signals is totally ignored.

If we want to understand the Human-Computer Communication – we first have to understand the Human-Human communication

Very rapidly, psychologists, pedagogues (educationalists), sociologists and especially cognitions-scientists were animated to apply this theory to (human) communication processes in a broader sense.

Communication (from lat. communicatio = "Communication, conversation") is generally the understanding (exchange of information) between people, people and machines or between machines.

Telecommunication

Multimedia-Communication

Communication can be used for a one-sided or mutual exchange of information. If this information occurs in the form of text, speech and music, pictures and videos, it is referred to as **telecommunication.** Enhance this telecommunication extended by the possibility of **interaction** and „true" **multi-media communication** is achieved

OSI Open Systems Interconnection – a Working Group of ISO

If systems implement international standards (OSI) enabling them to communicate with other systems which support equivalent standards, they are referred to as **Open Communication** Systems.

Communication is every exchange of information with definable information content (Message).

Communication is a **process** which includes the following elements:

- Sender,
- Information (the "communication") and
- Receiver.

The communication is expressed through symbols in a medium and transmitted by a channel. A successful communication is possible, when the symbols employed are accessible to both participants.

Fig. 1.16 A Communication becomes first possible, if sender and receiver are in the possession of a suitable character set

3.1 Semiotics as a Foundation

The evolution and, in particular, the spread of unambiguous **symbols** were an necessary postulate for the transfer of information, as for example in sign language, speech, writing, light signals etc.

Mankind's earliest and to date most important "Symbol System" is the spoken word (language). Pictures were the early pre-forms of writing. People first expressed their ideas with cave drawings. The first figure systems and later the oldest known writing systems in Mesopotamien, Egypt and China were developed from these drawings (Pictograms).

Semiotics is defined as the **Science of Signs.** It was recognised as a separate science at the beginning of the 20th. century due to the works of CHARLES SANDERS PIERCE (1839–1914) and FERDINAND DE SAUSSURE (1857–1913).

According to PEIRCE (in 1931) the basis of the communication process is a **linguistically** and **culturally** determined (established), but *still evolving* **interpretation of signs.**

Fig. 1.17 Charles Morris (1903–1979) divided the die Semiotics in Syntactic, Semantic and Pragmatic

> Semiotics is the basis of the exploration of subject and operation modes of communication processes. Semiotics is subdivided into Syntactics, Semantics and Pragmatics.

Building on the works of PEIRCE, CHARLES WILLIAM MORRIS developed a sign theory (Semiotics), with a social-psychological emphasis, on the background of behaviourism (See volume 2).

He divides semiotics into three disciplines: Syntactics, Semantics and Pragmatics.

Syntactics (pertaining to syntax) describes and analyses the inner formal relationships between the different symbols of a sign system and attempts to find reasonable and permissible character strings.

Semantics examines the relationships between symbols and objects, e.g. the subjects to which the symbols relate. Every symbol has an **meaning** and *"designates"* an object. In this case the "object" need not necessarily be physical, the term can also be used to refer especially to terms, thoughts, ideas etc.

Pragmatics examines the relationships between symbols and those using them. A symbol is employed in order to produce an **effect;** pragmatics deals with this application.

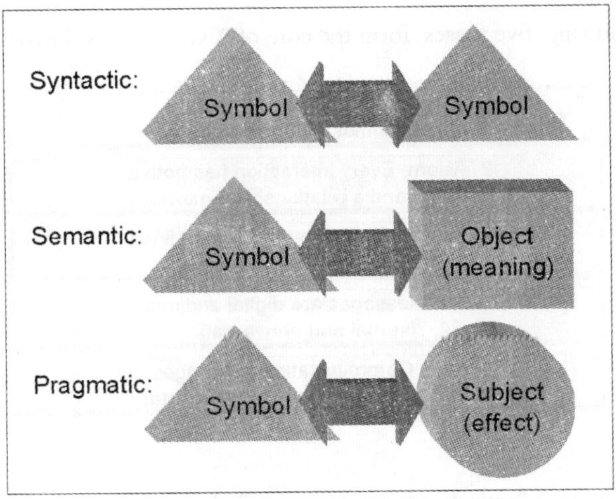

Fig. 1.18 Semiotics is subdivided into Syntactics, Semantics and Pragmatics

3.2 Processes of Communication

3.2.1 Three levels of communication

All communication processes between sender and receiver work on three layers. The lowest layer (the foundation or base) describes the purely syntactic layer: the physical transmission of signals. The middle layer compromises the meaning of the signals, while the effect is incorporated into the third level:

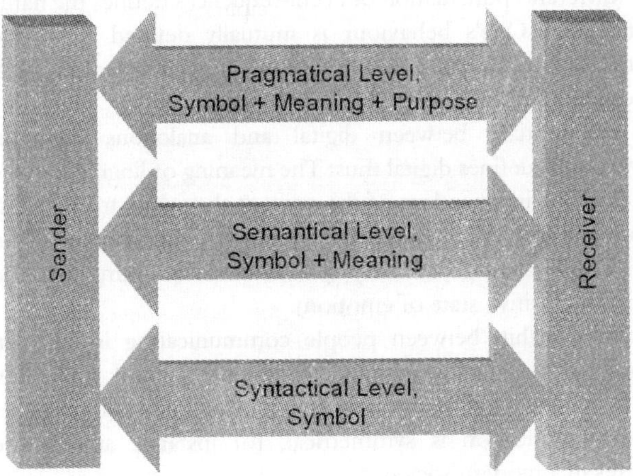

Fig. 1.19 The three levels of communication between sender and receiver

3.2.2 Axioms of Communications

The following five theses form the core of WATZLAWICK'S Theory:

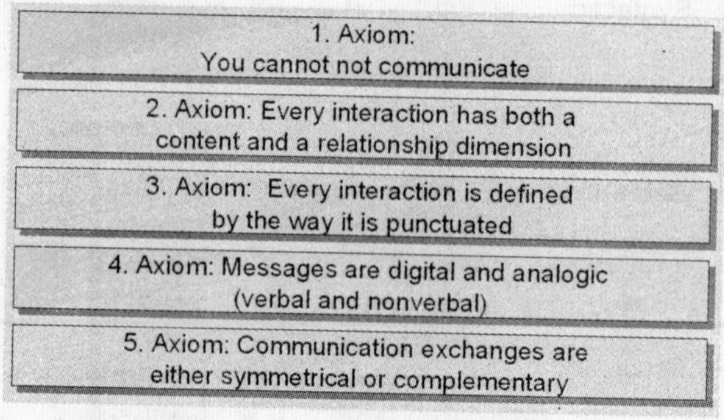

Fig. 1.20 The five pragmatic axioms of Watzlawick

Fig. 1.21 Watzlawick (born. 27. 7. 1921 in Villach, Austria), since 1960 Member of the Mental Research Institute (Palo Alto), since 1967 Lecturer at Stanford University [W4]

- One cannot "actively not communicate": Anyone attempting to inform a conversational partner of their intention not to communicate – has already communicated.
- Communication has a textual or material aspect (content) and a relationship aspect: Not only the content of a statement but also the tone, expression and the manner of delivery, – whether due to positive or negative emotions – is decisive in the interpretation made by the addressee.
- In particular if the "channels" of communication disagree (if for example a friendly content is sent in an unfriendly manner), this can lead to interpretation problems for the addressee or to a so-called "connection gap" ("drop" or "slump").
- The (different) punctuation of event sequences defines the nature of the relationship: One's behaviour is mutually defined as a reaction to another's behaviour, which can lead to pathological cycles with increasing alienation.
- We differentiate between digital and analogous communication. WATZLAWICK defines digital thus: The meaning of linguistic signs (terms, sentences) is independent of the content they refer to. Whereas analog communications bear a direct relationship to their content. (This is valid for for body language, mimicry, gesticulation: for example a smile usually expresses positive state of emotion).
- The relationship between people communicating is symmetrical or complementary. An upright social relationship exists between students and their professors (complementary communication). Between peers, the communication is symmetrical, for instance among friends or spouses in a modern society.

Every relationship has individual advantages and disadvantages for the communication

Digital communication has a complex, versatile logical syntax with, however, insufficient semantic for the field of relationships. **Analogous communication** does have this potential but lacks the logical syntax necessary for unambiguous communication.

WATZLAWICK advocates a system theory based on the assumption that every communication represents an integrated continuity.

A linear sender and receiver pattern cannot deal with these requirements:

Also, the communicants exist within an interacting environment, within which "Feedback" is produced which can, if negative, lead to pathological cycles of communication.

WATZLAWICK also advocates so-called "Radical Constructivism“. This is an epistemology (Theory of Knowledge) based on the premise that an objective reality does not exist: Everything we accept as "reality" is actually the result of our own subjective perceptions.

The understanding of other people is a rather unlikely case, it is much more probable that they do not understand if itself everyone means to have understood the other one

The practical starting point for WATZLAWICK'S *communication theory was the faulty communication of mentally ill people, schizophrenic patients and their families.* WATZLAWICK *applied the paradoxes of linguistic communication forms he had discovered to normal communication and came to the surprising result that such communication paradoxes also occur in the everyday life of very normal people – and were the cause of misunderstanding.*

According to WATZLAWICK everyone lives in his own, self-constructed, inner world, which he accepts as reality and assumes that everyone else also conceives the same reality.

If the communicant's differing awareness of reality (of which they are unaware) lead to a communication conflict, they either become confused or assume that the behaviour of the other is at fault.

This conflict situation can not be solved by the people themselves because they are too rooted in their own interpretation of reality.

WATZLAWICK intentionally exaggerates of course. Without knowing his precise background information and correlations, we must deal with his theories cautiously. Nevertheless, it makes particular sense to be aware of his theories and their relevance to multimedia.

3.3 Types of Communication

It is possible to differentiate between four types of communication:

- Human-to-human communication, with the special case of
- Human-machine-human communication,
- Human-machine communication and
- Machine-machine communication.

3.3.1 Human–Human Communication

Human-to-human or Person-to-person communication is the type of communication by which people communicate directly with each other. This can be, for instance, the direct exchange of information, a discussion of specific ideas or negotiations in a conflict situation.

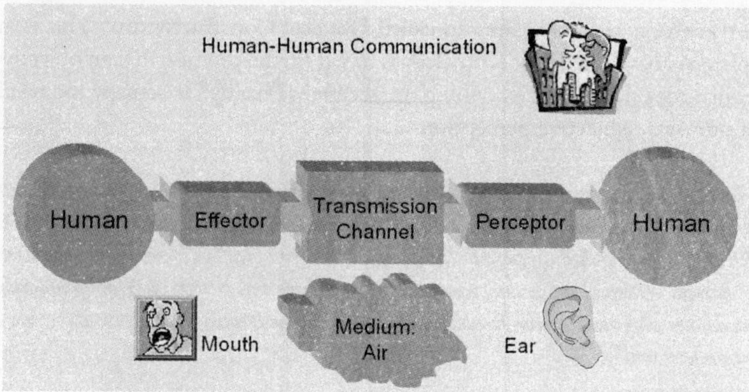

Fig. 1.22 The structure of the human-to-human communication

Human-to-human communication *(Person-to-person)* is known as **inter-personal communication** and represents an important and basic **social communication.**

---

inter-personal = between humans

Inter-personal communication is effected through two different (mutually comparable) kinds of symbol systems:

Proxemics, Example: In Europe mourning people wear black clothes during a funeral – in Japan white clothes

- **verbal-linguistic** (vocal), for example language or sounds (laughter, snoring ...) and
- **nonverbal-non linguistic** (nonvocal), for example signals (flashlight signals), signs (flags), symbols and pictures (icons), (gestures, mimicry and gesticulation (kinesics), communicative dimension of the human proximity behaviour (proxemics) and culturally dependant behaviour, for example mourning (grief).

Communication between humans is effected directly through interactive gesticulation, mimicry, sounds and language. Both sender and receiver must draw from the same set of symbols – to understand each other.

If we switch a machine, such as a telephone, into the communication we obtain a human-machine-human communication.

3.3.2 Human-Machine-Human-Communication

This kind of communication is called **indirect communication.** The essential difference to person-to-person communication is that the information is carried, via an transmission channel, through the intervening machine from the sender to the receiver.

Computers established themselves in Human-machine-human Communication by virtue of their *universal adaptability*.

This kind of communication is widely distributed on the Internet, for example in eMail, IRC (Internet Relay Chat), Internet-telephony (IP-telephony) or tele-conferences.

Classical examples of this type of communication, apart from Internet, are for instance telephone conversations, fax (facsimile telegraphy) and of course the evergreen "letter" when produced either on a computer or a typewriter. Very few letters are still written by hand.

eMail, Chat, IP-Telephony, Tele conference

The medium, over which the communication is transmitted, is of far less importance than the person or persons for whom the communication is intended.

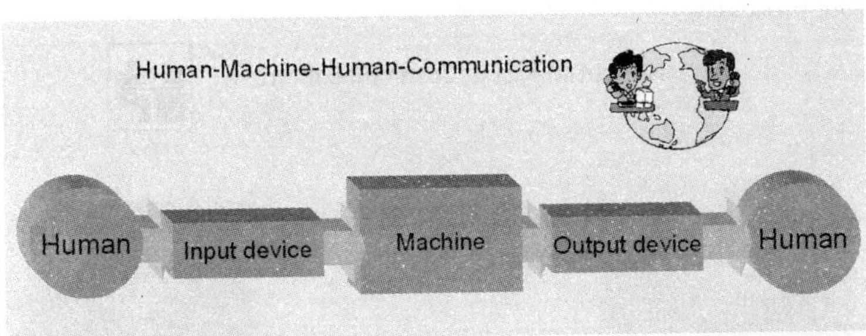

Fig. 1.23 The information from human to human passes through the "intermediator" machines

3.3.3 Human–Machine Communication

Human-machine Communication is the communication between a human and a machine (Computer). This kind of communication is particularly widespread in Internet and Intranet.

HCI
Human-Computer Interaction is an field of increasing importance and will be covered in volume three of „Basics Multimedia"

In computer science (IT/Informatics) the term HCI (Human–Computer Interaction) is generally used. HCI concentrates on the:

- organization,
- implementation and
- evaluation

of interactive information systems (IIS), and is supported by **Software Ergonomics** and **Usability.**

Typical examples for this are data bank queries (query/answer) or ITS (Intelligent Tutoring Systems). The user appropriately formulates the question, for example by entering search keys (strings of characters or numerals) into an input mask or screen, and the computer "answers" the inquiry.

Communication between humans and machine is both more complicated and more expensive because a high level of competence is necessary on the part of both sender and receiver. The human user must have additional skills (operating) in order to be able to decode messages.

The human-to-machine interface is also known as the „user interface" or „Computer–Human Interface" (CHI) and defines the „user view". For the average user this view is all of the system he sees (they believe it to be the system) and should be adapted as closely as possible to human thought and work processes.

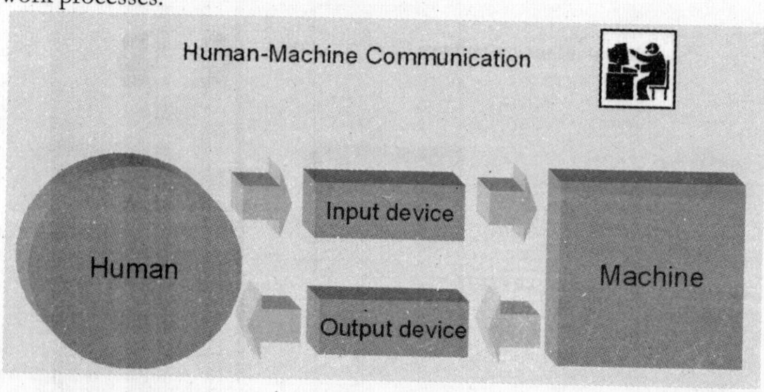

Fig. 1.24 In human-machine communication cognitive processes, such as perception, thought and learning, are particularly important

For example: in the following fields people are superior to computers:

- Sensitiveness for weak visual and auditory stimulation.
- Recognition of periodically varying, complex and fuzzy stimulation (for example: language).
- The ability to solve individual problems creatively.

Whereas computers are superior to people in the following fields:

- Detecting uniquely defined signals.
- Measuring, counting, computing and formal, logical operations.
- unfatiguable performance even with high signal density and distraction.

Performance = speed and quality with which a computer handles jobs

3.3.4 Machine–Machine Communication

Machine-to-machine communication is a type of communication with which two or more computers exchange data amongst themselves (without direct human intervention).

The term should not, however, disguise the fact that the communication is for the ultimate benefit of humans.

EDI, Electronic Data Exchange

A typical example of machine-to-machine communication is EDI, a system enabling computers to exchange financial and business documents without direct human intervention. For example: offers, receipts, bills etc. The files have a homogeneous format corresponding to a previously specified standard. They are machine-readable which makes it possible for the data to be processed automatically.

EDI is an **Electronic Commerce** application, with which *formalized* and *structured* files are exchanged between business partners.

Formalized files are file where the exact order in which information may appear is pre-specified.

An advantage of EDI lies in the fact that the workflow can be optimised due to automation and simplification. Initially individual enterprises developed their own EDI-standards, which soon led to compatibility problems.

The standard EDIFACT offers a series of international standards, for example, EDIFACT: Electronic Data Interchange For Administration, Commerce and Transport.

4 Module Summary

Multimedia Systems are interactive information systems. The principles of **Information Processing** (EDP) apply: Information is the result of physical signals varying in time or space. The physical carriers are the signals. The information lies in the *alteration* of a signal. Knowledge is applied information. A bit is the *smallest* quantity of binary information.

The mean information content of an information is termed **Entropy.** Redundancy, although reducing the information content, increases the reliability. The **Channel Capacity** is the maximum **Information Flow** that can be transmitted through a **Communication Channel** without error (for example: an *analog telephone* has a channel capacity of approximately 50 kbps).

SHANNONS interpretation of the term **Information** only really deals with the the concept of technical-mathematical communication: The meaning of the symbols is neglected. In order to understand and particularly to design multimedia information systems it is extremely important to be acquainted with the fundamentals of human communication. Communication is every exchange of information with a determinable content (News). We are dealing here with a *process* in which a **sender** and a **receiver** transmit a communication (message) over an information channel. A successful communication is only possible if the symbols used are accessible, and intelligible, to *both* sender and receiver.

Semiotics is defined as the Science of Signs and is divided into **Syntactics** (symbol ↔ symbol), **Semantics** (symbol ↔ meaning) and **Pragmatics** (symbol ↔ effect).

All communication processes between sender and receiver work on *three layers.* The lowest layer (the foundation or base) is the purely **syntactic layer**: the *transmission* of signals. The middle **semantic layer** compromises the *meaning* of the signals, while at the highest **pragmatic layer** the *effect* of the message on the receiver is registered.

It is possible to differentiate between *four types of communication*: **Human–to–Human Communication** (e.g. gestures, mimicry, sound, symbols or language) with the *special circumstances* of **Human–Machine–Human communication** (e.g. chat, eMail, IP telephony, teleconferencing), **Human–Machine communication** (Human–Computer Interaction, HCI; particularly important for the design of *interactive* multimedia systems) and **Machine-Machine Communication** (for example Electronic Data Exchange – EDI).

5 Module Supplement

5.1 Literature

5.1.1 Books in English

BERGER, T. (1971): *Rate Distortion Theory.* Englewood Cliffs (NJ): Prentice Hall.

GALLAGER, R. G. (1968): *Information Theory and Reliable Communication.* New York: Wiley.

HAMMING, R. W. (1986): *Coding and Information Theory.* London: Prentice Hall.

PIERCE, J. R. (1980): *An Introduction to Information Theory: Symbols, Signals and Noise.* 2nd Ed. New York: Dover.

SHANNON, CLAUDE E.; WEAVER, WARREN (196[illegible]): *The Mathematical Theory of Communication.* 2nd Ed. Urbana, Chicago, London: University of Illinois Press.

SWETS, JOHN A. (1964): *Signal Detection and Recognition by Human Observers.* New York, London, Sydney: Wiley.

5.1.2 Articles in English

HUFFMAN, D. A. (1952): A Method for the Construction of Minimum Redundancy Codes. *Proceedings of IRE,* No. 40, 1098-1101.

MAX, J. (1960): Quantizing for Minimum Distortion. *IRE Transactions of Information Theory,* Vol. IT 6, 7-12.

SHANNON, C. E. (1949): A Mathematical Theory of Communication. *Bell System Tech. Journal,* Vol. 27, 379-423 (Part I), 623-656 (Part II).

SHANNON, C. E. (1959): Coding Theorems for a Discrete Source with a Fidelity Criterion. *IRE Conv. Rec.,* Part 4, pp. 142-163.

5.1.3 German Books

BATESON, GREGORY (1984): *Geist und Natur: eine notwendige Einheit.* 2nd. Edition Edition. Frankfurt am Main: Suhrkamp.

BEUTH, KLAUS; HANEBUTH, RICHARD; KURZ, GÜNTER; LÜDERS, CHRISTIAN (2000): *Nachrichtentechnik (Elektronik 7).* Würzburg: Vogel.

CHARWAT, HANS JUERGEN (1992): *Lexikon der Mensch-Maschine-Kommunikation.* Munich, Vienna: Oldenbourg.

GEISER, GEORG (1990): *Mensch-Maschine-Kommunikation.* Munich, Vienna: Oldenbourg.

GOERTH, JOACHIM (1982): *Einführung in die Nachrichtentechnik (Teubner-Studienskripten, 91).* Stuttgart: Teubner.

HASEBROOK, JOACHIM (1995): *Multimedia-Psychologie: eine neue Perspektive menschlicher Kommunikation.* Heidelberg, Berlin, Oxford: Spektrum. 1-17.

HENZE, ERNST; HOMUTH, HORST (1974): *Einführung in die Informationstheorie.* Braunschweig: Vieweg.

HERCZEG, MICHAEL (1994): *Software-Ergonomie: Grundlagen der Mensch-Computer-Kommunikation.* Bonn, Paris, Reading (MA): Addison-Wesley.

HERTER, EBERHARD; LÖRCHER, WOLFGANG (1994): *Nachrichtentechnik: Übertragung, Vermittlung und Verarbeitung (Studienbücher der technischen Wissenschaften).* 7th. Edition. Munich, Vienna: Hanser.

HESSELMANN, NORBERT (1983): *Digitale Signalverarbeitung: rechnergestützte Erfassung, Analyse und Weiterverarbeitung analoger Signale.* Würzburg: Vogel.

JOHANNSEN, GUNNAR (1993): *Mensch-Maschine-Systeme.* Boston (MA): Kluwer.

KRESS, DIETER (1977): *Theoretische Grundlagen der Signal- und Informationsübertragung.* Braunschweig: Vieweg.

MITTENECKER, ERICH; RAAB ERICH (1973): *Informationstheorie für Psychologen: Eine Einführung in Methoden und Anwendungen.* Göttingen: Hogrefe.

OBERLIESEN, ROLF (1982): *Information, Daten und Signale: Geschichte technischer Informationsverarbeitung.* Reinbek bei Hamburg: Rowohlt.

SCHÖNRICH, GERHARD (1999): *Semiotik (Reihe: Zur Einführung).* Hamburg: Junius.

UECKERT, H.; RHENIUS, D. (1994): *Komplexe menschliche Informationsverarbeitung.* Bern, Stuttgart: Huber.

WATZLAWICK, PAUL (1969): *Menschliche Kommunikation: Formen, Störungen, Paradoxien.* Munich, Zürich: Piper.

WATZLAWICK, PAUL (1976): *Wie wirklich ist die Wirklichkeit?* 3. Edition. Munich, Zürich: Piper.

WATZLAWICK, PAUL; BEAVIN, J.; JACKSON, D.D.: (1990): *Menschliche Kommunikation.* 8th. Edition. Bern: Huber.

WOSCHNI, EUGEN G. (1988): *Informationstechnik: Signal, System, Information.* 3. Auflage. Berlin: Verlag Technik.

ZEHNDER, CARL A. (1998): *Informationssysteme und Datenbanken (Leitfäden der angewandten Informatik).* 6th. Edition. Stuttgart: Teubner.

5.1.4 Articles in German

HOLZINGER, ANDREAS (1999): Information und Licht: Der Mensch als Informationsverarbeitungssystem. *Wissenschaftliche Nachrichten,* 109, 1/99, 34-39. Vienna: BMUK.

UMSTÄTTER, WALTHER (1998): Über die Messung von Wissen. *Nachrichten für Dokumentation,* 49 (4), 222-224.

ZEMANEK, HEINZ (1973): Philosophie der Informationsverarbeitung. *Nachrichtentechnsiche Zeitschrift (NTZ),* 26 (11), 543 - 560

5.1.5 Journals

IEEE Transactions on Information Theory | ISSN 0018-9448; electronic: 0018-9448 | IEEE Institute of Electrical and Electronics Engineers

Information and Computation | ISSN 0890-5401; electronic: 1090-2651 | Academic Press Inc.

Information and Software Technology | ISSN 0950-5849; electronic: 0950-5849 | Elsevier Science Ltd.

Information Communication and Society | ISSN 1369-118X; electronic: 1369-118X | Taylor & Francis Ltd.

Information Retrieval | ISSN 1386-4564; electronic: 1386-4564; combined: 1386-4564 | Kluwer Academic Publishers Group

Information Society | ISSN 0197-2243; electronic: 1087-6537 | Taylor & Francis Ltd.

Information Systems Journal | ISSN 1350-1917; electronic: 1365-2575 | Blackwell Science Ltd

Information Systems Research | ISSN 1047-7047; electronic: 1047-7047; combined: 1047-7047 | INFORMS Institute for Oprations Research

Information Technology and People | ISSN 0959-3845 | MCB University Press Ltd

International Journal of Cooperative Information Systems | ISSN 0218-8430 | World Scientific Publishing Co.

JIT – Journal of Information Technology | ISSN 0268-3962 | Taylor & Francis Ltd.

Journal of Information Science | ISSN 0165-5515; electronic: 0165-5515; combined: 0165-5515 | World Wide Subscription Service - Bowker Saur

Journal of Information Technology for Teacher Education | ISSN 0962-029X | Triangle Journals Ltd.

Journal of Intelligent Information Systems | ISSN 0925-9902 | Kluwer Academic Publishers

Multimedia Information and Technology | ISSN 1466-190X | Association for Information Management

Multimedia Systems | ISSN: 0942-4962; electronic: 1432-1882) | Springer Verlag KG

Multimedia Tools and Applications | ISSN: 1380-7501 | Kluwer Academic Publishers Group

New Review of Hypermedia and Multimedia – Applications and Research | ISSN: 1361-4568 | Taylor Graham Publishing – Journal Department

Problems of Information Transmission | ISSN 0032-9460 | Plenum Publishing Corporation

5.2 Internet Links

Up-to-date Internet Links for this module can be found on the homepage of this book **www.basiswissen-multimedia.at** (in English and German) under Volume 1: Technology, Module 1: Information and Communication Supplement.

5.3 Examination Questions

Question-Type 1: Yes/No (Dichotomy) :

01	Surprising, rare or new events have small information content.	❐ Yes ❐ No	
02	Information with the probability of “1” has the information content of “0”.	❐ Yes ❐ No	
03	Redundancy always means a loss of information and is therefore undesirable.	❐ Yes ❐ No	
04	The channel capacity is dependent on the information source and the transmission channel.	❐ Yes ❐ No	
05	SHANNON’S Theory of the Communication recognises the importance of the symbols used.	❐ Yes ❐ No	
06	Syntactics describes and analyses the relationships between different symobols.	❐ Yes ❐ No	
07	According to WATZLAWICK, every communication has an aspect of content and an aspect of relationship.	❐ Yes ❐ No	
08	Communication via eMail is assigned to the field of human-machine-human communication.	❐ Yes ❐ No	
09	Human-Machine communication is easier due to the fact that competence in communicating is less importnt.	❐ Yes ❐ No	
10	Software-ergonomics and usability are important fields of research within HCI.	❐ Yes ❐ No	

Question-Type 2: Multiple Choice:

01	In our modern information society ... ❒ a) ... 75 % of employees work with information, not with material. ❒ b) ... 50 % of the production costs are booked to information. ❒ c) ... computer science and information technology are basics. ❒ d) ... we live increasingly in a Society of Knowledge.	
02	Information is ... ❒ a) ... a statement or message that tells something new. ❒ b) ... a space or time variant series of physical signals. ❒ c) ... the same as knowledge – forward looking and probabilistic. ❒ d) ... a modification process that leads to an increase at knowledge.	
03	The information content of a message ... ❒ a) ... according to SHANNON, includes the meaning of the information. ❒ b) ... is smaller the bigger the surprise value. ❒ c) ... with discreet signs, is the result of the entire character set *s*.. ❒ d) ... is dependent on the occurrence probability of the signs.	
04	In the information theory ... ❒ a) ... a higher entropy value means a greater insecurity. ❒ b) ... redundancy means a desired information increase. ❒ c) ... redundancy means an unwanted information reduction. ❒ d) ... redundancy means a decrease in the mean information content.	
05	The channel capacity ... ❒ a) ... is the maximum flow of information *F* transmittable over a channel. ❒ b) ... of an analog telephone is approximately 300 kbps. ❒ c) ... is determined by the bandwidth *B*. ❒ d) ... is independent of the characteristics of the information source.	
06	Semiotics ... ❒ a) ... deals exclusively with human speech. ❒ b) ... examines the relationship between symbols in the sub-division Pragmatics. ❒ c) ... examines symbols and their importance on the semantic level. ❒ d) ... is the basis of research into communication.	
07	According to WATZLAWICK ... ❒ a) ... every form of *relationship* has an influence on human communication. ❒ b) ... every communication has a content and a relationship. ❒ c) ... there is no such thing as an "objective reality". ❒ d) ... a linear transmitter-receiver model is the basis of communication.	
08	HCI ... ❒ a) ... is fundamentally more extensive than other forms of communication. ❒ b) ... deals with usability and software ergonomics. ❒ c) ... handles cognitive processes. ❒ d) ... concentrates on machine intern communication.	

5.4 Answers

Correct answers to Group „Question Type 1":

01 No; 02 Yes; 03 No; 04 No; 05 No; 06 Yes; 07 Yes; 08 Yes; 09 No; 10 Yes;

Correct answers to Group „Question Type 2":

01 a) b) c) d); 02 a) b) d); 03 c) d) ; 04 a) d); 05 a) c) d) 06 c) d); 07 a) b) c); 08 a) b) c)

5.5 Hands-On: Exercises

- Set up a chart showing the theories of SHANNON and WATZLAWICK in tabular form. Which differences do they have? Which characteristics do they share?
- Search for information about the term „Information" in the Web. Compare the different viewpoints and definitions.
- Look around you. Which sources are information in your vicinity? Determine their channel capacities and bandwidths!

5.6 Themes for Debate

- One person takes the role of SHANNON, another the role of WATZLAWICK. Discuss the advantages and disadvantages of your approach. Allow the „public" to ask questions during your debate.
- Discuss the aspects of the information theory and it's application to your language. What would be the result of all characters/symbols being equally necessary, no redundancy.
- Speculate about the future of communication. Which new forms of information and communication will exist in the future and what do the current problems originate.

5.7 Timeline: Information and Communication

800 B.C.: Torch telegraphy as communication method in Greece.

500 B.C.: AISCHYLOS describes Greek fire telegraphy.

490 B.C.: Persia has an organized communication system (Torch telegraphy).

350 B.C.: AENEAS describes a hydraulic synchronous telegraph.

100 A.D.: The Romans have a functioning „Internet", the cursus publicus: Information is sent over distances of up to 300 km (approx. 190 miles) in 24 hours (Relay system).

1450: GUTENBERG: Beginning of the information age.

1665: First periodic news paper in Paris.

1794: Fast communication: Optical telegraphy (CHAPPE Brothers).

1837: COOKE and WHEATSTONE test pin telegraphy.

1844: SAMUEL MORSE develops the morse code for telegraph communication.

1876: GRAHAM BELL receives a patent for speech transmission (Telephone).

1897: MARCONI succeeds in the first radio-telegraphic communication.

1920: The world's first public radio broadcasting in Koenigs-Wusterhausen (Germany).

1935: The world's first regular, public channel service in Berlin.

1941: The world's first program controlled computer from ZUSE (Germany).

1956: First educational Television Programme in Chicago (with final examination).

1962: The first communications satellite TELSTAR I goes into orbit.

1970: Information transmission via optical fiber cables.

1980: Public Picture Transmission Systems (BTX, German for Bildschirm-Text).

1981: Increasing ownership of personal computers (PC's)

1982: Informations system MUPID (Austria).

1983: Start of the first European communications satellite (ECS).

1984: First electronic newspaper.

1985: First video conference.

1990: Begin of the digital car phone.

1992: Multimedia-Systems on CD-ROM.

1995: Exponential growth of the world wide web (WWW) proving as the greatest information system in the history of mankind.

2000: Broad-band satellite communication.

5.8 Glossary

ASCII **A**merican **S**tandard **C**ode for **I**nformation **I**nterchange is the most common format for text files in computers and on the Internet. In an ASCII file, each alphabetic, numeric, or special character is represented with a 7-bit binary number (a string of seven „0" or „1"). 128 possible characters are defined.

Alphabet is a set of letters or other characters with which one or more languages are written esp. if arranged in a customary order, for example: the latin alphabet (ABC), Morse alphabet (wireless transmission), ASCII-Text (Computer text), Flag alphabet (Nautical), sign language (Deaf), Braille alphabet (Blind).

Baud was the prevalent measure for data transmission speed until replaced by a more accurate term: bits per second (bps). One baud is one electronic state change per second. Since a single state change can involve more than a single bit of data, the bps unit of measurement has replaced it as a better expression of data transmission speed. Baud was named after the French engineer, BAUDOT. It was first used to measure the speed of telegraph transmissions.

bit **bi**nary digi**t**, smallest unit in digital technology („0" or „1").

bps **b**its **p**er **s**econd, transmission speed, also: bit/s.

Byte **b**inar**y** digit **e**ight, information unit (1 Byte = 8 bit).

CCITT Comité Consultatif Internationale de Télégraphie et Téléphonie; now also known as the ITU-T (Telecommunication Standardization Sector of the International Telecommunications Union), is the primary international body for fostering cooperative standards for telecommunications equipment and systems. It is located in Geneva (Switzerland).

EDI **E**lectronic **D**ata **I**nterchange.

Entropy originally a term in Thermodynamics. In data communications, the term entropy refers to the relative degree of randomness. The higher the entropy, the more frequent are signalling errors. Entropy is directly proportional to the maximum attainable data speed in bps (bits per second). Entropy is also directly proportional to noise and bandwidth. The entropy in a signal is inversely proportional to compressibility; the greater the entropy, the smaller the factor by which the data can be compressed. Entropy also refers to disorder deliberately added to data in certain encryption processes.

HCI **H**uman-**C**omputer **I**nteraction, sometimes called CHI (Computer-Human Interaction), but the „Human" should come first.

ISO International **S**tandards **O**rganization.

Pragmatics a branch of semiotic that deals with the relation between signs or linguistic expressions and their users.

Redundancy is the part of a message that can be eliminated without loss of essential information („longwindedness"). Used for fail safe operation and error detection.

Semantics is a branch of semiotics dealing with the relations between signs and what they refer to and including theories of denotation, extension, naming, and truth.

Semiotics is the theory of signs and symbols that deals with their function in both artificially constructed and natural languages and comprises syntactics, semantics, and pragmatics.

Sign is a fundamental linguistic unit that designates an object or relation or has a purely syntactic function.

Signal is the physical carrier of information. Signals are physical measurements for example light impulses, voltage alterations, etc. Signals are transmitted always through an energetic process.

Symbol can be an act, sound, or object having cultural significance and the capacity to excite or objectify a response.

Syntactics is a branch of semiotics that deals with the formal relations between signs or expressions in abstraction from their signification and their interpreters.

Unicode is an entirely new idea in setting up binary codes for text or script characters (Unicode Worldwide Character Standard). Refer to ASCII.

Workflow is a term used to describe the tasks, procedural steps, organizations or people involved, required input and output information, and tools needed for each step in a business process (used in EDI-Systems).

Module 2: Signals and Coding

„The recent development of various methods of modulation such as PCM and PPM which exchange bandwidth for signal-to-noise ratio has intensified the interest in a general theory of communication."

Claude E. Shannon on page 1 in his famous work [10]

Learning objectives

Now we know what information and communications is, and are familiar with the basics of the information theory. With this knowledge we can now turn our attention to the actual **physical carriers of information** – the signals. We shall clarify the difference between **analogue** and **digital,** learn about **digital signal processing** to the extent necessary for the study of multi media and investigate for instance the Pulse Code Modulation (PCM), what it is and why this PCM coding is so fundamental.

Analogue/Digital

Digital Signal Processing (DSP)

PCM-Coding

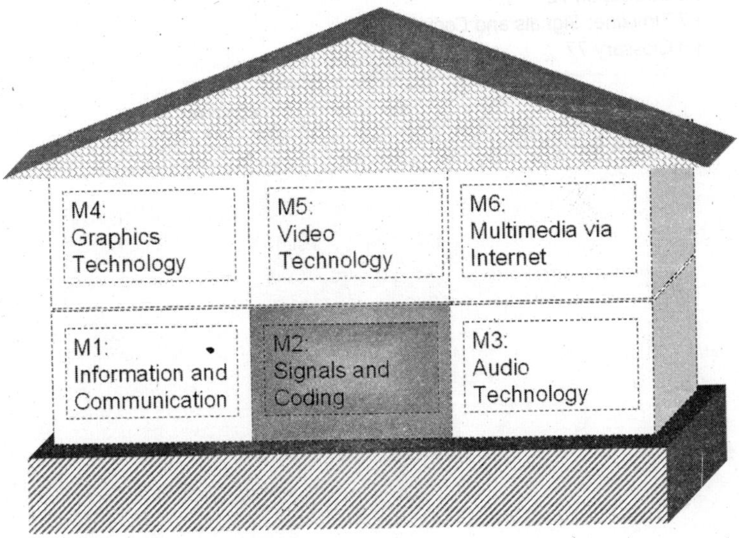

In the last twenty years **digital technology** has achieved an unsuspected victory. Although analogue technology is still important for interfaces, we need only consider sound reproduction; there is hardly a field today, which is not dominated by digital technology.

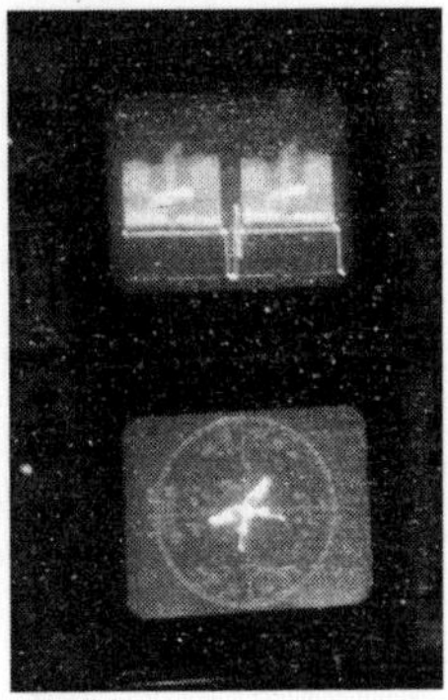

Fig. 2.1 Signals are the physikal carrieres of information (above: Oscilloscope shows a TV-signal, below: Vectorscope, displays the colour signals)

Today, we usually just refer to a computer when we mean a digital computer. Unlike the analogue computer (e.g. operational amplifier, OPA), the digital computer only manipulates digital values, which are displayed by two discrete, strictly distinguishable signals. All programs and data are internally stored in the form of binary signals – either 0 or 1 (code). In principle a digital computer consists of the connection of a number of singular function units (logical gates and Flip-Flops).

> Multimedia Information Systems (MMIS) are based on **digital** computers, however due to the application of *multimedia,* both analogue **and** digital technology in these systems is important.

In order to understand both technologies, the difference between analogue and digital must first be clarified.

A basic knowledge about signals is required to be able to understand the "route" from analogue signals to digital signals.

1 Signals

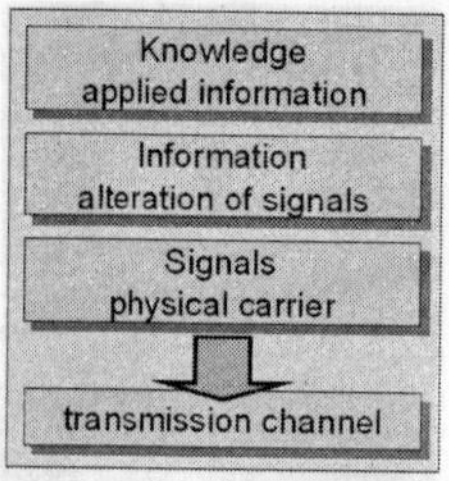

Fig. 2.2 Signals are the carriers of information

In Module 1, we defined the term „Signal" to mean the physical carrier of information. In Multimedia we are dealing with both analogue and digital signals.

Signals contain both information dependent and information independent features.

We call the information dependent features of a signal **„signal parameter"**.

Parameter = characteristic quantity in processes

All signals are dependent on **time** *(t)*, this is an essential quantity in information technology.

The signal, which is uniquely assigned to the information, is named **„desired signal"** – to differentiate from **interference signals** (drop-ins).

Signals can be classified according to their external form. Since this classification can be dependent on both their **signal parameters** (amplitude) and their **time dependence** (time), *four* possible subdivisions result:

continuous = uninterrupted extension in space, time, or sequence; discrete = consisting of distinct or unconnected elements or values: noncontinuous

- continuous amplitude and continuous time („pure" analogue signal),
- discrete amplitude and continuous time (quantized signal),
- continuous amplitude and discrete time (sampled signal),
- discrete amplitude and discrete time (a „pure" digital signal).

An *analogue signal* is a signal, which is **continuously varying, both in time and amplitude.** A *digital signal* is a signal consisting **only of encoded discrete characters.**

The field, which describes what happens during the processing and transmission of signals, is called **system theory** (signals and systems).

For systems and signals you can refer to [W7] and [W8]

A **„system"** consists of a quantity of mutually coupled „Elements". A system responds to applied **input** signals, and its response is described in terms of one or more **output** signals. We determine generally between an anlogue system which is processing continous time signals **(CT System)** and a digital system which is processing discrete time signals **(DT System).**

It must be emphasized here that non-determined (incidental/random) signals are decisive in information technology. The basis for the (mathematical) handling of these signals forms the probability theory.

1.1 Types of Signals

1.1.1 Continuos Amplitude and Continuos Time

If a continuous process (occurance) is displayed over a continuous period, we speak of a „pure" analogue signal.

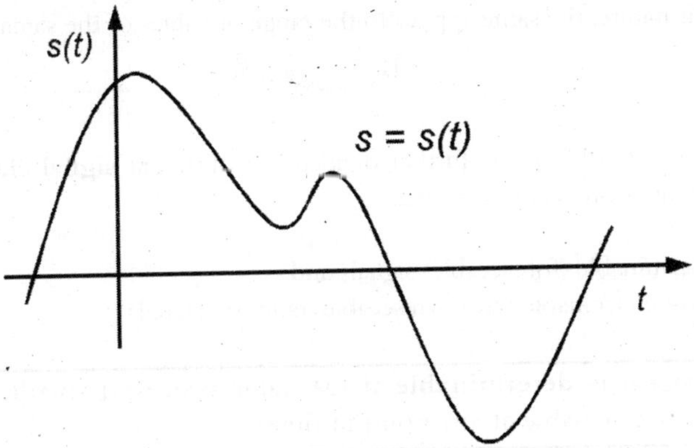

Fig. 2.3 An analogue signal has a continuous *s* over *t*

The term „analogue" = comes from the old-Greek „analogos = meaning proportionate calculation". Signal comes from the latin „signalis = meaning in order to give a sign in a certain way". Since analogue signals are important in multimedia-systems (audio and video), we must study them in more depth.

Generally, analogue signals are represented mathematically:

$$s = s(t)$$

s (any) signal parameter (for example a voltage $v(t)$)
t time

In the signal $s = s(t)$, the time t is the **independent** variable and the amplitude s the **dependent** variable.

The s stands for any signal, s(t) (pronounced „s dependent on t"), and indicates the dependence on the time t.

In information technology (IT) s can be either an electric voltage v(t), an electric current i(t) or a mechanical sound pressure p(t).

s_{max} = Peak Value
$s_{(t1)}$ = Instantaneous Value

The expression s_{max} is called **peak value.** The expression $s(t=t_1)$, or short $s(t_1)$, is called the **instantaneous value** (pronounced: s at the place t_1).

Since signals are virtually always recorded over a limited period, particularly in multimedia systems, the time variable t covers a real interval as a definition domain of the respective signal:

$$t \in [t_0, t_n] \subset \Re$$

Since amplitudes (electric voltage, mechanical pressure etc.) are also limited, by their nature, the same applies to the range of values of the signal:

$$s \in [s_{min}, s_{max}] \subset \Re$$

Analogue signals can be further divided into different **signal classes.** A priority division occurs between:

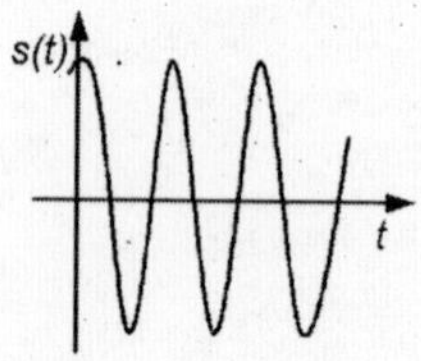

Fig. 2.4 A perodic signal in form of an harmonic sinussoidal

- determinable (foreseeable) signals and
- non-determinable (non-foreseeable, random) signals

A signal is **determinable** if the value process is mathematically calculable at any point in time.

The determinable signals are sub-divided into:

- periodic signals and
- non periodic signals.

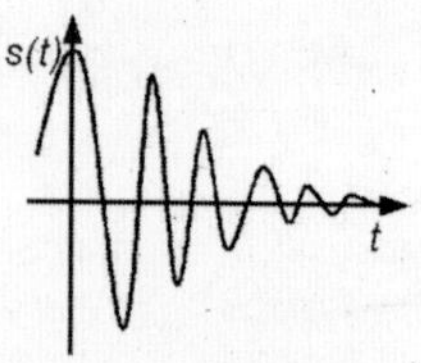

Fig. 2.5 A non periodical signal: transient decay curve

Periodic signals are, for example, harmonious frequencies. The best example being the well-known harmonic (or sinusoidal) oscillation defined by:

$$s(t) = s_{msx} \cdot \sin((\omega t) + \varphi)$$

ω angular frequency ($\omega = 2\pi f$)
φ phase shift (deviation from the origin)

According to JEAN BAPTISTE JOSEPH FOURIER *(1768–1830), periodical signals can be assembled as the sum of harmonic frequencies. A sum of sine- and/or cosine-shaped signal components (in a mathematical line, the so-called Fourier series) to be put together (Fourier factorization).*

Non-periodic signals can be either:

ECG
Elektrocardiogram

- **quasi-periodic** (for example ECG) or
- **transient** (for example a oscillating pendulum, see figure 2.5).

The non-determinable signals are, from the informational theoretical point of view, the most important. Due to their „random behaviour" they have been designated **stochastic.**

Fig. 2.6 Steady state wideband noise

The most common random signal known is called **noise.**

Experimentally, it is possible to make television interference both audible (noise) and visible by unplugging the antenna.

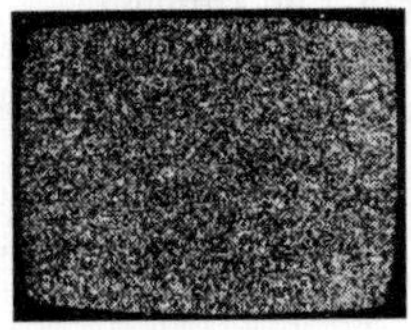

Fig. 2.7 We can make noise visible on a TV screen by unplugging the arial (antenna)

A summary results in the following possibilities:

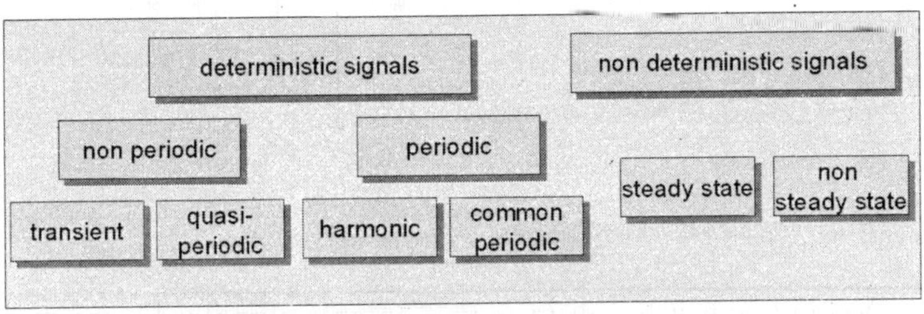

Fig. 2.8 Grouping of different types of signals

1.1.2 Discrete Amplitude and Continuous Time

If, instead of admitting an infinite number of functional values, the signal parameter is divided into a finite quantity of discrete intervals, an analogue symbol can be converted to an amplitude quantized signal.

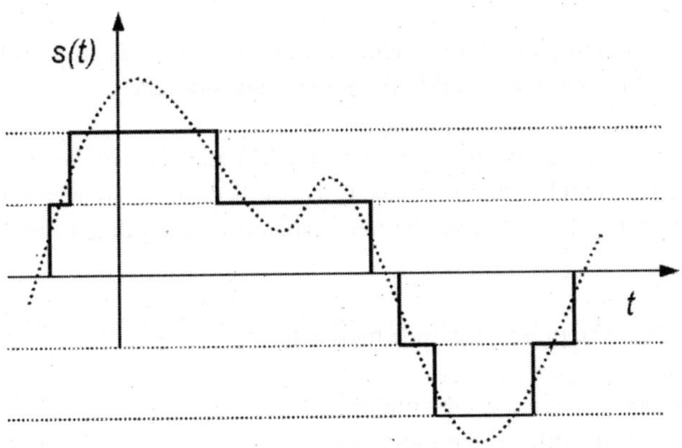

Fig. 2.9 This signal is still continous in time (CT), but discrete in amplitude

The recording level indicator on a magnetic tape recorder is a good example of an practical application of this type of signal.

1.1.3 Continous Amplitude and Discrete Time

When an analogue signal is **sampled** at specific, discrete times we receive a sample signal.

Fig. 2.10 Through sampling at specific discrete times we get a „sampled signal“

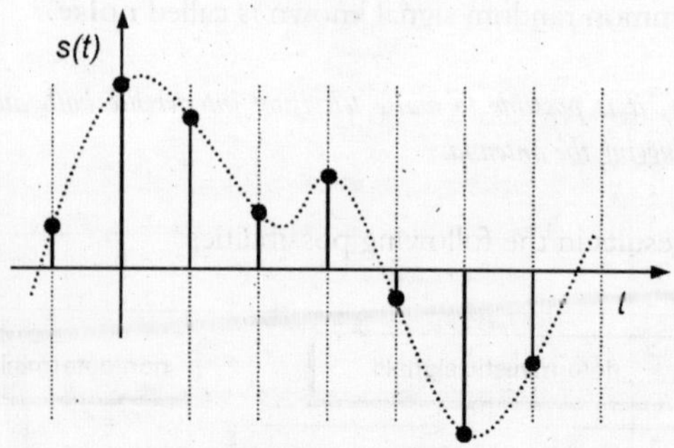

Difficulties arise during the sampling which we will discuss later.

A continuous value, discrete time **sample signal** is known as a **Pulse Amplitude Modulation** (PAM). This signal only occurs as an intermediate stage before coding and is very sensitive to interference.

Mathematically a time truncation occurs, when the analogue signal

$$s = s(t)$$

through sampling at discrete values of time t_1 ... t_n takes amplitude values, that may be continuous within the signal value domain.

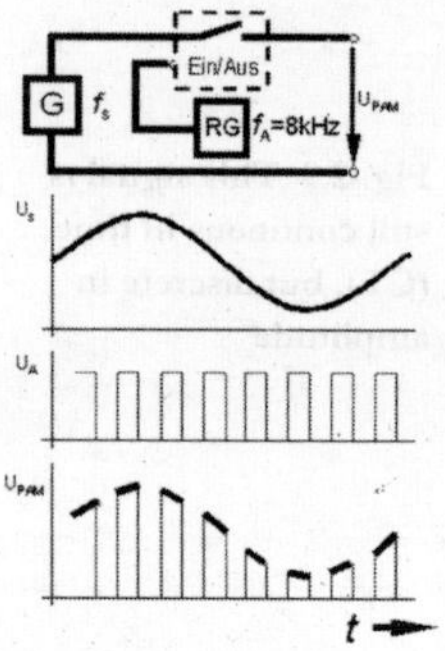

Technically the generation of such a PAM-Signal can be done by an **analogue switch** (circuit breaker) controlled by a square-wave signal generator (fig. 2.11). The switch opens and closes according to the sampling rate f_a.

Fig. 2.11 One possibility for the technological realization of a PAM-signal (refer to text)

Qualities of the pulse amplitude modulation:

- NF signal sources can be multiplexed,
- high bandwidth for the signal necessary,
- interference-prone (Information is in the amplitude).

The pulse amplitude modulation (PAM) serves in practice for another pulse modulation procedure as a preliminary stage.

1.1.4 Discrete Amplitude and Discrete Time

If an analogue signal is sampled, amplitude quantized and encoded in binary form, we receive a („pure“) digital signal.

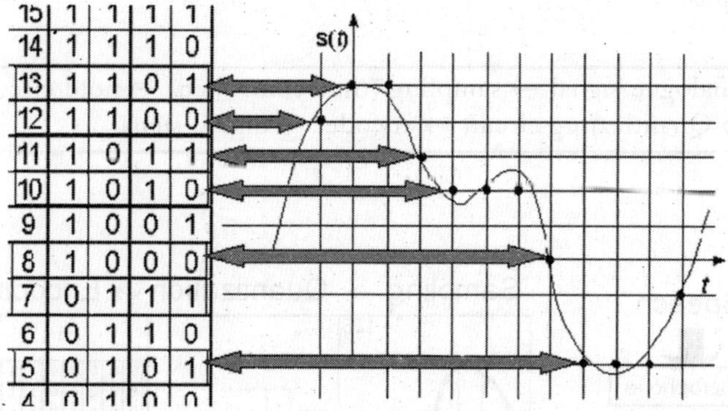

Fig. 2.12 Through encoding of the sampled values into binary data words a „pure“ digital signal is the result

The binary digital technology is based on a **binary logic:** Values are represented through binary digits „0“ and „1“.

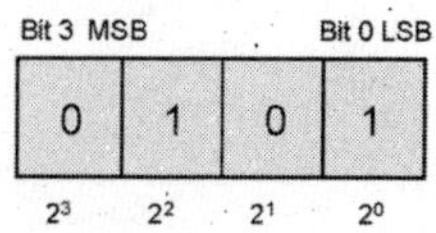

Fig. 2.13 A 4-bit-data word: the most and the least significant bit

In our example the samples are represented by data words with 4 bit word size. In case of limitation to positive integer numbers, the greatest realizable numerical value is given by the following binary digit (binary number) of the word size w in bit:

$$Z_{max} = 2^w - 1$$

In our example (4-bit-data length) the number of the representable characters is $2^4 = 16$, thus the greatest realizable numerical value is $16 - 1 = 15$.

The number of representable characters is 2^w

The possibility to transfer analogue signals into digital signals is generally called **„digitizeability“** and is to be understood as a basic phenomenon of our 21st century („digital age“): digitizing any acustical and optical element into a binary „0/1“ language (with two amplitude values) and thus making the information machine processable.

This „0/1“ language is to be seen as a (maybe as last) common denominator of all media phenomena and is the basis for a total convertibility of all conceivable data and the „convergence“ of the media already existing today and also the basis e. g. for the generation of virtual worlds (see Virtual Reality in module 6).

1.2 Digital Signal Processing (DSP)

For good online sources on DSP refer to [W9] and [W10]

Before analogue signals (for example from a microphone) to be able to be processed in a digital computer, these analogue signals must be turned in a digital signal. This digitalization occurs through sampling, quantization and encoding.

Analogue signal → sampling (time controlled) → hold circuit → Quantizating circuit → encoder → digital signal

---

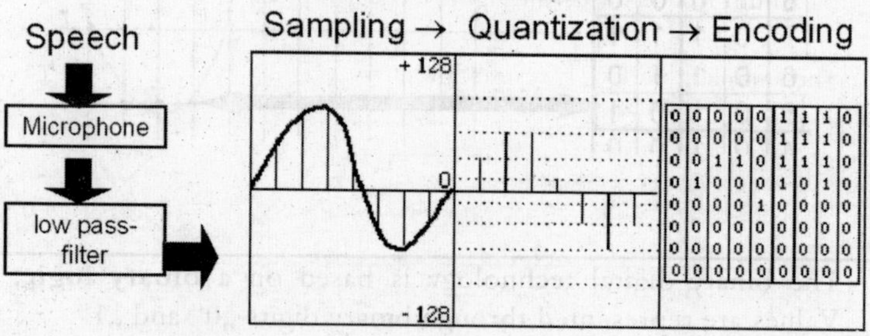

Fig. 2.14 The steps sampling – Quantizating – encoding, for example within an audio aplication

1.3 Sampling and Quantization

The transforming into discrete amplitudes occurs through sampling of the input signal *s(t)* in the time period of $n \times T_s$, near which T_s indicates the distance between two samples.

For example at a sampling rate of 16 kHz this means a respective distance of the next samples of 62,5 ms.

Sampling: „signal samples are taken from the signal in regular time intervals.

The sampled signal exists now only at the sampling spots. Important during the scanning process is, that the sampling theorem is kept by SHANNON.

Quantization: A division of the amplitude range occurs into N range, and every sample is characterized by the number of the range into which it falls.

1.3.1 Sampling Theorem

The sampling theorem of SHANNON states that the sampling rate must be **more than twice as large** as the maximum frequency of the signal to be sampled.

If the highest frequency present in the input signal is f, then in order to be able to reconstruct the signal from its sampled values it must be sampled at a frequency greater than 2f. Shannon and Nyquist

It must be valid therefore:

$$f_a > 2 \cdot f_{max}$$

f_a Sampling frequency
f_{max}: maximum frequency of the signal to be sampled

Thus the sampling period T_s results into:

$$Ts = \frac{1}{2 \cdot f_{max}}$$

If the sampling theorem is not kept, it comes in the signal to unintentional distortions during the scanning, thus also results in a signal corruption (alienation).

These unintentional distortions causes „wrong (alias) frequencies“ and are the cause for image interferences (edges) or audio disturbances (buzz).

false (alias) frequency

Example Music CD: Due to the fact that the maximum audio frequency (Module 3) of the human being is at about 20 kHz, the employed sampling rate must be twice as large - in order to guarantee optimal music quality: 44 100 hertz at 16 bit (= 65 536 possible samples).

1.3.2 Aliasing

When a signal is *under-sampled* (refer to fig. 2.15), the so called **aliasing effect** occurs. This can result in overlapping of the spectrum being repeated periodically, exactly when:

undersampling → aliasing (alienation)

$$f_s < 2 \cdot f_{max}$$

The single discrete time values of the sampled signals can be represented only into data words of finite word size. This means of course that every analogue value can be resolved only with a *finite accuracy* which is combined directly with the data word length. The permissible amplitude range is divided up into a finite number of discrete amplitude ranges.

low pass filter = let low frequencies pass and damps higher frequencies

In practice signals with frequency components are pre-filtered above half of the sampling rate by a **low-pass filter.**

Such a filter has therefore the name **antialiasing-filter,** sometimes also called **presampling-Filter**.

Fig. 2.15 When the sampling rate is too low, the signal is „alienated" what we call aliasing (below)

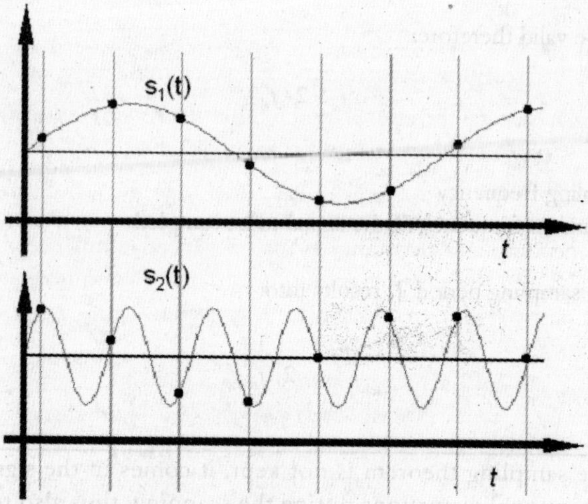

1.3.3 Quantization Noise

Since a signal with continuous amplitude (analogue signal) is factorized during the digitalization into values of a finite value domain, it results inevitable in **rounding errors.**

Since the error magnitudes occurs statistically uniform distributed, they can be interpreted as noise and are called „quantization noise".

Originally the sound impression caused by statistical variations of the air pressure was designated as „noise". Generally every statistical disturbance of signals is designated with the term „noise".

In particular with signals, which are related in an even numbered proportion to the sampling rate, an unpleasant „tonal" noise occurs. The error rate is not anymore stochastic, but it follows the phase locking of the signal.

The frequency chosen for the sampling (the bit number of the digitalization) determines the size of the quantization noise. The higher the bit number, the higher the signal signal-to-noise ratio and the lower the quantization noise.

2 Coding

What is Coding for? Signals and codes are the fundamentals of digital signal processing. Audio and video signals, which are the basis of the multimedia technology, must be processed and encoded. In this chapter we begin by discussing the general basics of encoding. Specific applications (ADPCM, GSM etc.) are dealt with in module 3, chapter 4: „The Representation of audio in Computers" and in module 4, chapter 4: „Compression concept".

Fig. 2.16 Samuel Morse (1791–1872) Pioneer of Coding

Used in everyday speech the term encoding is generally equated with encrypting. In general the term is used to refer to an expression that follows **fixed rules,** (such as Morse Code for example, Fig. 2.16) and the earlier telex tape symbols.

Coding (encoding and decoding) is also a general term in digital signal processing (DSP) and encompasses the concept of compression (refer to module 4, chapter 4).

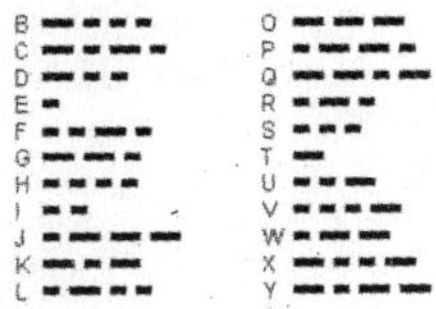

Fig. 2.17 The classic „Morse-Code" is a code with variable word length; the characters are represented by long and short electrical pulses

In computer science, code is the form in which a program is created. In other words it is the setting down of instructions or information in a specific format (a „programming language" such as Fortran, Java, C++ etc.) and known as source code.

However, in communication theory the word coding has a completely different meaning: The sampling at discrete periods, amplitude quantizing and finally encoding of analog signals (from lat. codicillus = „secret letter").

Formally, the term coding is understood to mean the depiction of one language by another. This means: the characters or signs of a (source) alphabet are transposed, one to one, into the signs of another (object) alphabet (e.g. 15 → 1111). In this case the resulting character-string is known as a **word.** The total of all words in the object alphabet are referred to as **code.**

If the code words are all the same size, it is known as a fixed word length code, the alternative, variable length word code, contains adjustable length words (example: Morse Code). Codes with variable word lengths have the advantage that the more common symbols or characters can be given shorter codes, thereby reducing the actual amount of data to transmit.

The DIN 44 300 standard defines the term Coding as follows:

See www.iso.org for the equivalent international standards

> Coding is a regulation for the unambiguous assignment of one character set to another character set.

There are innumerable coding possibilities, for example BCD (Binary Coded Decimals), 8-4-2-1-Code, Aiken Code, Stibitz Code ...

The **PCM Coding** (Pulse Code Modulation) has a basic and increasing importance in the digital transmission technology.

The introduction of wide-area digital networks (ISDN) and digital mobile telephones (cell-phone) have made PCM to the most important value- discret coding method.

The basic advantages of PCM are:

- an almost complete **suppression of interference** is possible due to the exclusive transmission of pulses, (which must not of course have a higher amplitude than the original PCM signal),
- through the use of exclusively digital basic technology the production of PCM circuits is **economical,** and
- the digital output signals are available **directly** for the processing in digital circuits.

As an only disadvantage of PCM the large transmission bandwidth can be mentioned.

Technically four kinds of PCM can be distinguished:

Details of PCM Coding in Module 3 Audio technology

- **Linear PCM** – same quantization intervals, higher resolution, low noise, but however, higher data rate
- **Dynamic PCM** – non constant quantization intervals, with small signals small incremental steps (for example logarithmic)
- **DPCM** (Differential-Pulse-Code-Modulation) – mostly only small changes between the samples, differential coding with less bits, reference points in fixed distances; Problem: blatant alternations of the signal level (slope overload)
- **ADPCM** (Adaptive DPCM) – loophole: foresighted encoding: to provide more bits if required for differences (and to reduce after that again = adaptive)

Principle of the PCM: A PAM-signal (refer to chapter 1.1.3) appertains to the discrete time, but continous amplitude signals: Infinitesimal analogue values exists. Every value is put into an amplitude class by amplitude quantization (discretization).

Since there is a final number of these classes, every class can be expressed through binary numbers (encoded).

If this code now is sent about a transmission channel serially, the receiver needs only to distinguish between exactly two analog values: „0“ and „1“.

Example: Using within a speech channel a sample rate of f_a = 8 kHz there can be taken an analog sample at every 125 ms (every 1/8000 Hz). Using 2^8 (=256) amplitude levels this results in 8-bit data words with a data rate of 8000 1/s × 8 bit = 64 kbps. Since the bandwidths of the available transmission channels are usually larger, the duration of a bit can be chosen smaller. A free period arises from that up to the transfer of the next data word. Within this „time gap“ data words of other channels can be transmitted. The historical interesting PCM-30 system of the European postal administrations (in 1975) for example used 32 channels: Using of 32 channels within a „frame“ of 125 ms, results in a data rate of 8000 1/s × 8 bit × 32 = 2,048 Mbps.

The basic idea of the DPCM format: At a sampling rate of 8 kHz a very „dense“ series of samples stands for disposal, because for f_s = 8 kHz a sampling-distance of T_s = 125 ms results. We assume that the consecutive samples distinguish from each other only insignificantly. The idea now seems obvious that we transmit only the **differences** instead of the whole samples. The differences needs to be transmitted only with a reduced resolution. This leads to the DPCM = difference pulse-code-modulation.

The basic idea of the ADPCM format: Since the statistical qualities of a signal (for example a voice signal) can change continuously, the „profit“ with the DPCM procedure is indeed relatively small. From that the idea to recalculate the predicator coefficients in specific intervals (in short distances of about 10 ms) arose, so that these can „adapt“ to the most current signal in each case. Therefore this technique is called ADPCM = Adaptive Difference Pulse Code Modulation.

During the selection of the correct encoding method it depends very much on the kind of the application. In audio technology (see module 3) for example we are dependend very much onto the subjective hearing-impression of the human being. The contentment of the listeners stands in this case in the foreground. Mathematical calculations are fundamental indeed and helpful, however, but not always very reliable: The voice quality plays for some applications no big role, instead of this, however, a lower data rate.

3 Module Summary

Signals are the physical carriers of information. All signals are time dependend, actually the **time** t is an essential quantity in Multimedia.

Multimedia systems are based on digital computers and work basically with **digital signals,** but processes, however, also **analogue signals** (e. g. audio signals, audio input/microphone and audio output/loudspeaker).

If a continuous function is recorded over a continuous period, we receive an **analogue signal.** If the value range is predeterminable, the signal is *deterministic*. However, **non deterministic** signals are most important for information purposes. Through their non deterministic behaviour they are also called **stochastic.**

If an analogue signal is partitioned in a finite number of discrete intervals, we obtain an **amplitude quantized** signal (for example the recording level indicator at cassette tape recorders).

If an analogue signal is sampled at specific discrete points of time, we obtain a **sampled signal.** This continous amplitude and discrete time signal is called **Pulse Amplitude Modulation (PAM)** and serves as a preliminary stage for other pulse modulation procedures (e. g. in mobile phones).

Only if an analogue signal is sampled **and** is amplitude quantized **and** the samples are encoded, we obtain a „genuine" **digital signal.**

The **sampling theorem** is to be kept in this case: The sample rate must be more than twice as large as the maximum signal frequency must be. If the sampling theorem is not kept, it results in unintentional distortions (for example aliasing).

A **code** is the amount of all words of a target alphabet which are used when mapping from one language to another (simply: substitution of one word by another word)

Encoding is a regulation for the unambiguous assignment of a character set to that of another character set (for example Morse code).

The **PCM-coding** has basic and increasing importance in digital transmission systems (for example mobile multimedia). Through exclusive transfer of impulses an almost complete **noise suppression** is possible.

4 Module Supplement

4.1 Literature

4.1.1 Books in English

ALKIN O. (1994): *Digital Signal Processing: A Laboratory Approach Using PC-DSP.* London: Prentice-Hall.

GLISSON, T. H. (1987): *Introduction to System Analysis (McGraw-Hill series in electrical engineering, networks and systems).* New York: McGraw-Hill.

HAMMING, R. W. (1986): *Coding and Information Theory.* London: Prentice Hall.

OPPENHEIM, ALAN V.; SCHAFER, RONALD W. (1975): *Digital Signal Processing.* London: Prentice Hall.

OPPENHEIM, ALAN V., ED. (1989): *Applications of Digital Signal Processing (Prentice-Hall Signal Processing Series.* Englewood Cliffs (NJ): Prentice-Hall.

OPPENHEIM, ALAN V. ; SCHAFER, RONALD W. (1989): *Discrete-time signal processing.* Englewood Cliffs (NJ): Prentice-Hall.

SOLIMAN, SAMIR S.; SRINATH, MANDYAM D. (1998): *Continous and discrete signals and systems.* 2nd Ed. Upper Saddle River (NJ): Prentice-Hall.

SWETS, JOHN A. (1964): *Signal Detection and Recognition by Human Observers.* New York, London, Sydney: Wiley.

4.1.2 Articles in English

DEL CORSO, D.; C. SANSOE (1999): Exploiting new technology for education: teaching signal integrity in computer science curricula. *Microprocessors and Microsystems,* Volume 23, Issue 5, 25 October 99, 265-279.

HUFFMAN, D. A (1952): A Method for the Construction of Minimum Redundancy Codes. *Proedings of IRE,* No. 40, 1952, 1098–1101.

MASTEN, M. K.; PANAHI, I. (1997): Digital signal processors for modern control systems, *Control Engineering Practice,* Volume 5, Issue 4, April 1997, 449-458.

TESCHER, ANDREW G. (1999): Multimedia is the message. *IEEE Signal Processing Magazine,* Volume 16, Issue 1, January 99, 44-54.

WANG, WENDY X.; BLOSTEIN, STEVEN D. (2001): Video image transmission over mobile satellite channels. *Signal Processing: Image Communication,* Volume 16, Issue 6, February 2001, 531-540.

4.1.3 Books in German

BORUCKI, LORENZ (1977): *Grundlagen der Digitaltechnik (Leitfaden der Elektrotechnik; Bd. 10.* Stuttgart: Teubner.

HERTER, EBERHARD; LÖRCHER, WOLFGANG (1994): *Nachrichtentechnik: Übertragung, Vermittlung und Verarbeitung (Studienbücher der technischen Wissenschaften).* 7. Auflage. München, Wien: Hanser. 164-195.

HESSELMANN, NORBERT (1983): *Digitale Signalverarbeitung: rechnergestützte Erfassung, Analyse und Weiterverarbeitung analoger Signale.* Würzburg: Vogel.

SCHUMNY, HARALD (1978): *Signalübertragung: Lehrbuch der Nachrichtentechnik und Datenfernverarbeitung.* Braunschweig: Vieweg. 132-151.

4.1.4 Articles in German

BAUER, FRIEDRICH L. (1998): Historische Notizen: Zuse, Aiken und der einschrittige Übertrag. *Informatik-Spektrum,* Volume 21, Issue 5, 279-281.

FRANZ, ELKE; PFITZMANN, ANDREAS (1998): Einführung in die Steganographie und Ableitung eines neuen Stegoparadigmas, *Informatik-Spektrum,* 21, 4, 183-193.

ZAISER, W. (1963): Pegelangaben in der Übertragungstechnik. In: *NTZ, Nachrichtentechnische Zeitschrift,* 16, 1963, 137-142 & 461-463.

4.1.5 Journals

Analog Integrated Circuits and Signal Processing | ISSN 0925-1030 | Kluwer

Applied Signal Processing | ISSN 0941-0635 | Springer-Verlag

Digital Signal Processing | ISSN 1051-2004 | Academic Press

IEEE Transactions on Signal Processing | ISSN 1053-587X; electronic:1053-587X | IEEE Institute of Electrical and Electronics Engineers

IEEE Signal Processing Magazine | ISSN 1053-5888; electronic 1053-5888 | IEEE Institute of Electrical and Electronics Engineers

Multidimensional Systems and Signal Processing | ISSN 0923-6082 | Kluwer

Signal Processing | ISSN 0165-1684 | Elsevier

4.2 Internet-Links

Up-to-date Internet Links for this module can be found on the homepage of this book **www.basiswissen-multimedia.at** (in English and German) under Volume 1: Technology, Module 2: Signals and Coding Supplement.

4.3 Exam Questions

Question-Type 1: Yes/No (Dichotomy)

01	A "pure" analogue signal maps continuous functions of events continuously.	❐ Yes ❐ No	
02	In a signal $s. = s(t)$ the time t is the dependent variable and the amplitude s is the independent variable.	❐ Yes ❐ No	
03	A signal is said to be deterministic, when the information content is a maximum.	❐ Yes ❐ No	
04	Deterministic signals are more important for information systems than non-deterministic signals are.	❐ Yes ❐ No	
05	Stationary broadband noise is a stochastic signal and can be factorised according to FOURIER in separate signals.	❐ Yes ❐ No	
06	Pulse amplitude modulation (PAM) is a continuous and time-discrete sampling signal and is sensitive to interferences.	❐ Yes ❐ No	
07	With a digital signal the samples are coded into data words in a "two value" (binary) logic.	❐ Yes ❐ No	
08	The sampling theorem of SHANNON says that the sampling rate must be at least twice as large as the maximum signal frequency.	❐ Yes ❐ No	
09	In case of lower sampling the alias effect occurs, which leads to overlapping in the spectrum.	❐ Yes ❐ No	
10	A great advantage of PCM is that through the exclusive transfer of impulses a good noise suppression is achieved.	❐ Yes ❐ No	

Question-Type 2: Multiple Choice

01	A digital signal ... ❐ a) ... is a discrete amplitude and discrete-time signal. ❐ b) ... consists only of coded, discrete signs. ❐ c) ... is virtually always deterministic. ❐ d) ... has the time t as signal parameter.	
02	Non-deterministic signals ... ❐ a) ... are worthless for communication. ❐ b) ... are called "stochastic" due to their "accidental behaviour". ❐ c) ... are, for example, stationary noise. ❐ d) ... can be represented on data display terminals.	
03	A continuous amplitude, discrete-time sampling signal ... ❐ a) ... is also called a pulse code modulation (PCM). ❐ b) ... is interference-prone because the information is in the amplitude. ❐ c) ... can be implemented simply through an analogue switch. ❐ d) ... is generated by scanning and amplitude quantization.	
04	Possible errors with digital signals arise from ... ❐ a) ... ignoring the sampling theorem. ❐ b) ... under-sampling. ❐ c) ... over-sampling. ❐ d) ... mapping the data words in infinite accuracy.	

05	Coding in information systems occurs mainly ... ❒ a) ... with specific codes, for example by using AIKEN, STIBITZ and so forth. ❒ b) ... with PCM. ❒ c) ... with PAM. ❒ d) ... with PDM.
06	Qualities of the PCM are ... ❒ a) ... almost complete suppression of interference. ❒ b) ... almost complete suppression of peak impulses. ❒ c) ... the use of analogue basic technology. ❒ d) ... that the sampling theorem may be ignored.
07	PCM ... ❒ a) ... is based on a PAM with subsequent coding. ❒ b) ... is the most important discrete amplitude coding technology. ❒ c) ... needs high data rates. ❒ d) ... is applied in many variations.
08	PAM ... ❒ a) ... serves as a practical substitute for PCM. ❒ b) ... is technically difficult to implement. ❒ c) ... only needs small bandwidths. ❒ d) ... is not prone to interference.

4.4 Answers

Correct answers to Group „Question Type 1“:
01 Yes; 02 No; 03 No; 04 No; 05 No; 06 Yes; 07 Yes; 08 No; 09 Yes; 10 Yes;

Correct answers to Group „Question Type 2“:
01 a) b); 02 b) c) d); 03 b) c); 04 a) b) d); 05 b) 06 a); 07 a) b) c) d); 08 a) b) c)

4.5 Exercises

- Compare different coding possibilities. Compare their similarities/ differences and advantages/disadvantages (pros and cons).
- Search for information regarding "coding" on the Internet. Compare different viewpoints and definitions.
- Look around your direct environment: Which devices use analogue signals and which use digital signals?

4.6 Discussion

- Starting from SAMUEL MORSE'S deliberations, discuss the importance and significance of different coding methods.
- Discuss SHANNON'S sampling theory. Look for possibilities for the avoidance of the problem.
- Speculate about the future of signalling technology. What significance will digital signals have in the future? Will we be entirely "immersed" in a digital world?

4.7 Timeline: Signals and Coding

200 B.C.: The Romans employ fire codes as alarm signals.

180 B.C.: POLYBIOS develops a differentiated fire telegraph coding.

1844: MORSE introduces his coding for communication on the Washington-Baltimore telegraph line.

1854: BOURSEUL formulates and describes the technical problems for the transfer of electrical audio signals.

1872: Multiplex procedures according to BAUDOT.

1874: Time-division multiplex method by EDISON'S twofold telegraphy.

1909: Four phone signals on one cable (Phantom circuit).

1925: Picture telegraphy.

1929: First transmission of television signals.

1937: REEVES' (ITT) PCM coding starts the signal transmission revolution.

1945: First electronic digital computer ENIAC at MIT (USA).

1957: Sputnik shock: The interest in digital signal processing increases.

1965: First minicomputer PDP-8 from DEC (Digital Equipment Corporation).

1970: INTELs first microprocessor for digital signal processing.

1971: Optical fiber system with multimode fiber (Glas fiber).

1975: German post begins to use the PCM 30 E system.

1980: Beginning of the digital transmission system in the telephone network.

1981: Circuit-switched digital network (DATEX-P) packet switching in Germany.

1987: Begin with ISDN pilot projects in Germany.

1989: ISDN in 79 German cities.

1992: GSM signal standard for digital mobile phones.

1996: Digital signal transmission for television (HDTV).

2000: Signal transmission over wideband information network.

4.8 Glossary

Aliasing is the generation of a false (alias, distorted) frequency along with the correct one when doing frequency sampling. For images, this produces a jagged edge, or stair-step effect. For sound, it produces a buzz.

Fig. 2.18 After the German physicist Heinrich Hertz the unit of frequency (1/s) is named [W11]

Analogue connotes any continually changing process and is also used to describe a circuit or device designed to handle such analogue signals. The opposite is digital or discrete.

Digital describes technology that generates, stores, and processes data in terms of two states: „0" and „1". Thus, data transmitted or stored with digital technology is expressed as a string of 0's and 1's. Each of these state digits is referred to as a bit.

DSP Digital signal processing is a science and technology relating to the creation, modification and manipulation of signals using digital elements.

Hertz (Hz) named after HEINRICH HERTZ (German physicist); a unit of frequency (of change in state or cycle in a sound wave, alternating current, or other cyclical signal) of one cycle per second (1/s). It replaces the earlier term of „cycle per second (cps)." 1 kHz = 1 000 Hz; 1 MHz = 1 000 kHz etc.

LF Low Frequency (up to 20 kHz)

PAM **P**uls **A**mplitude **M**odulation

PCM **P**uls **C**ode **M**odulation

Quantization a process by which an analogue signal is converted into digital samples of finite precision.

Quantization noise errors through reduction of resolution.

Sample rate frequency at which a signal is sampled. Measured in samples per second.

Signal-to-Noise Ratio (SNR) both in analog and digital communication this is a measure of signal strength relative to background noise (in Audio-technology called "dynamics"). The ratio is usually measured in decibels (dB). If the incoming signal strength in microvolts is V_s, and the noise level, also in microvolts, is V_n, then the SNR in decibels is given by the formula:

$$SNR = 20 \cdot \log \frac{V_s}{V_n}$$

Communications engineers always strive to maximize the SNR. Traditionally, this has been done by using the narrowest possible receiving-system bandwidth consistent with the data speed desired.

stationary A system (signal) is stationary (fixed), when the time variations of the system measures is constant (do not confuse with "static").

stochastic from Greek „stochastikos" guess at, random; involving a random variable, involving chance or probability: probabilistic

Module 3: Audio Technology

„"The idea in my compositions for orchestras
with computers is as follows:
The understanding of music should be a stage
in a psychological journey,
whereby it centres around the question of what music is.
I attempt to experience different relationships."“

TOD MACHOVER at the First European Software Festival 1991 in Munich

Learning Objectives

Now we are familiar with the basics of information and communication and understand signals and coding. Now we turn to the first "interesting" medium in a multimedia system: Audio. We will discover the basics of **psychophysics,** human **hearing** and **audio technology** and review different **audio file formats.**

Hearing

Sound Technology

Audio File Formats

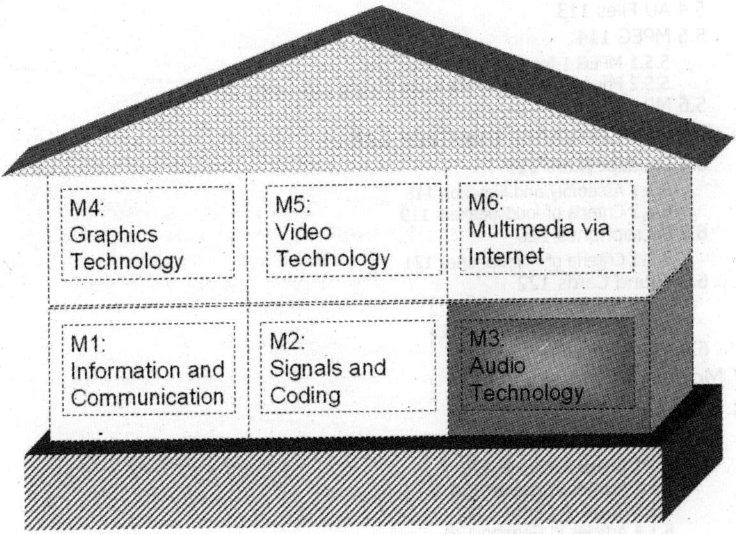

A first essential and technically relatively light to achieve augmentation of multimedia information systems (for example multimedia teaching programs) as opposed to classical information systems (for example hypertext books) is the fabrication of notes, sound effects, noises, and in particular language and music. We refer to this under the title of **audio**.

Fig. 3.1 Audio improves the motivation of computer programmes

For example audio makes it possible, through the inclusion of assorted "auditory backgrounds", to add a specific atmosphere to a screen contents (e.g. dynamic, relaxation etc.). Under special consideration of media specific features these effects can be carried over to multimedia systems.

Fig. 3.2 „Listening to the world"

In order to acquire the best possible understanding of the use of such auditory components, we need, however, a solid grounding in the basics and knowledge of the nature of these phenomena and, of course, knowledge about how humans perceive them. In particular – building on the preceding module 2 "Signals and Coding" – how these can be transformed into bits and bytes and be represented on a digital computer.

Design and Didactics in Volume 3

We review only the technological and psychophysical rudiments of the audio technology here and will extend this knowledge to didactic and software specific design principles in volume 3 "Multimedia Design".

1 Audio Basics

1.1 From Acoustics to Audio Technology

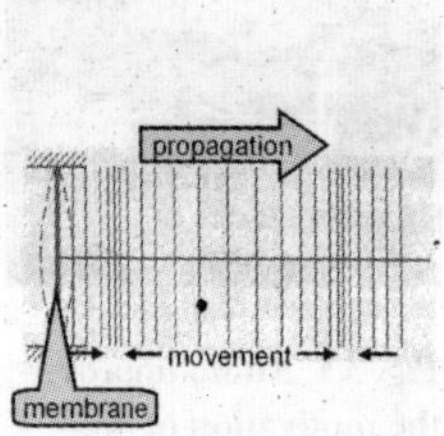

Fig. 3.3 Sound travels as a longitudinal wave

Acoustics is the study of mechanical oscillations (the science of sound). In air sound travels with a speed of approximately 1200 km/p.h. (330 m/s), that is Mach 1 (at sea level).

Sound consists of **mechanical oscillations,** which travel in the form of longitudinal waves (fig 3.3).

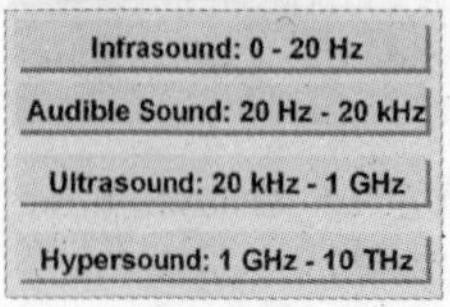

Fig. 3.4 Only audible sound is relevant for Multimedia-Systems

Sound can be sectioned into different frequency ranges (fig 3.4):

Infrasound at 0 ... 20 hertz, audible sound at 20 hertz ... 20 kHz, ultrasound at 20 kHz ... 1 GHz and hypersound at 1 GHz ... 10 THz.

Naturally, only the field of audible sound is important for common multimedia systems, although infrasound could have some effects.

Acoustic signals are pressure wave variations (Effective sound pressure changes) which can spread out in solids, liquids and gases. In a vacuum no audible signals can travel.

Audio (lat. audire = „hearing") is a collective term for all signals in the frequency range of audible sound, as for example noises, chimes, sounds and music. Of course this also includes human language and song. Most multimedia systems employ themedium of audio in the form of music or vocal information.

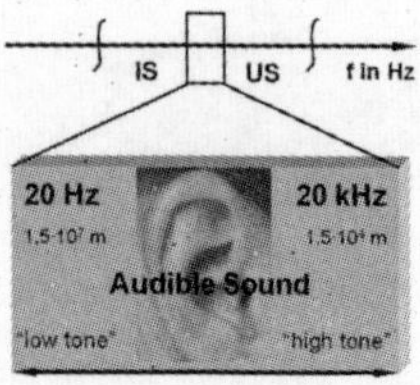

Fig. 3.5 Sound is audible for humans in a range from 20 Hz to 20 kHz. Below is the area of infrasound (IS), above the area of ultrasound (US)

Audio signals are the signals in the audible sound field (fig 3.5) which can be heard by people.

Physically it is a matter of **audible sound** in the Frequency range between approx. 20 Hz to 20,000 Hz (20 kHz).

Audio Technology deals with the processing of audio signals. Important aspects are the fundamentals of acoustics, psychophysics, digital audio and for example the processing of music with MIDI (Music Instrument Digital Interface).

Synthetic and analytical language processing is becoming an increasingly important field.

1.2 Psychophysics

Objective outer world versus subjective inner world

Psychophysics is an inter-disciplinary subarea of perception psychology, which deals with the relationships between the objective (material) world and the subjective (psychological) world. (fig 3.6).

Hereby, it is matter of the connection between physically measurable stimulation (for example effective sound pressure) and the human objective sensation (e.g. sound sensation) and subjective perception (e.g. sound perception).

Humans possess specialized sense organs for different kinds from physical stimulation: for example the ears for **sound stimulation** (audible signals), the eyes for **light stimulation** (optical signals). Each of these sense organs have specialized receptors.

The **receptors** serve as signal transformers and change the physical stimulation (sound, light) into chemical-electric signals (hearing, seeing).

The electric excitation signals are transfered alone nerve strands to the brain. For the each different sense there are **specialized areas** (Brain regions). There the sensations and the resulting perceptions arise first.

The sense organs only serve as **signal transformers.** The sensations arise in the **brain region** which is specialized for the corresponding sense.

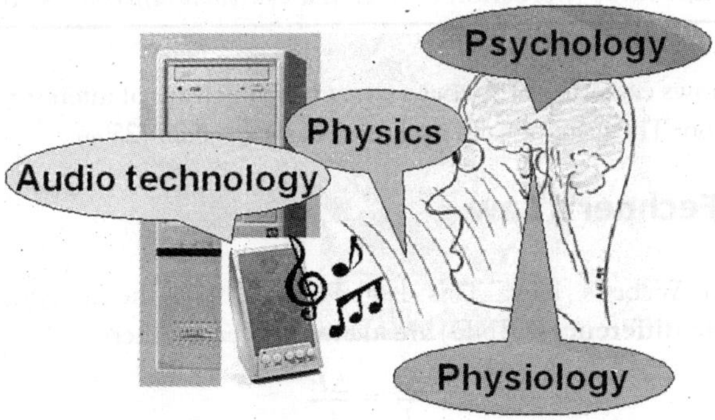

Fig. 3.6 Audio is the cooperation between audio technologie and psychophysics that combines elements of physics, psychology and physiology

The painstaking distinction between stimulation, sensation and perception is important:

stimulus

The physical excitation of a sense organ is **stimulus** and causes a **response.** Every stimulation needs a specific threshold; the sensation level (stimulus threshold), in order to become effective. On exceeding this specific threshold (pain threshold) pain receptors are also stimulated.

sensation

Sensation is a neurophysiological process (Hearing, sight, smell etc.), that is first caused by a stimulation.

perception

Finally, **Perception** is the cognitive recognition of the coordination between feelings as a reflection of the objective-real environment, and self (inner world). Perceptions are dealt with intensely in volume 3 of "Basics Multimedia: Design".

The following three **basic laws of psychophysics** are important:

1.2.1 Weber's Law

Wilhelm Weber (1804–1891)

This law is fundamental and states that a stimulation increase must always be a specific fraction of the initial stimulation:

$$\frac{\Delta I}{I} = c$$

Audio-Frequency (pitch) c = 0,003 (0,3 %)
Audio-Intensity (volume) c = 0,09 (9 %)
Video-Luminosity (brightness) c = 0,016 (1,6 %)

Fig. 3.7 Weber's constants for the sense of hearing and sight

I stimulation intensity
c Weber's Constant

The relative divergence threshold is constant, while the absolute divergence threshold increases with the stimulation intensity: A stimulation must *increase or decrease* by a specific constant value (percentage) so that a *noticeable difference* is "felt".

Fig 3.7 shows examples of Weber's constants which are of interest to us. For comparison: The taste of saline solution has a $c = 0.25$ (25%).

1.2.2 Fechner's Law

Fechner (1860)

Based on Weber's Law: This law assumes that the individual, **just noticeable differences,** (JND) are identical to each other::

$$\frac{\Delta I}{I} = \frac{\Delta E}{E}$$

I Stimulus Intensity
E Strength of Sensation

In this equation we replace Δ through *d*, and receive:

$$\frac{dI}{I} = \frac{dE}{E}$$

An integration of both sides of this equation gives:

$$E = c \cdot \ln(I) + C$$

A squared increase of the stimulus strength (geometrical progression) leads to a linear increase of the strength of sensation (arithmetical progression)

C ... Integration Constant

This is the famous (original) Fechner's law, often also (not quite correctly) called Weber-Fechners Law. It states:

A logarithmic increase of the stimulus strength leads to a linear increase of the strength of sensation.

However, this is not a universal law since it does not apply to extremely small or extremely large stimulus strengths.

1.2.3 Stevens' Law

STEVENS (only 100 years later) went even further than FECHNER:

He does not take divergence thresholds and so determine the sensation strength, instead he measures the sensation directly.

Stevens Law (power law) is therefore universal and describes the correspondence between the strength of stimulus and sensation:

$$E = I^k$$

k Sense Constant
(e. g. Volume *k* = 0,67; Brightness *k* = 0,33)

k-Values are considered as international standards

The k-values are regarded as standard for the organization of work places, where the precise observation of minimum intensity signals fluctuations is important.

The psychological importance of these laws is reviewed more exactly in volume 3, now we return to the actual audio technology.

More details in Volume 3 „Design"

1.3 Audio Technological Fundamentals

1.3.1 Tone

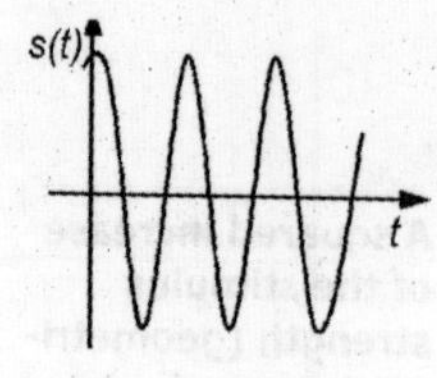

Fig. 3.8 A single harmonious oscillation is called a tone.

ATone can arise through the vibration of a material (e.g. a violin string, a loudspeaker membrane, refer to fig. 3.3), whereby, **air fluctuations** are caused and transferred as longitudinal pressure waves through the air.

With an electro-acoustic sound transformer (Microphone, see chapter 6) these sound pressure changes can be transformed into corresponding electric analog signals and finally into digital signals for multimedia systems.

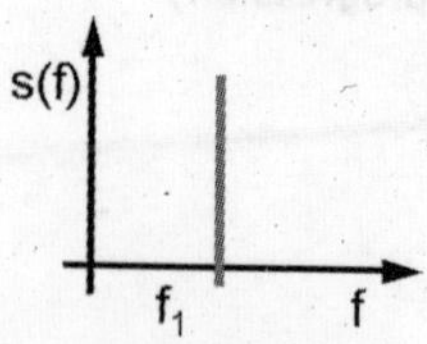

Fig. 3.9 The same tone in the Frequency spectrum: only one Frequency

A Tone is a **harmonious oscillation** of a single audio frequency (see figures 3.8 and 3.9).

The qualities of a tone are the **frequency** (Pitch) and the **amplitude** (Volume).

In music the sum of the keynote (tonic) and the overtones is also called a tone.

Harmonic scale: the scale formed by the series of harmonics of a fundamental note

A tone is not naturally "there" immediately, but requires a certain "build-up" time (fig 3.10) or **transient period**.

The transient period consists of two parts: **Attack**, until the tone reaches its maximum volume, and **Decay**, until the tone has built up to a quasi-fixed state (**Sustain Level**). Also a tone does not die away to the end of the excitation phase immediately, but requires a certain fading time (**Release**):

Fig 3.10 shows the basic time elapsed of a tone amplitude strength.

Fig. 3.10 A tone is not immediately *there* neither does it immediately *cease*: der Amplitude strength time elapse:

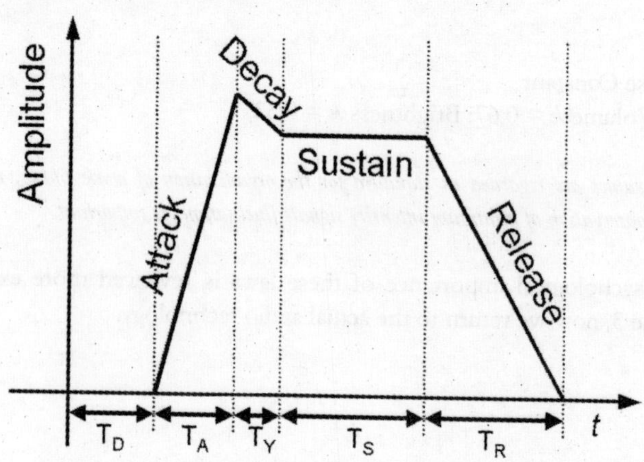

1.3.2 Sound

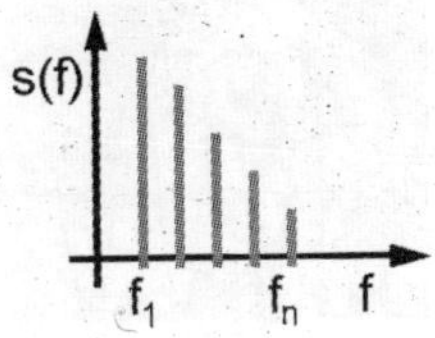

Pure notes *rarely occur naturally*. When we refer to composite oscillations in physics we mean a sound that can be split into a **fundamental oscillation** *and* **harmonic oscillations** (fig 3.11). For the psychophysical sensation of a sound *(from a musical point of view: a note)* the *structure of the overtones* is decisive. For a "noise" the spectrum of intensity is *not linear,* but a broadbanded with a strongly varying amplitude process (fig 3.12), whereas for a "bang" the *spectrum of intensity is broadbanded and constant over a wide frequency range* (fig 3.13).

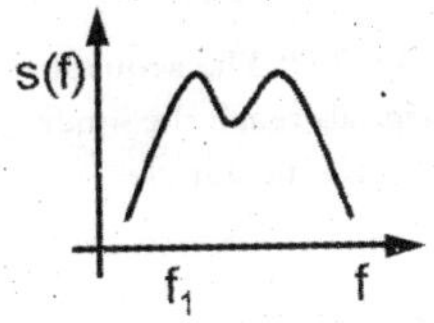

Fig. 3.12 „noise"

1.3.3 Score

We call the fixed sequence of notes, values and timing for music a *score.* This is an important **representation of information** in music, which was introduced around 1650, is also employed in multimedia-applications. The most important components of the score can be seen in fig. 3.14:

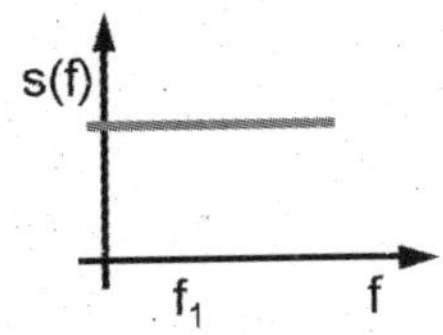

Fig. 3.13 „bang"

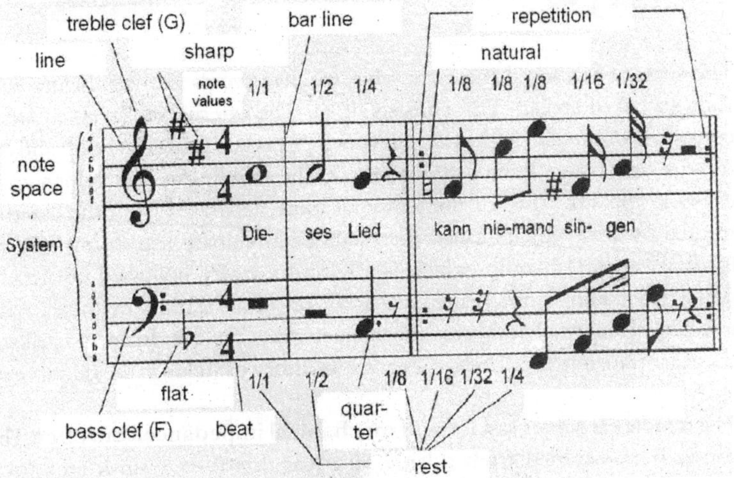

Fig. 3.14 The score, introduced in 1650 is also valid for multimedia systems (Jarz (97), 200)

Fig. 3.15 The score is an important information form

The **scale** is a *fixed sequence of notes within an Interval* (fig 3.16). There are different scales with different numbers of notes and steps. **Harmony** is developed by the *chronological interrelation of individual notes.* Notes sounding after each other are scales, two simultaneous notes are called an **interval** and three notes an **accord**, and the combination of musical notes in chords – harmonic. The **tempo** determines the *rate of the chronological sequence* of notes and also the duration of individual notes. The **beat** determines the numeric relationship between stressed and unstressed timing. The **dynamics** is the volume rating for chronological sequence of single notes. In music, the steps of these dynamics have been given italian terms (from ppp – pianissimo possible, as softly as possible to fff – forte fortissimo, as loud as possible). Note: The interval is the difference of pitch between two musical sounds or notes, either successive (in melody) or simultaneous (in harmony).

Fig. 3.16 Piano Keyboard with the C Major scale. The black keys mark the half-tonés (Veit (96), 37)

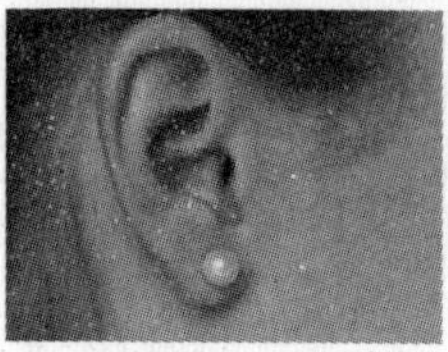

Fig. 3.17 The acoustic signals reach the inner ear via the auricle

Fig. 3.18 From physical reality to psychological perception

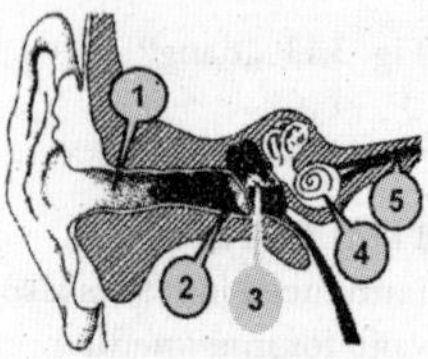

Fig. 3.19 A sectional drawing of the ear (see text)

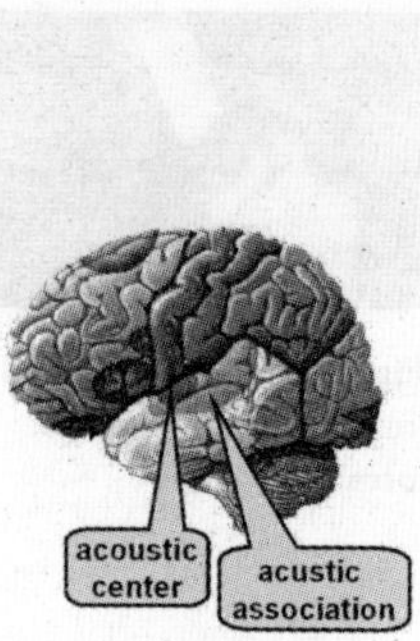

Fig. 3.20 The acoustic centre lies in the upper part of the temporal lobe

2 Our Ear as acoustic Sensor

2.1 Ears and Hearing

Mechanical oscillations are guided via the "acoustical system ear" to so called "hair cells" in the inner ear, converted there into electric signals and then sent on to the corresponding brain area by the auditory nerve.

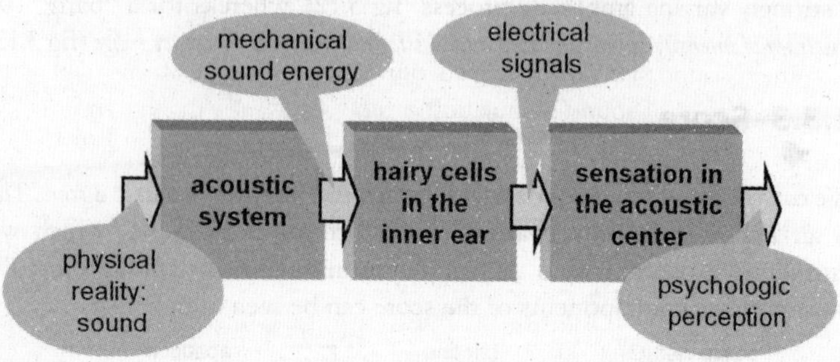

The sensations caused there are what we perceive as hearing. Figure 3.19 shows a cut of an ear: This consists of: (1) The external ear (auris externa), consisting of the pinna (the portion which projects outside the head) and the meatus or passage leading thence to (2) the middle ear, or tympanum, a cavity in the substance of the temporal bone, separated from the external meatus by a membrane called the membrana tympani (ear drum); (3) the internal ear, or labyrinth, which is a complex cavity hollowed out of the bone. The audio signals mainly reach our organ of hearing by the external ear. The effective sound pressure changes cause the **ear drum** to oscillate, these are transmitted to the inner ear by **auditory ossicles** in the middle ear.

The middle ear serves as a form of **mechanical impedance converter**: The sound is transmitted from a large area (ear drum) to a small area (oval window). The lever construction of the auditory ossicles (Hammer, anvil and stirrup) increase the power transmission to the membrane of the oval window. The optimum lies in the range of 1 to 2 kHz.

A "transient wave" arises from these oscillations in the Cochlea, where the hair cells are. The wave causes a mechanical shift **(décollement)** of these cells (in the nm range) activating electric action potential in the fibres of the corresponding auditory nerve.

This nerve signal stimulates the corresponding area in the brain; **the acoustic centre** in the upper part of the temporal lobe (fig 3.20). Here the sense and perception of hearing are first formed (fig. 3.20).

2.2 Psychophysics of Hearing

For the forthcoming design of multimedia-systems the following questions are of interest:

- How sensitive is the ear sense organ really? Can we hear sounds at any level? **sensation**
- How exact is the perception of our hearing organ? How small are the differences in sound stimulation within our range of awareness? **perception**
- Which sound simulation attracts our attention the most? We can sense any number of sound stimulation or only a few? **attention**

To begin with, we review the following **sound qualities**, which are coded by the hair cell for forwarding to the brain via the acoustic nerve:

Remember: Sound is the sensation produced in the organs of hearing when the surrounding air is set in vibration in such a way as to affect these

- Sound frequency (pitch),
- Sound pressure level (SPL),
- Sound intensity (loudness, volume),
- Sound direction (localization),
- Displacement of the acoustic source (distance) and
- Tone quality (Harmonic oscillations, timbre).

2.3 Subjectivity and Selectivity of Perception

The objective (physical) world consists of atoms, molecules and electro-magnetic oscillations. Our perception, however, is subjective. We do not feel atoms or oscillations, but colours, odours or musical notes – entities that in fact do not exist in our external, physical world at all.

objective versus subjective

A specific type of psychological sensation ("feeling") corresponds to each of these physical stimulations and for every type of these stimulations there is a specialized sense organ – such as the ear for acoustic waves.

Sensations ("feelings") do *not* arise in the sense organs, but in the brain. These are dependent on excitation in specific regions of the brain and are not possible if this areas are missing, or the contact to them is broken.

Selectivity is noticeable in as much as that, only when the sound waves lie within a frequency range of approx. 20 Hz to 20 000 Hz is our "awareness" of them activated. The upper-threshold can fall with increasing age down to values from 5 000 Hz (Presbyakusis).

The selectivity of the perception refers also to the strength of stimulus: The stimulation within these quality thresholds must have of course a certain minimum strength so that we become aware of them. On the other hand the simulation may not exceed a certain maximal strengths, however, else we register this as pain (see sound intensity, chapter 2.3.2).

2.3.1 Sound Frequency (Pitch)

The theoretical range of human hearing is approximately 20 Hz to 20 kHz. Equal frequency proportions are registered as equal pitch differences (Example: The frequency ratio 2:1 is experienced as an octave in all frequencies).

The classification of pitch by the human ear is, to a large extent, proportional to the sound frequency.

wow: Fluctuations in pitch in reproduced sound that are sufficiently slow to be heard as such in long notes

The perceptibility threshold from relative pitch fluctuations. is dependent on the frequency and the strength. For instance, this amounts $\pm$ 0,3% of the audio frequency at medium sound turn-off levels.

To scale the sensed pitch, the frequency range of the sound sensed is subdivided logarithmically into **octaves.** Each doubling of the tone frequency is equivalent to an octave step.

The **octave** (in the chromatic scale) is subdivided into twelve tone ranges with constant frequency ratios.

The pitch difference between neigh boring tone intervals amounts to a continuous half-tone step 1: 1.0595 (12th root of 2); for a whole tone step 1:1.1222 (6th root of 2)

Fig. 3.21 The half-tone steps c1 to c2 with concert pitch (to tune instruments)

Ton	c1	cis1	d1	dis1	e1	f1	fis1	g1	gis1	a1	b1	c2
Frequenz Hz]	262	277	294	311	330	349	370	392	415	**440**	466	464

Fig. 3.22 The half-tone steps as musical notes

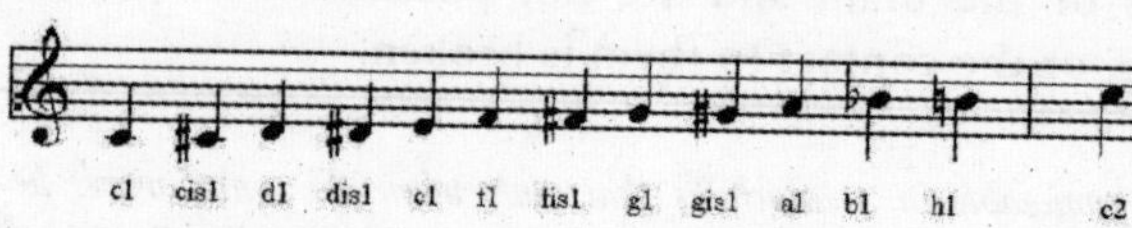

The standard tuning tone **(concert pitch a1)** relevant to tuning musical instruments is f = **440 Hz.**

2.3.2 Sound Pressure Level

Fig. 3.23 „Bel" after Graham Bell (1847–1922): Originally, the "Bel" was named after Alexander Graham Bell (1847–1922); however, as acousticians proved that the subjective power of differentiating sound lay by approximately 1/10 of this value, the dB was introduced

The "pseudo-unit" Decibel **(dB)** was introduced as a useful aid for the handling of **amplifiers** and **attenuators** *(the decrease in amplitude of an electrical signal or current)*. The basic idea being to specify **levels** (ratios) logarithmically rather than directly. The dB values are referred to as levels (fig. 3.23).

Decibel is not a genuine unit, but a reference that the indicated numerical value expresses the decimal logarithm of a ratio. A dB value can however, become a "genuine unit" if a basic value is agreed upon and a physical size is indicated in multiples of this basic value.

The introduction of a logarithm has many advantages: As a rule, signal levels travel over many orders of magnitude (fig 3.24). The logarithmic representation of these values, this frequently wide range of numbers become considerably *simpler to handle*.

The **decibel (dB)** only indicates the **ratio** between two sizes as a **level**, with *no measurement*.
However, given an agreed reference unit, a measurement relevant size can also be stated logarithmically.

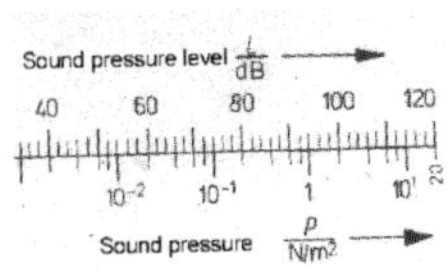

Fig. 3.24 Example of a convertion of sound pressure level using a nomograph (cf. Veit, 96, 30)

Conform with the Weber-Fechner Law (see 1.2.1) the sound pressure level is defined as follows:

$$L_s = 20 \cdot \log\left(\frac{p}{p_0}\right)$$

p_0 Sound pressure reference $2 \cdot 10^{-5}$ Pa
L_s Sound pressure level (SPL) in dB

1 Pascal (Pa) = 1 N/m²

The reference sound pressure of $2 \cdot 10^{-5}$ Pa corresponds to the effective sound pressure of a sine-wave tone with a frequency of 1000 hertz, just within the **human hearing threshold**. This value is called the **audibility threshold.**

From a sound pressure level of approximately 120 dB the sound becomes intolerably loud (pain threshold): Sustained excessive sound pressure levels are damaging to hearing ability.

Through the change over from the unit [Pa] to the pseudo-unit [dB], a relatively good adaptation to non-linear human hearing is possible. None the less, a specific volume measure (sound intensity) was introduced to take into consideration the subjective nature of our sense of loudness (see next page).

2.3.3 Volume Levels (Sound intensity)

Whether we consider a sound is loud or not is, of course, subjective but it is also dependent on the level of sound pressure (as discussed in 2.3.2.) and its frequency spectrum.

Two notes (sinusoidal signals) with the same sound pressure level but different frequencies do not seem equally loud.

The connection between volume and sound pressure level and its relevance to hearing (so-called equal sound level curves) was indicated by FLETCHER & MUNSON in 1933 (fig. 3.25) and internationally introduced in 1961 as an ISO recommendation (DIN 45 630):

Fig. 3.25 Equal sound level curves (Isophone) from Fletcher und Munson (x-axis: Frequency, y-axis: sound pressure level). Veit, 96, 124

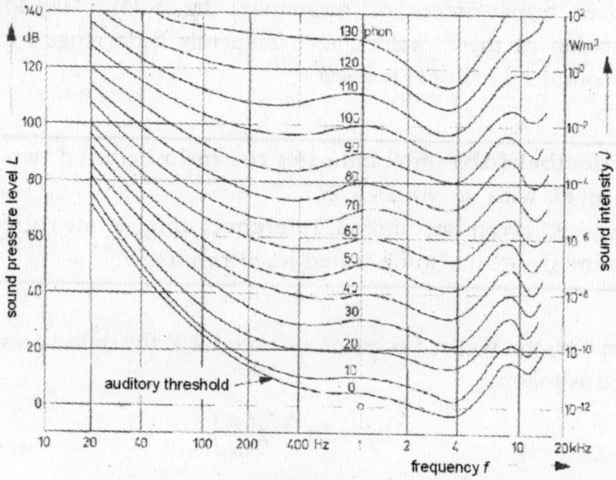

In order to be able to judge these subjective volumes quantitatively, some specific psychophysical sizes were introduced next to the purely physical sizes:

Phon: A unit of loudness level, defined so that the loudness in phons of any sound is numerically equal to the intensity in decibels of a pure 1000 Hz tone judged to be equally loud

Volume levels in Phon

The volume level L_N in **phon** is employed as a measure of the subjective volume , whereby the determination of the volume is ascribed to a subjective comparison with the sound norm of 1 kHz.

The use of the unit phon is an attempt to reproduce the subjective sense of volume. A single curve of the "Curves of Equal Loudness" has a fixed phon value (see fig. 3.25).

40 Phon at 1000Hz = 40 dB; 40 Phon at 50 Hz = 65 dB

For example: a 40 phon tone at a frequency of 1 kHz corresponds to a sound pressure level of 40 dB; however, a 40 phon tone at a frequency of 50 Hz is equivalent to a sound pressure level of 65 dB.

The sound pressure level in dB (Chapter 2.3.2) is physically and uniquely measurable. This is not true in the case of human volume level comparison measurements since this involves subjective mean values of measurements taken from different people. Therefore, electronic filters are installed in sound level meters marked with A, B and C.

The **filter A** is built to correspond to the phon curve.

Modern sound level meters almost always use this filter alone. The volume level measured is given the name **dB(A)**. Values used to indicate volume levels for environmental control or traffic (for specific driving conditions) are also given in dB(A).

The ear's volume range is between 20 µPa (limit of audibility = 0 phons) and 20 Pa (pain threshold = 130 phons). The hearing has the *highest sensitivity* of all sense organs: at the limit of audibility an energy equal to 5 · of 10^{-18} W is sufficient.

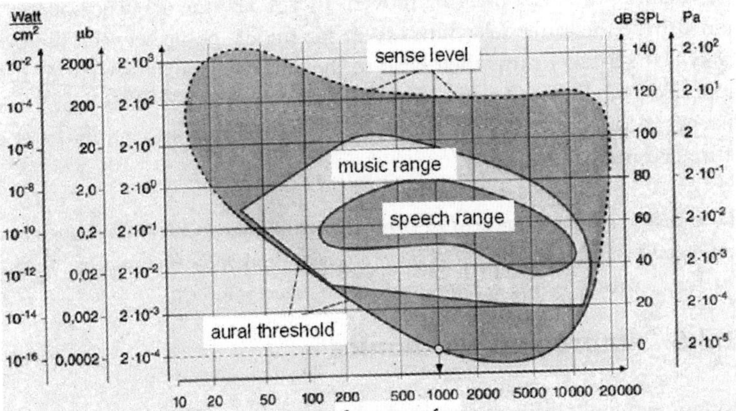

Fig. 3.26 auditory sensor range of people with normal hearing

The sensitivity of the ear is greatest at 3500 Hz.

The sonorousness (loudness) is measured in sone. A sinusoidal wave tone (f = 1kHz) at a sound pressure level of 40 dB was assigned the basic value of 1 sone. A sound felt to be *twice* as loud has a sonorous value of 2 (+10 phon), one four times so loud 4 sone and so on.

The unit sone is of far more importance in acoustic metering technology than in sound studio technology. For example in the results of quality control tests for computer hard disks the noise interference level is often given in sones.

2.3.4 Direction of Sound (Localisation and Distance)

Acoustic figure see Volume 3

Stereophonic hearing is made possible by reverberation, sound absorption, sound shadows, signal times and the directional sensitivity of the exterior ear. In this manner information can also be obtained about the size of the surrounding room the nearness of obstacles. Blind life forms are able to evade obstacles when they hear, self-made, reverberated sounds ("Bat effect").

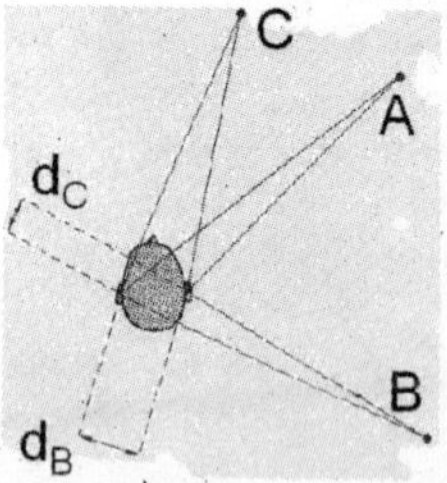

Fig. 3.27 A sound source is localized by differences in delay, volume and echo (explanation in text; Herkner (92), 77)

The source of sounds within a room are only localizable through "stimulation information" **in both ears simultaniously** (binaural hearing).

For example the accuracy of click noises lies at approx. 3° (use of delay times, volume and sound shadows).

In order to determine the *difference in delay times of sound stimulus*, the signals must be compared with each other in the brain. If we compute this time difference, we receive quite amazing results. In order to receive direction information, the head must be moved. In fig. 3.27 the acoustic sources **A** and **B** have the same delay times d_C at the middle point between the ears. Only if the listener turns their head to the left, the acoustic source **A** then appears to be displaced to the side and d_C becomes bigger: This enables the listener to recognise that the source of the sound **A** is, in fact, in front of them and not behind.

These volume differences are used by stereo systems in order to convey the impression of stereophonic sound. The greater the volume difference between the loudspeakers, the closer the sound source appears to be to the side where the noise is loudest.

2.3.5 Timbre and Harmonics

Fortunately sinusoidal notes almost only occur in books about music or psychology, in acoustics labs and sometimes by bad synthesizers ... not however in nature." John R. Pierce, 1989

Sounds not only differentiate in pitch and volume, but also through the amplitudal ratio of harmonic oscillations (overtones) to fundamental oscillation (keynote).

It is only possible to recognize, and differentiate between, musical instruments (Oboe, clarinet) and different peoples voices with the aid of the timbre of sound.

The "character" of a sound results from its harmonic content. Sounds appear bright or even shrill if the high frequency components or partial tones are more strongly apparent than the low frequency ones. Alternatively, if deep partial tones dominate then the tone quality appears to be dull and dark.

3 Human Speech

3.1 Fundamentals

Language is a form of information exchange based on auditory signals. The voice signals are received by the auditory perceptor i.e.: ear and sent to the brain (hearing centre) to be interpreted as a series of signs.

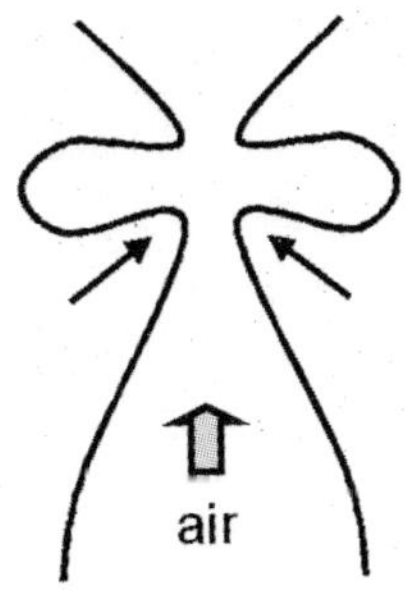

Fig. 3.28 If the vocal cords take through the airstream in frequency vibrate, the voice lips (Arrows) also

Humans have been accustomed to using **language** as a communication media for thousands of years. As an agent of communication the **voice** is directly aligned to our hearing abilities. Similar to a wind instrument (for instance a flute) the voice is also produced in the wind-pipe (trachea). This musculo-membranous tube extends from the larynx to the bronchi, and is surrounded by gristly (or in birds often bony) rings, which convey the air to and from the lungs. The air travels through an aperture (glottis) at the upper part of the windpipe and between the vocal chords, which, by its dilatation and contraction, contributes to the modulation of the voice. The resonance is provided by the throat and the oral and nasal cavities. A large number of muscles make a wide range of vocal variations possible (registers). By changing the form of the tube (fig 3.28) high notes (formants) are added, at almost the same fundamental frequency, causing different sounds, such as vowels, to emerge (fig. 3.29). The muscles for regulating the vocal cords and the **rima glottis** (the passage in the glottis between the vocal chords and the arytenoid cartilages of the larynx) are controlled from the motor-sensitive cortex by signals from the **vagus nerve.** The primary acoustic centres within the motor-sensitive cortex control the secondary areas of the cerebral cortex (Broca speech centre).

see Volume 2 Brain areas

A malfunction of the Brocasche area causes a speech impediment, i spite of intact primary acoustic centres (motoric aphasia). A malfunction of the secondary area of the auditory paths (Wernicke Areal) causes a loss of language comprehension. (sensory aphasia).

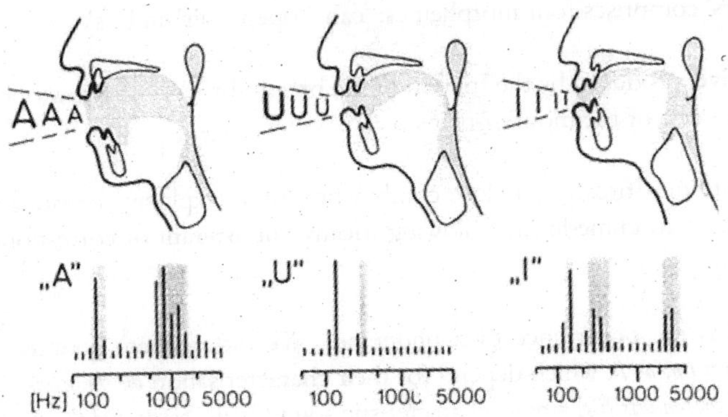

Fig. 3.29 Spoken vowels are differentiated, at almost the same master frequency, through the added high notes (Formanten); Silbernagl & Despopoulus (83), 325

3.2 Vocal Output

Auditory Parameters

The generation of a synthetic language has been achieved with digital computers. The resulting language is understandable but frequently sounds unnatural, which of course it is. Some telephone enquiries are already being answered by these machine languages.

> Intelligibility is a basic requirement, however, sounding natural increases user acceptance.

Before we can begin to concentrate on voice frequency processing, we must clarify some central terms (auditory parameters):

Fundamental frequency is the lowest periodic signal fraction of voiced sounds in the speech signal.

(C. Wernicke *Grundriss der Psychiatrie (1896) II. 126)* The more complicated hallucinations which are conceived by the patient to be 'voices'–verbal auditory hallucinations–are known as phonemes.

Phoneme is a phonological unit of language that cannot be analysed into **smaller linear units** and that in any particular language is realized in non-contrastive variants. Although its exact nature is disputed, and the existence of an abstract phonemic level (and hence the abstract phoneme as a constituent of morphemes) is controversial in phonological theory, the phoneme remains a standard taxonomic unit in the description of speech. The phoneme of structural linguistics is sometimes called the autonomous or taxonomic phoneme by generative phonologists, and distinguished from the systematic phoneme. The (UK) English language differentiates 44 phonemes.

Allophone (or sometimes called phone) is the term for any of the variants It is common practice to write phone symbols between square brackets and phoneme symbols between oblique brackets. Thus [t] and [th] are allophones of the /t/ phoneme.

Morpheme marks the smallest meaningful morphological unit of language, one that cannot be analysed into smaller forms. An expression such as 'can openers' comprises four morphemes: 'can', 'open', '-er' and '-s'.

Fricative, produced by the friction of the breath through a narrow opening between two of the mouth-organs.

Affricate or affricative, a close combination of an explosive consonant or 'stop' with an immediately following fricative or aspirant of corresponding position.

Sound is the occurrence of a phoneme. We differentiate between *voice consonants (m, w, l)*, which depend for their characterisation *on the speaker* and *voiceless consonants (f,s)* whose characteristic sound is *independent of the speaker.*

Sounds are spoken, not phonemes.

A more complete division of sounds is:

- **Vowel** (e.g. a,e,i,o,u (see fig., 3.30) and in some languages y),

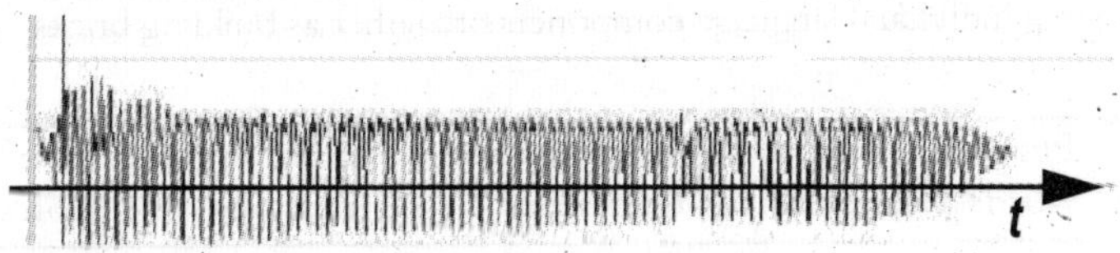

Fig. 3.30 The vowel „a“ display as a signal

- **voiced consonants** (as m in Multi),
- **fricative voiced consonants** (as w in Worm),
- **fricative voiceless consonant** (as s in case),
- **explosive consonant** (as c in cat, or d in don't fig 3.31),

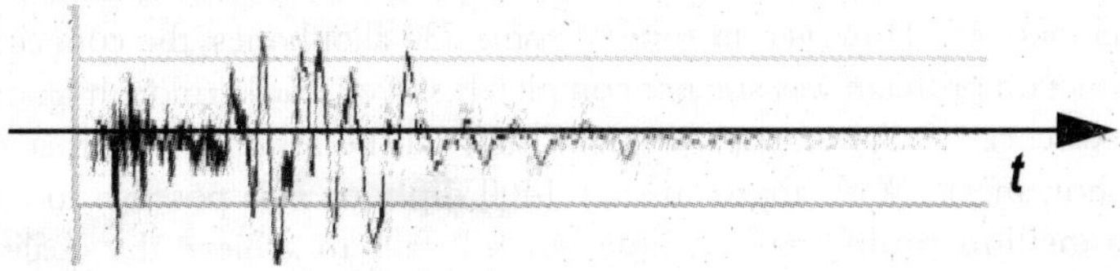

Fig. 3.31 The explosive consonant „k“

- **affricative consonant** (as in the German pf).

Diphthong (or diphon) is the union of two vowels pronounced in one syllable as in week or the combination of a sonantal with a consonantal vowel as in boy. ("ch" and "th" are consonantal diphthongs).

Prosody is the melody of speech, and depends on the semantics of the language; for instance: A question is notable for the "raised" ending of the sentence.

In the theories of FIRT, *prosodies include the class of 'suprasegmental' features such as intonation, stress, and juncture, but also some features which are regarded as 'segmental' in phonemic theory, e.g. palatalization, lip-rounding, nasalization. In volume 3 "Design" we will review the formative parameters to be considered by the representation of voice signals in computers. Here will only deal with the technological aspects.*

Formative parameters for speech signals see Volume 3

We can differentiate between four standard types of voice output for multimedia applications:

- a) reproductive voice rendition,
- b) periodic sound concatination,
- c) sound concatination within a frequency range and
- d) speech synthesis.

a) The simplest procedure is **reproductive voice rendition**. The language elements necessary for the respective multimedia system are simply spoken by a person, recorded, coded (for instance with PCM) and replayed whenever required.

b) Voice output by means of **periodic sound concatination** is achieved by linking individual language components together as building bricks.

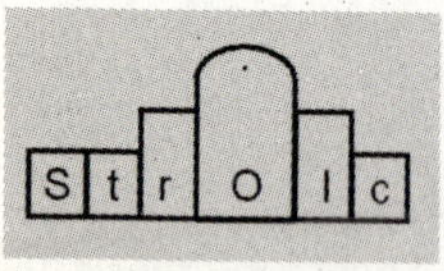

Fig. 3.32 Concantation of single phonemes

Periodic sound concatination attempts to put together sounds, words and sentences from syllables or fractions of syllables.

In the manner, it is possible to make a an almost unlimited vocabulary with only a few phonemes (fig 3.32). However, the connection between the individual phonemes proved problematic. To help solve this problem, the phoneme were put back in to the their natural environment - the allophones. However, in spite of some 230 allophones, the connection or junction problem was still not completely solved, furthermore it ignores the existence of diphonemes (a sound that can be assigned to either of two phonemes). With approximately 1400 **diphons** it is possible to ease the **transition problematic** a little but still fails to achieve the quality of a natural sound (fig 3.33).

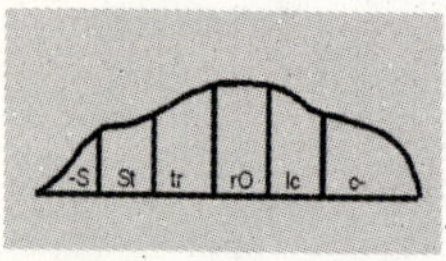

Fig. 3.33 Concantation of diphons

The best voice output quality is achieved when the whole spoken word is saved.

---

c) With voice output by means of **sound concatination within a frequency range** the **formant synthesis** is often used. A **formant** is the partial tone of a sound and a concentration of energy in the voice signal spectrum. Through a synthesis (connection) the human language tract is simulated by electronic filters. Characterizing criteria are the **mean filter frequency** and the filter bandwidth. For the voiced sounds a pulse signal with the language master frequency is chosen. Unvoiced sounds are simulated by a **noise generator**.

Linear Predictive Coding constitutes a further possibility. The human speaking tract is reproduced over a multi polar **lattice filter**. The vocal cords are simulated by a noise generator and a tone generator.

The speaking tract can also be reproduced over a mechanical **thermionic valve model** together with a **digital wave filter**.

d) **Speech synthesis** (fig 3.34) constitutes the possibility of transforming printed text into an audible signal. There are a number of applications in which the vocabulary to be produced must be virtually unlimited. One example being a "reading machine" for the blind. The written text is scanned in followed by a character recognition (OCR) application. The resulting test is converted into language. Since the written original can contain arbitrary text, it is not possible to record this in advance. In this case, the language must be put together from a limited number of **sound elements**, limited by the physiology of the human articulation tract.

OCR, optical character recognition

Speech synthesis in the result of two steps: (fig 3.34):

- First, a translation of the text into a phonetic transcription using a lexicon (via software). Here the user has the possibility of continually expanding and correcting this lexicon.
- Second, the phonetic transcription is converted into an acoustic voice signal (via hardware).

Speech synthesis via Software and Hardware

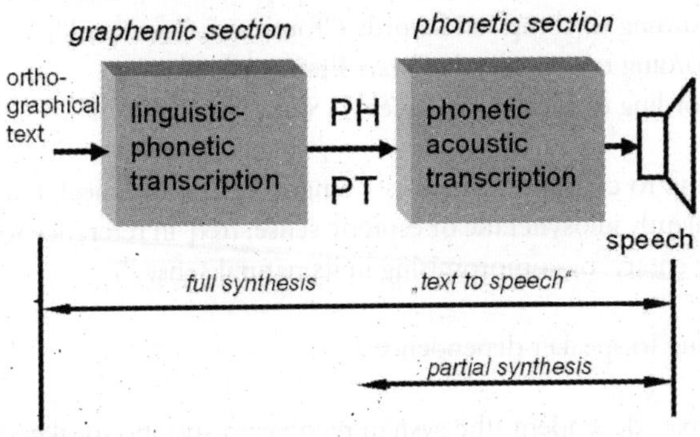

Fig. 3.34 The principle of speech synthesis;

Semantics constitutes a large problem: frequently correct pronunciation can only be insured when additional knowledge is available concerning the full contents of the completed sentence.

3.3 Speech Recognition

Humans can recognise respective speakers and their characteristics very well from hearing a language, even to extracting disturbing background noises. An unconscious correction of recognized grammatical errors and of background noises occurs in the brain.

This is possible because many mistakes due to grammatical and lexical rules are recognizable from the **context.** In a system for voice data entry a considerable expenditure must be invested in order to achieve an acceptable recognition rate.

- Speaker recognition: Speech content is **unimportant**, individual speaker differences are evaluated.
- Speech recognition: Speech content is **important**, speaker variety is complicating.
- Speaker analysis: Speech content is **unimportant**; it is important HOW something is said. (Analysis of the state of mind and the Intention of the speaker).

We are only concerned here with speech recognition. With ASR speech recognition **(automatic speech recognition)** we understand the computer based transformation of spoken language in text.

Speech recognition can be roughly subdivided:

1) into the form (complexity) of the statement:

- a) according to individual words ("stop", "further", "now", ...),
- b) according to compound words ("fourteen", "weekend"),
- c) according to commands ("start Framemaker"),
- d) according to simple sentences ("I want to end Word"),

e) according to complex sentences ("language, in a technical, constructive, or conveniently idiosyncratic or esoteric sense; freq. in reference to language 'unparliamentary' or compromising in its natural sense.")

2) according to speaker dependence:

- a) speaker dependent (the system recognizes specific speakers),
- b) speaker adaptive (the system adapts to new speakers during work),
- c) speaker independent (the system recognizes arbitrary speakers).

3) according to the interference source:

- a) undisturbed (laboratory conditions),
- b) real, normal environmental noises,
- c) high noise level (factory floor, ...).

4) according to the vocabulary extent:

- a) small (up to 100 words),
- b) medium (100 ... 2,000 words),
- c) high (2,000 ... 100,000 words).

A speaker-dependent individual word recognition is easiest to realize with a small vocabulary and a low noise level.

A speaker independent speech recognition of fluid language, with a large vocabulary and a strong interference source is the most difficult.

With speech recognition various mistakes can occur:

- Confusion: The selection of a wrong word from the vocabulary;
- Rejection: A spoken word is not assigned to any word in the vocabulary
- Incorrect recognition: A word not connected with the vocabulary or a background noise lead to a (false) recognition of a word.

Current speech recognition programs work with a learning phase and a working phase:

In the **learning phase** the user speaks the a given vocabulary. Every word is analysed in order to derive parameters from the voice signal representing the word in order to a saving and intensification of the particular features of a word. From the parameters a **attribute vector** is then compiled. Each vector represents a word and is stored as attribute vector data.

Attribute vector in data storage

During the working phase, the speech recognition software determines words and sentences (fig 3.35) from the spoken language.

Fig. 3.35 Working phase of speech recognition

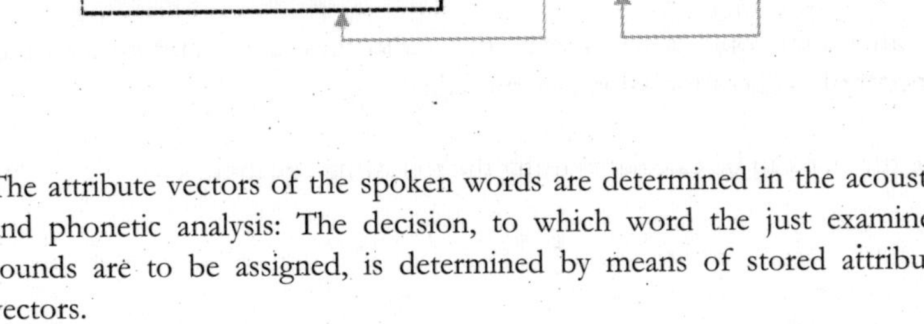

The attribute vectors of the spoken words are determined in the acoustic and phonetic analysis: The decision, to which word the just examined sounds are to be assigned, is determined by means of stored attribute vectors.

Mostly a word can not be determined unambiguously, but only a list of possible words constructed and arranged according to probabilities. The syntactic analysis can eliminate mistakes from the preceding phase and restructure the list of possible words.

syntactical Analysis

Also the semantic analysis helps to eliminate any remaining mistakes. By means of higher priority rules, it influences the syntactic analysis.

semantical Analysis

4 Computer representation of audio

After reviewing the basics of the digital signal processing in module 2 "Signals and Coding", we can now apply our knowledge directly onto the field "Audio" and expand these, first of all, by the field "Coding Audio Signals". Then we will look at the most important audio file formats.

4.1 Raw Sound Data

An analogue, steady and continuous audio signal, made for example, by a musical instrument, can not be directly reproduced in a digital computer directly. The signal must first be sampled, quantized and coded (Module 2).

Three components must be taken into consideration during the digitalization of audio signals:

- Scanning frequency, amplitude, sound channels (mono or stereo).
- For multimedia three standard sampling frequencies can be used:
- 11.025 kHz, 22.05 kHz, 44.1 kHz.

Audio CDs are scanned with 44.1 kHz. This appears at first to be far beyond the human hearing range. However, according to the sampling theory of Shannon and Nyquist (see module 2, 1.3.1) the portable bandwidth is only half the sampling rate.

For Studio quality 48 kHz and for High End DVD 96 kHz are used

With a sampling rate of **44.1 kHz** frequencies of 0 to 22.05 kHz can be registered. This lies very close to the human hearing range (20 Hz – 20 kHz).

An important topic is the size of the audio files and therefore also the concept of data compression (see module 4).

The file size can be calculated using the following equation:

$$F = c \cdot s \cdot t \cdot b$$

F Filesize

c Number of channels (mono c = 1; stereo c = 2)
s sampling rate in Hz
t Time in seconds
b Number of bytes (8 bit = 1 Byte; 16 bit = 2 Byte)

The following picture shows us the most important possibilities used:

Quality	*b*	c	*s* in kHz	*F* (*t*=60s)
Studio	2	4	48,00	23 MB
CD (ISO 10149)	2	2	44,10	10,5 MB
HQ Speech	2	1	44,10	5,25 MB
PC-Quality	1	2	44,10	5,25 MB
MM standard	2	2	22,05	5,25 MB
Low-End-PC	1	2	22,05	2,5 MB
LQ-Quality	1	2	11,00	1,3 MB
LQ Speech	1	1	11,00	650 KB

Fig. 3.36 The high demand on memory space shows the importance of the topic „compression“

Fig. 3.36 shows impressively the increasing size of sound files. Therefore, in spite of continually greater hard disk storage capacity, procedures for the reduction of data are still necessary.

For example:

- Downsampling at 22 kHz or 11 kHz,
- Reduction of the resolution to 1 byte,
- dispense with stereo,
- data compression (e.g. ADPCM, MPEG).

4.2 PCM for digital audio

As discussed in module 2, the Pulse Code Modulation received its name because the analogue audio signal is first chopped up into individual time packets (pulses) and then digitalized. At the time this method was developed magnetic tape was the only economical recording medium available.

Therefore PCM sound program signals were recorded by PAL at a rate of 50 ... 60 images/s and NTSC recorded as audio frames with video tape recorders on normal **video-tape.**

This method was also taken over as PCM-1630-Standard for audio CDs. Also the DAT recording is based on PCM coding. In the PC sector, PCM can be found under WAV file sub format.

Warning: Since PCM recordings can detect and recognise sampling depth and sampling rate, check for the existence of a corresponding transformer by direct data exchange.

ISDN-telephony also use the PCM format. A sampling frequency of 8 kHz and a resolution of 8 bit is used. With these rates one achieves a data rate of 64 kbps or 8 kByte/s for ISDN. With the aforementioned values for sampling rate and resolution a very good articulation can be achieved, however, the data rate necessary is no longer modern.

As already mentioned, a further example of the application of PCM is represented by the WAV Format which is frequently employed in the PC field. Although, in principle, arbitrary sampling rates and bit depths can be stored in WAV format, frequently a sampling rate of 44.1kHz and a resolution of 16 bit is used here. When these possibilities are fully exploited, high-quality photos can be made. The data rate needed and the corresponding memory requirements are, however, considerable: A data rate of 172 kByte/s are needed for a stereo-signal.

4.3 ADPCM for Digital Audio

The reduction of the bit rate with DPCM (see module 2) is disappointing for voice signals. The reason lies with the attributes of a voice signal.

We have studied some voice signals, and discovered that the waveforms can change considerably according to the sound. From this, it is possible to draw the conclusion that a better estimate can be achieved by adjusting to each new waveform as it becomes available.

The recommendation of the CCITT G.721 describes a procedure for the compression of typical 64-kbit/s audio signals (codes in μ-law, a-law or linear) on 32 kbit/s. It is generally known as the Adaptive Differential Pulse Code Modulation (ADPCM).

The procedure with ADPCM is based on the similarity (not equality!) of adjacent signals. It attempted to anticipate future signals on the basis of the previous signal response using predictor coefficients.

Every 20 ms a recalculation of the predictor coefficients occurs

In actual use this adaptation is so carried out that a recalculation of the predicator coefficients is made at short, regular periods of time (of equal length) usually every 20 ms.

Due to the continuous adaptation this coding-procedure received the name Adaptive Difference PCM = ADPCM.

Now the values turn out much better: per sample one can save approx. 4 from 8 bits, or alternatively up to 12 bits per 16 bits. The bit rate for a system with a sampling rate of, for example, 8 kHz and a resolution of 8 bit is reduced to 32 kbps.

Many sound cards support the storing of WAV FILEs in the ADPCM format. If we take as an example a sampling rate of 44.1 kHz and a resolution of 16 bit, we receive a data rate of 43 kByte/s for a stereo signal. Compared to the initial PCM the data rate has been lowered to a quarter. However, the quality of ADPCM is not as good as PCM.

ADPCM Encoder

Basically, the encoder uses the functions of the decoder, in order to "foretell" the signal response. First of all, possible logarithmic input values are transformed into linear input values (uniform PCM). The so "re-quantized" values are then weighted with a corresponding offset (dependent on the implementation of the quantisizer). This offset is used in order to position the uniform PCM values within the quantization strip.

This enables the ADPCM Encoder to **adapt** the pattern of the signal by varying the number of the quantization and/or forecast stages (predictor steps). The output signals are then only transmitted only differences. This is the reason why theses numbers are coded together, within the ADPCM output signal, in order to hold independent implementation of the used quantisizer and predictor compatible.

The corresponding implementation of the quantisizer depends mostly on the input signals to be expected.

A short introduction to the IMA Algorithm follows. Other algorithms are described in the recommendation G.721 or G.723 or described in the CD-I (Compact Disk Interactive Audio Compression Algorithm).

IMA Algorithm:

This algorithm achieves a compression of 4:1. Its Speed results from the simplicity of his predictors.

IMA Interactive Multimedia Association

The forecast value is simply the previous audio sample. Therefore this step is designated **non-adaptive.**

The adaptation first takes place in the quantization block, whereby the three bits of the number of quantization stages of the just quantized signal point, as an index, to a table. The value listed there is subtracted and acts as index in a second table. This is stored for the next iteration.

The value from the second table is then the new number of quantization steps of the next sample. This procedure is completely reversible, and thus no additional information is needed within the resultant bit stream.

Additionally, the ADPCM procedure offers possibilities for Error Recovery: With bit errors within the packed data stream only individual samples within their respective quantization stage are falsified.

ADPCM decoder

The decoder applies, first of all, the Inverse Adaptive Quantizer to the output signal and reconstructs the difference signal. With the aid of the difference signal and the Adaptive Predictor the sample is reconstructed and transferred from the uniform signal to a normal PCM signal.

ADPCM is used also in the digital telephony (ISDN) since it is suitable well for the transfer of language. The compression means are in this case synchronized with the frequency range prevailing with the telephony.

ADPCM is suitable for speech transmission

ADPCM is employed by computer Sun also directly from the audio hardware. Programs employing ADPCM and ADPCM are to be ported also onto other platforms and on contemporary computers without hardware commitment coding and decoding bar.

4.4 GSM-Standard

GSM (Global System for Mobile Communication) is a Europe wide (digital) car telephone standard that makes international **Roaming** ("To roam about in the net") possible.

The GSM norm defines a mean radio frequency of 900 MHz (e.g. D-Network). GSM 1800 (e.g. E-network) is a standard that is based on the GSM standard but lies in the 1,8 GHz in frequency range.

ETSI = European Telecommunications Standards Institute in Nice

In the GSM network different language and date services are integrated which have different standardization levels.

The standards for a pan-european car telephone were summarized in the European Telecommunications Standards Institute GSM 06.10.

GSM is based on digital transfer in **time multiplexing** with eight channels per broadcast carrier, a bandwidth of 200 kbps and a speech coding of 13 kbps.

GSM is a recommendation by the European Telecommunications Standards Institute for language compression and is used, for example, in the telephone D-Network; highly integrated circuits are therefore available. GSM can be only be implemented with a high software expenditure.

The GSM coding procedure is based on the **Linear Prediction Coding**, is mathematically complex and can only be represented in a basis-diagram in a strongly simplified form (See reference for more information; Examples [W18]).

With LPC, *voiced sounds* are described by means of lower resonance frequencies. Individual samples are *linearly dependent* and are predicted, *as a weighted sum*, from former values.

LPC = Linear Prediction Coding

Many sound cards support the storage of WAV files in the GSM format. If we take, as an example, a sampling rate of 44.1 kHz and a resolution of 16 bit, we receive a data rate of 18 kByte/s for a stereo signal.

However, the quality is far worse with GSM than with PCM or ADPCM.

4.5 μ-Law Coding

The μ-law Transformation is an audio compression technology internationally standardised by the CCITT (Comité Consultatif Internationale de Télégraphique et Téléphonique) is their Recommendation G.711 in 1969.

G.711 (CCITT) μ-law and a-law

Assumed is a logarithmic conversion and a transformer resolution of 13 bit that is reduced to 8 bit after the transformation. The transformation itself occurs using the 13-to-8 bit and 8-to-13 bit tables defined in the recommendation.

Through this kind of the transformation, the coding is adapted to the logarithmic hearing properties of the human ear.

A smaller coding resolution corresponds, qualitatively, to the higher quantization resolution.

The transformation can be described mathematically as follows:

$$y = 255 - \ln(1+x) \text{ for every } x = 0$$

$$y = 127 - \ln(1+x) \text{ for every } x < 0$$

x represents a rated (normalised) signal value between 0 and 1. Resulting values are therefore in the 0 ... 255 range.

μ-law-Coding in North America and Japan a-law in Europe

Die μ-law-Coding is used generally in North America and Japan for the transfer with ISDN. There are routes which do not allow a continual transfer of zeros - since the bit rate disappears.

The μ-law-Coding, according to G.711 is employed, for example, in Telecom ISDN Networks in Europe. This uses other 13-to-8 bit convertion tables and values between -128 and 127.

With an ISDN Connection there is only one coding and one decoding so that the limitation of 8 bit at 8 kHz appears less reasonable. Nevertheless the hardware and software manufacturers continue to adhere to it for the following reasons:

- 8-bit-PCM-Codecs are available as highly integrated elements,
- ADPCM is to be integrated into the ISDN,
- Existing hardware and software solutions (digital knots, available hardware, fitted software) can no longer be reconfigured to other data capacities and sampling rates.

μ-law is not suitable for high quality audio

The G.711 format is not, however, suitable for the high-quality audio recording, audio processing and audio transfer.

While no plans are currently known of attempts to change the existing format, a 8/13 compression rate is totally insufficient for such high volume data as music on CD.

However, since it mostly a question of the transfer of speech or data streams, which are limited by the capacity of the available cables, this format is none-the-less often employed (e.g. for coding audio signals for ISDN cables and for the transfer of audio data with H.261 and SMP).

5 Audio File Formats

5.1 Overview

A number of very different audio files formats have been developed, each depending on the available computer systems, however, only a few managed to cross over and only a *very few* are suitable for the internet.

With regard to the transfer of audio files we differentiate between static files stored locally on a personal computer, and streamed files, which are transmitted sequentially (one after the other) but played in real-time, which is particularly important for the internet (see Module 6).

Before we review individual audio file formats in detail, a first glance over of the most important formats, in order to get a first impression:

File names	File extensions	Origins	Pros	Cons
Apple Interchange File Format	.AIFF	Flexible Sampling-Format from Apple	any Sampling-Rate	no tempo- and time information
Sun-Audio	.AU	Sampling-Format from Sun and NeXT	very common with JAVA	extremely big
Music Instrument Digital Interface	.MID .MIDI	for Music on the Computer „Postsckript for Audio"	small and platform independent	synthetical Sound production
Diverse Amiga Formats	.MOD .NST .WOW .FTK .TT	Sampling-Formats from Amiga	many different sound possibilites	not very flexible
MPEG Audio Layer I+II	.MPG .MP2	Moving Pictures Expert Group (ISO + IEC)	good quality	high calculation times
MPEG Audio Layer III	.MP3	Fraunhofer Institute for Integrated Circuits (IIS) Erlangen (Germany)	good Quality in the Internet, psycho-acustical Compression	before replay a decoding is necessary
Real Audio	.RA .RAM .RM	RealNetworks, Seattle, USA	real Streaming	Data can only be reproduced with a player
Wavelet	.WAV	Microsoft sampling format	Standard very common	very big
WMA	.wma	Windows Media Audio	lower bitrate then MP3	Data can only be reproduced with a player

Fig. 3.37 An overview on the most important audio file formats

The two most important audio formats for multimedia in the PC field are Wave and MIDI. They have in common that the sound information is stored in coded form and the replay quality is generally quite good.

However, both formats differ fundamentally in the way that the sound information are coded.

In principle, a Wave file stores the form process of the sound, a MIDI file on the other hand the musical content.

5.2 Wavelet (WAV) Files

The short form WAV, is simultaneously the file extension (filename.wav), and stands for Wavelet ("small wave").

It was initially developed in the eighties by Microsoft and IBM as a binary audio file and can also be used on Apple computers.

Under LINUX a replay is possible with, for instance, the program "playwav".

A WAV file is a "digital copy" of the effective sound pressure at the microphone during the recording, or during the re recording of an audio CD. WAV files can include any sound event and are not limited to music as MIDI files.

The WAV format (actually RIFF WAVE) conforms with the RIFF (Resource Interchange Format) defined by Microsoft for the Windows operating system.

RIFF
Resource
Interchange Format

The RIFF format is a modification of the IFF format, made necessary because the standard was not kept. Other than by IFF, the data are stored in the Little Endian format of the Intel processors. The distribution in chunks corresponds however to the IFF format.

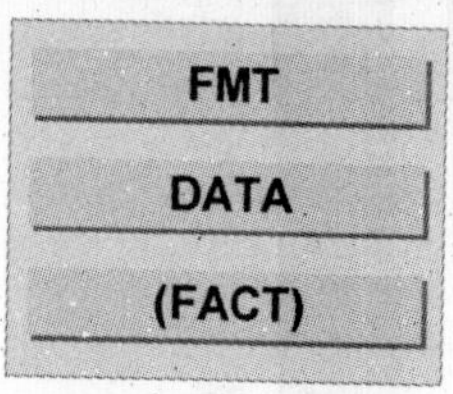

Fig. 3.38 The „chunks" in a WAV file

The uppermost chunk of every RIFF FILE (the chunk which covers the whole file) always carries the identification "RIFF" and the first 4 bytes of the data area show the type of file. WAV files carry the internal identification "Wave".

In general a WAV file is expected to **contain this data, unannotated, in the PCM format**. A Standard WAV format contains, as a rule, two chunks (fig 3.38): A format chunk containing the parameters of the audio data (format type, number of channels; 1 or 2, sampler rate, byte rate, bytes per sample and bits per sample) and a data chunk containing the audio data in PCM format.

If PCM is not used, a FACT chunk contains the information on the recording format employed (fig. 3.38).

5.3 MIDI file format

Before we discuss MIDI, we must define our terms:

- MIDI is a *standardized* data format for the operation and control of electronic music instruments and music effect devices,
- a hardware interface, which conforms to this *standard*,
- a general term for all music which conforms to this standard.

5.3.1 General Information

The music industry has used the MIDI as a standard since 1983. It makes a transfer of coded music signals between computers and electronic music instruments possible.

MIDI
Music
Instrument
Digital
Interface

With this **sequencer technology,** either short analogue sound sequences (for example striking a piano key, plucking a guitar string) are digitalized or digital sounds (with a MIDI instrument) directly created.

A sequencer is an editor for MIDI musical compositions. With this, a MIDI musical composition can be shown as a score or as a MIDI event history and edited. Also the assignment of individual voices to an instrument can be changed and modifications in tone are possible.

MIDI is the most compact representation of music data which a natural reproduction allows.

Strictly speaking we should not use the definition "MIDI is especially for music and computers" but rather "MIDI is for remote control of music instruments" since this is the point which makes the MIDI format special. The "small size" of these files results from this.

MIDI for remote control of music instruments

Instead of the actual samples MIDI uses an instrument related representation.

The coding contains three basic facts:

- the volume,
- the master frequency and
- the name of the instrument.

With MIDI it is possible for the coding to include 10 octaves (128 notes).

When a piano key is pressed on a MIDI instrument, then

- the beginning of the note,
- the typing force and at the release of the key, and
- the end of the note

is transmitted.

As a standard value for the memory space required one can approximate: about 10 minutes of music requires 200 KB of MIDI dat. This order of magnitude is considerably under the 105 MB (!) required for scanning with 44 kHz.

---

piano = 0
trumpet = 56

In the MIDI standard 128 different instruments are defined, whereby in the **General MIDI Standard** a specific number is assigned to every instrument. For example that one is assigned "0" to the piano, the trumpet is addressed with the number "56".

In the MIDI standard 16 channels can be simultaneously active. An instrument needs either one channel (for example a trumpet) or several channels (for example a guitar) according to type. One synthesizer per channel is needed.

5.3.2 Technical MIDI basics

The MIDI Interface is based on the RS 232 C interface with a five point DIN socket. The data transfer occurs in an 8-bit width per MIDI byte with two additional control bits. According to specification, the MIDI interface must have a Universal Asynchronous Receiver Transmitter (UART), with a standardised input is galvanically separated from the entry socket by an optocoupler.

5.3.3 Advantages of MIDI

Some great advantages result, especially for the music field :

pros: multi-platform compatible,
small,
ideal for composing

- MIDI files are multi-platform compatible, this means, they can be employed on different operating systems,
- MIDI files are comparatively small, and
- MIDI corresponds exactly to the classical composing procedure (Recording with notes and creation with different instruments and their particular sound qualities).

5.3.4 Disadvantages of MIDI

Of course there are also some disadvantages:

- Without good instruments no good sound, due to the synthetic sound generation (FM synthesis),
- no language or other noises - as for example with WAV files - possible, and
- MIDI files sound different on different systems, according to devices used, (WAV files also supply the same result).

cons: synthetic sound, no speech, sound different on different systems

5.4 AU Files

The Audio Files with the File ending ". au " were developed in 1986 by the Sun company for Sounds in the operating system of the Sun-3-Computer and are currently used mainly for Java.

Unlike applications Java-Applets make the sounds possible. The output possibilities are limited to sampled sounds, which must be available in AU format, however. A sample places the AU format – from the Sun-System – in format 8 bit mono, sampling rate 8 kHz, m-law-Compression.

Unfortunately, the playback of WAV files, as usually done in Windows, is not currently supported by Java. However, there is a line of freeware and shareware tools for sound processing, with which conversions can be carried out between the different formats (for example: CHRIS CRAIG'S GOLDWAVE).

The output of an AU FILE can occur in two different ways. The first is, **class Applet** makes the *method play* available, with which a sound file can be loaded and played:

- public void play (URL url);
- public void play (URL url, string name);

The parameter can either be the URL of a sound file or the combination of URL directory (path) and file name (see module 6).

Usually one of the Applet methods: **getCodeBase** or **getDocumentBase** is em,ployed to pass the directory-URL:

These supply an URL of the directory from which the Applet was started and/or in which the current HTML-page is:

- public URL getCodeBase();
- public URL getDocumentBase();

The disadvantage of this procedure is that the sound file must be reloaded with every call. In the second variation AudioClip called, which produces an object which can any be played as often as required:

public getAudioClip(URL url, string name);

AudioClip makes the three means available play, loop and stop:

public void play();

public void loop();

public void stop();

Play starts the previously loaded sound file and plays it exactly once. Loop also starts it; plays the sound file, however, in an endless loop until a stop is called. It is also possible to play more than one sound simultaneously. So for example, a background melody can be played, in a loop, over and over again without the output being affected by additional sounds.

5.5 MPEG

MPEG stands for Moving Pictures Expert Group (review module 2 „Signals and Coding"). MPEG defines codec (coder/decoder) standards for audio and video data (for a more detailed overview refer to module 5, chapter 4.2).

The major advantage of MPEG compared to other audio coding formats is that MPEG files are much smaller for the same quality. This is because MPEG uses very sophisticated compression techniques.

5.5.1 MPEG 1 for Audio

We will see in Module 6 a comparison of different file sizes

For CD Audio a digital audio signal with a sampling rate from 44.1 kHz per channel is recorded and stored in 16-bit-samples (packets). The sampling rate is therefore, according to the sampling theorem (cf. module 2, chapter 1.3.1), more than double the audio bandwidth of high-quality audio. This takes more than 1,4 Mbit however, for one seconds time of stereophonic sound.

MPEG audio compression reduces the sound data by approx. factor 12 without noticeably forfeiting the high quality. Compression factors of 24 and more can still achieve a considerably better audio quality than with mere reduction of the bandwidth (for example from 44.1 kHz to 22.05 kHz).

"Perceptual Audio Coding" achieves this, by means of removing inaudible (for human ears) elements.

5.5.2 Principle of the MPEG Audio Coding

The goal of this standard is to take a studio format recording of 1.5 Mbps and reduce this to 384 kbps, while retaining a compact disc quality – at the same time, even lower data rates of 192 kbps to 112 kbps an equally acceptable quality must also be achieved.

Human hearing is more sensitive to acoustic disturbance than human sight is to visual interference, e.g. noise and clicking are more disturbing than the flickering of an image.

Four modes of coding are differentiated:

- **Single Channel Coding** for monosignals,
- **Dual Channel Coding,** for example for coding bilingual monosignals (e.g. dual-channel tone English/German),
- **Stereo Coding** for coding stereo signals whereby both channels are separately coded,
- **Joint Stereo Coding** uses the data redundancy and data irrelevance between the two channels to achieve an even higher compression rate.

The digital input signal is separated into 32 uniform spectral components (frequency groups, tape sections).

Psychoacoustical Reduction of Audio Files through cancellation of irrelevant parts of the signal

This basic principle is equivalent to a sequence of events in human hearing (psychoacoustics). This event sequence is called **"time frequency range conversion"**.

Each spectral component is coded according to the perception (awareness) characteristics of human hearing. The final coding is carried out by one of three defined layers.

Masking – one Signal is "covered" by another signal

Both quantization and coding are implemented with the inclusion of a **masking threshold.**

By using the Fourier-Transform a signal can be transformed into the frequency representation

This masking threshold is computed from the psycho acoustical model, for each component individually, with the aid of the Discrete Fourier Transformation (DFT). The maximum permitted quantization error level, at which coding is still possible, is indicated, in this case – without the risk of this mistake being audible to human hearing.

Fig. 3.39 Function of an MPEG Audio coder

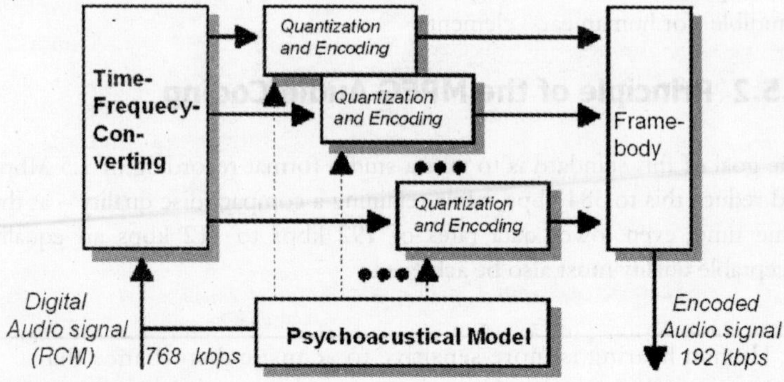

Three layers of the MPEG audio format are differentiated, with which effectiveness and compression rate increase but also complexity and expenditure also increases:

- **Layer I:** ("simple" implementation) 384 sampling points per frame; scaling before quantization; uniform quantization;
- **Layer II:** Frame with 1152 sampling points (24 ms at 48 kHz); uniform quantization corresponding to MUSICAM standard;
- **Layer III:** Frame with 1152 sampling points; modified DCT; non-uniform quantization.

5.6 MP 3

MP 3 is short for MPEG Layer 3 and not – as often stated – of MPEG 3 (there is *not* such format at all)

Audio MPEG layer III (in a word "MP 3") is an audio, format that allows a high compression rate of audio data with a very small loss of quality. The frequency coverage and the audio-frequency signal-to-noise ratio are maintained.

Possible losses are hardly audible even on "good" HiFi systems, presupposing that the files were corresponding well constructed originally.

The compression procedure is based on the elemental removal of all "inaudible" audio information. Many notes are overlaid by others; other notes are not notably hear-able at all, since they lie outside a specific frequency range.

The differences of the packed data to the original data are, however, disappearingly small and the amount of data economy enormous:

Stereo music can be reduced by up to a factor of 1 to 12.

This high compression offers many new possibilities. It is very simple to archive large amounts of music data – for example approx. 11 albums fit onto a single CD!

One Minute Music in MP-3-Format needs only approx. 1 MB memory – with CD-Quality

MP-3 files can be transmitted over the Internet considerably more rapidly, and therefore also at a lower cost, than, for example, the widespread, but many times larger, WAV files (see module 6).

This format was originally developed by the Fraunhofer-Gesellschaft (FHG) in Germany as a compression procedure for audio channels on Video CDs - similar to the American format AC-3.

Fig. 3.40 An Example for a MP-3-Player [W24]

A further advantage of the MP-3 format is that it is, what is known as a "Headerless File Format". MP-3 files do actually have a header but this is not absolutely necessary in order to play the file. The result of this is that any section out of the file, beginning, end or middle, can be extracted and played. This makes streaming of the MP-3 file possible (see module 6).

MP-3 files can be played with the Windows Media-Player, QuickTime from Apple and innumerable tools, shareware and freeware programs.

With mobile MP-3 players (about the same size as a cigarette packet), MP3 files can also be played on the move. Since MP 3 (currently) contains no copy protection mechanisms for this format, it is still very controversial in the music industry.

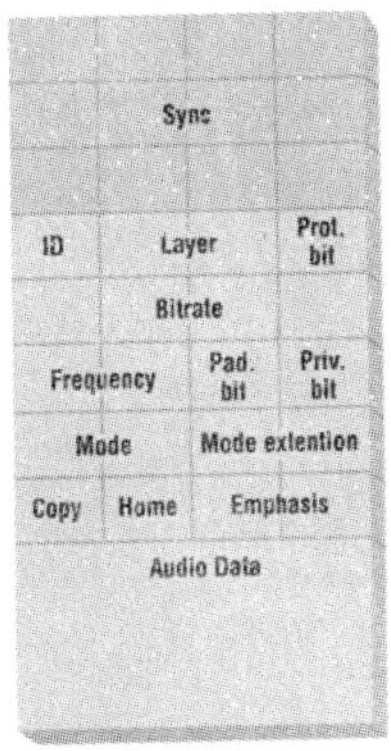

Fig. 3.41 Der Aufbau eines MP-3-Files [W25], [W26]

MP-3 employs an MDCT (Modified Discreet Cosine Transformation) on the output of the filter banks, which increases the resolution. As opposed to former procedures this results in the following advantages:

- Aliasing effects of the filter bank can be calculated out;
- The scale factors are combined in tapes (a tape contains several MDCT coefficients and has, approximately, the bandwidth of the human hearing range); and
- The quantization noise is reduced strongly.

The composition of a MP-3 file is shown in fig. 3.41 : The header is 4 bytes (32 bit) large and begins with "sync", which is followed by an ID bit (0 = MPEG-2 and 1 = MPEG-1).

6 Human-Computer Interface

In order to record, process and replay audio signals with a computer one needs, apart from a computer, a sound card ("audio adapter"), loudspeaker, microphone and where appropriate a compact disk drive (CD-ROM drive), plus, of course, the necessary software to control these hardware items. Fundamentally, audio signals can be displayed with the aid of a digital computer in four different ways:

- via digital-analogue conversion – the signals are already stored as a digital audio (on the hard disk),
- via synthesizers – the information from a MIDI file is sent to the sound cards synthesizer where they are executed,
- via the MIDI interface itself – the information from a MIDI file is transmitted to an external synthesizer, or
- sent via a CD-ROM disk drive.

The Sound card loudspeaker system virtually incorporates the interface between the human being and the computer. Therefore these human aspects must also be considered in the technological parameters.

Since the sound card and the loudspeakers form a unit, the quality of the overall system is determined by the worse of the two components.

Even the continuous advance of the technical components of these systems cannot ignore the existence of lasting **basic principles,** which we review in the following sections.

6.1 Loudspeakers

Piezo-buzzers were built-in to the first PCs and later mini loudspeakers that could send audible signals. At this time audio was still not a topic for personal computers, and the audible output was limited to attention-getting beep-codes for error recognition.

6.1.1 Assembly and Function

Loudspeakers basically are **electro-acoustic transformers,** which convert low-frequency electrical oscillations into audible mechanical oscillations.

In most loudspeakers the sound is made by a vibrating membrane or calotte and reaches the human ear via the intervening air.

6.1.2 Criteria of loudspeakers

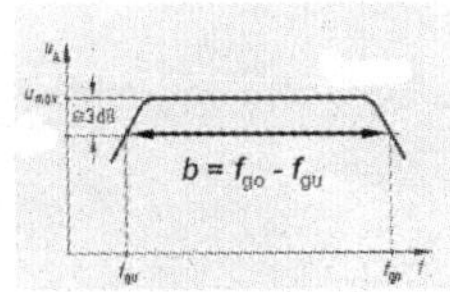

Fig. 3.42 The frequency response diagram. The bandwidth b identifies – as the difference of the upper limit frequency f_{go} and lower frequency f_{gu} – the transmission range

The **frequency response diagram** (fig. 3.42) indicates volume levels, with different frequencies and unchanging power.

The frequency response is experimentally picked up as follows: A tone generator feeds the appropriate speaker box, and a standard microphone records the volume levels with the respective frequencies. An ideal speaker box would have an almost linear frequency diagram with the lowest possible frequency under the limit and the highest possible frequency above the limit.

Actually, however, the human ear only notices variations of more than 3 dB, so that smaller deviations can be neglected.

The **Distortion Factor** is the difference between the fundamental oscillation and the harmonic oscillations. When a loudspeaker is provided with a sound signal, it should emit exactly this sound signal (in which case the distortion factor would be 0%). However, in practice unwanted harmonic oscillations are radiated. The strongest harmonic oscillations generally lay around two to three times the master frequency. According to the old HiFi standard DIN 45 500 (German industry standards) the distortion factor should not exceed 1%.

The **Efficiency** of a loudspeaker indicates the volume emitted by a specified power and is measured in dB W/m. Standard HiFi boxes have an efficacy of 86 ... 90 dB W/m. It is a matter of a relatively low efficacy. Sensitive HiFi boxes have an efficacy between 90 ... 95 dB W/m.

Fundamentally, the **Sound Performance Power** says nothing about the replay quality of a loudspeaker. It only becomes important when a little amplifier output power is available or the sound is to be heard throughout very large rooms.

Ohm = after Georg Simon Ohm (1867) the practical meter-kilogram-second unit of electric resistance equal to the resistance of a circuit in which a potential difference of one volt produces a current of one ampere

The **internal resistance** of a loudspeaker with alternating current (AC) is referred to as **Impedance;** it is measured in ohm, and must not be confused with the direct current (DC) resistance which can be measured with a multimeter and lies usually around 20% below the AC resistance.

Therefore: a box with an indicated impedance (AC resistance) of 4 ohm displays a DC resistance of 3,2 ohm.

In practice, it can be noted that the impedance of a loudspeaker changes considerably with increasing frequency.

Note: The impedance of boxes used must never be smaller than the minimum impedance of the amplifier used.

For example a 4-ohm speaker box should never be connected to an 8-ohm amplifier output. If the impedance of a box should be higher than the indicated impedance of the amplifier then, as a rule, only the output power of the amplifier is only reduced insignificantly.

The **Sinusoidal Load** is the sustained "strength" of a loudspeaker. It is tested by loading the system, for 48 hours, with an unchanging signal. According to DIN 45 573 this test should be completed without damage.

The term **Music Load** refers to the short-term "strength" of a loudspeaker, (for example 2 seconds long), without resulting in audible distortions or damage.

Elements can be found in every music signal, which either represent a short-term, very high stress (for example drum music). The **Pulse Load** of a loudspeaker mostly refers to a 10 millisecond long impulse.

The **positioning** of the boxes is important, the higher tones should be positioned at approximately ear height of the listener, and the box be tilted in the direction of the listeners' ears.

6.2 Microphones

Dynamic Microphones work according to the moving coil principle (dynamo). A membrane, which can be affected (set vibrating) by acoustic waves, is combined with a coil. This coil is immersed in the ring-shaped magnetic field of a strong permanent magnet. When the coil is moved by the acoustic waves in the magnetic field an alternating voltage is induced in the coil.

The alternating voltage is an exact "image" of the acoustic waves. Through suitable construction, it is possible to produce dynamic microphones with a relatively regular sensitivity in the entire audible frequency range. Qualitatively high-quality dynamic microphones are suitable for music recordings.

In **Electroide Microphones,** the membrane, together with the counter electrode, forms a permanently loaded condenser. Under the influence of an acoustic wave the membrane is bent, which alters the capacity of the microphone.

Because the microphone output must not be strongly loaded, an amplifier, switched to function as an impedance transformer, is installed into the microphone. Electrode microphones are employed as lapel microphones and as built-in microphones because of their small size.

Condenser Microphones (capacitive) function according to a similar principle as electroide microphones, are, however, considerably more complex. Condenser microphones are used as high-quality studio microphones.

Microphones are often installed directly into VDUs

6.2.1 Criteria of microphones

Microphones convert mechanical sound pressure fluctuations into analogue audio signals. Criteria are:

Sensitivity is the most important characteristic and indicates which effective alternating voltage a microphone yields, when it is exposed to a sound pressure fluctuation with the maximum of one Pascal (Pa). Typical microphones have a sensitivity of approximately 1 mV/Pa ... 10 mV/Pa. Often the sensitivity of a microphone is measured in relation to 1V/Pa and thus indicated in decibel (dB).

A sensitivity of -60 dB corresponds to 1/1000 × 1Pa / V = 1 mV/Pa.

A speaker with normal voice produces, approximately, an effective sound pressure of 0,1 Pa at 1 m distance. At a distance of 5 m from an orchestra an effective sound pressure of approximately 1 Pa is measured.

The output voltage of a microphone is very small. It must first be amplified by a factor of 1000 before it can be digitalized for further processing.

A further characteristic for microphones is the **directivity characteristic.** The sensitivity depends, according to the type and construction of the microphone, on the direction of the sound. Usual directivity characteristics are sphere, leg (beam) or cardioid.

Because there is a clear preferred direction with the beam and cardioid form, we speak of a directional microphone. In the preferred direction route there is full sensitivity. The directivity is also dependent on frequency.

6.3 Sound Cards

Fig. 3.43 A typical Sound Card

Sound cards (fig. 3.43) are plug-in boards for PCs, which are equipped with different interfaces and enable the input and editing of audio signals. There are various construction configurations. The following technical parameters are basic.

6.3.1 Sound Card Criteria

Output voltage at the line outlet. The usable signal voltage during the playback of a synthetic, digital signal (1 kHz test signal) with full modulation lies in the area of 1000 mV.

Linearity. This value specifies, how uncorrupted the volume signals ("quiet" – "loud") are after conversion by the ADC and DAC. Ideally, deviation should approach 0 dB, typical value lie around 0,1 dB.

Signal-to-noise Ratio. This is the difference between *wanted* (desired) signals and an interference signals (unwanted humming, static ...). The greater the interference signals are, the smaller the distance to the *wanted* signal is. Ideally, the signal-to-noise ratio should be infinitely high, typical values lie around 80 dB(A).

Harmonic distortion. As with HiFi systems, this value marks the non-linear distortion of a wave-form in which harmonics of the original frequencies are introduced into it. Ideally the distortion factor should approach zero, the german standard (from 1970) allows 1% (DIN 45 500) typical values today are much lower, approximately 0.02 %.

Dynamic. Specifies the useable dynamic range, as apposed to *static.* This is usually measured by gradually reducing the volume of the test signal until only interference can be heard. The greater the distance to complete modulation the better. Typical values lie around 80 dB.

Frequency Response. Specifies the frequency range and is a measure of linear distortions (Deviations from the frequency response). Recording and replay are declared separately and usually displayed graphically (see fig 3.42). The more linear the frequency range within the desired bandwidth, the better. Deviations can also be given in dB and ideally approach 0, typical values lie in the range of 3 dB.

Input voltage at the microphone input. Specifies the input voltage, which leads to full modulation of the (software-) modulation measuring device by 1000 Hz.

6.3.2 Sound Card Anatomy

Sound Blaster (SB) since 1989, compatible to AdLib MSC-1 of 1987

Die "Sound Blaster" sound cards, from the company Creative Labs, represents a "quasi-standard" due to their wide circulation, many manufacturers of other sound cards make their cards "Sound Blaster compatible".

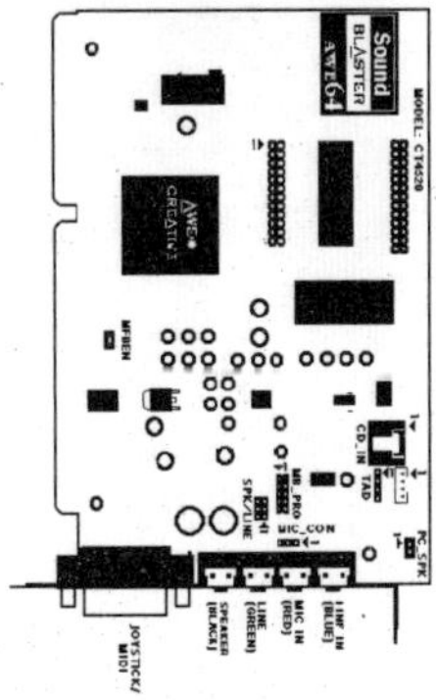

Fig. 3.44 A view on the board

A typical sound card creates sounds with an OPL-3-Chip (from Yamaha) according to the FM synthesis procedure. The OPL-4-Chip also supports the wave table procedure. A typical sound card with a view onto the circuit board is shown in fig. 3.44. The frequency modulation synthesis overlays several oscillations, in order to make different kinds of (synthetic) sounds. The **wave table procedure** draws on the original sounds of (genuine) instruments that have been stored in ROMs, which enable a production of far more natural music.

With the aid of an audio, input analog audio signals, with a data depth of 16 bit and a max. frequency of 22,05 kHz, can be digitalized (Sampling frequency 44.1 kHz). An additional MIDI connector makes the connection of synthesizers and other MIDI devices possible. Many cards have additional "3D Audio" abilities: Through an additional processor three-dimensional sound effects can be created by resonance and chorus. The fundamental function can be seen in the following block diagram:

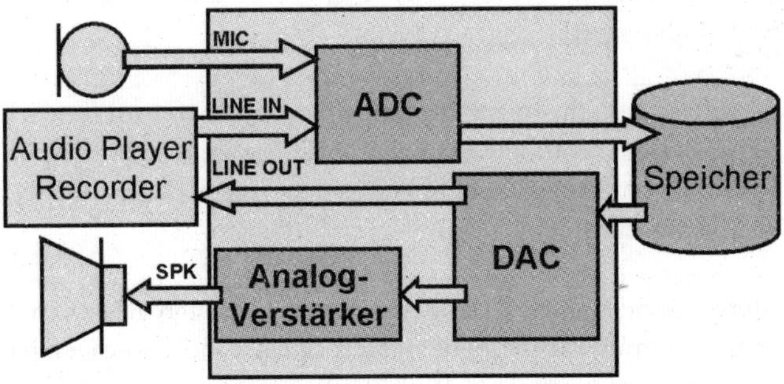

Fig. 3.45 Block diagram of a sound card

ADC Analog Digital Converter
DAC Digital Analog Converter

The analog signal sources; microphone, line in and CD (Analog output) are changed from ADC into digital signals that can then be sent to the digital signal processor. The digital signal processor can alter the digital input signals in various ways: Volume, tone quality, mixture and compression. The audio signals processed in this manner can then be transmitted, via a PC-

Bus, and stored as a WAV file. Stored WAV files are sent to the digital signal processor, which takes over for example, the replay volume setting. The altered replay signals are reconverted to analog by the DAC, so that they can be made audible in the loud speaker.

MIDI signals are recorded differently and replayed as WAV signals. A MIDI input device, such as a **keyboard**, makes a MIDI in data stream, which already consists of digital signals and can be stored as a MIDI file. To replay of MIDI files, the MIDI description language must be converted to equivalent digital audio signals. The **MIDI processor** intakes this. This extracts from a **Lookup Table**, the so-called **Wave Table**, how specific music instruments are copied. The digital audio signal is then influenced, in the digital signal processor, in volume sound etc.and sent to the loudspeakers via the DAC.

Simple sound cars work with FM synthesis instead of a wave table.

Most sound cards display a resolution of 16 bit and work with sampling rates of up to 44.1 kHz. Theoretically an SNR up to 90 dB and a frequency response up to 22 kHz is possible.

6.4 Mixer Consoles

A mixer console is used for synchronizing the signal levels of several audio signals from different sources with each other and merging them to a (resultant) audio-signal.

In the simplest case, the mixer has only one volume control for each audio-input. The total (the combined signal) is available at an audio-output. Inputs and the corresponding adjustment knobs (incorrectly designated regulators) are called **input channels**.

With stereo devices there is at least another two aggregate channels each with an own output, for the right and left signals, and a so-called panorama regulator for every input port. With the panorama adjustment device, the input signal gauge is distributed, left and right, in such a way that one can arbitrarily position the signal, according to the sound.

Larger mixers (mixer consoles) also offer the possibility of adapting every input signal with an own tone control (equalizer) to form several results according to personal preference.

7 Module Summary

Each kind of physical stimulation (e.g. acoustic vibrations) corresponds, in the brain, to a specific kind of psychological sensation (e.g. hearing). The coded sound qualities, that are provided to the auditory nerve for forwarding to the brain, are *sound frequency* (Pitch), *sound pressure level, sound intensity* (volume), *sound direction, distance* and *tone quality* (timbre). The subjectively sensed **volume** is not only dependent on the sound pressure level, but also on the frequency. The connection between volume and sound pressure level for the audibility range is shown by curves of same volume levels (audibility curves). Here, the **dB** only indicates the ratio. The **phon** unit attempts to depict the subjective volume.

Language consists of spoken sounds and is a form of information based on auditory signals. Multimedia systems *reproductive voice rendition* employ *sound concatination* in period/frequency ranges and speech synthesis. ASR (automated speech recognition) is based on the recognition of distinguishing characteristic vectors.

PCM, GSM and μ-Law are also employed for the coding of unrefined sounds.

The most important audio formats in the PC field are Wave and MIDI. A **WAV file** is a "digital copy" of the effective sound pressure at the microphone and it can contain every arbitrary sound event. **MIDI** (Music Instrument Digital Interface) is the most compact representation of music data; instead of actual samples, instrument related representation is used. The code contains volume, master frequency and identification of the instrument.

Furthermore **AU**, **MPEG** and *MPEG Audio Layer III* (in short MP3) are also frequently used.

The sound card loudspeaker system is an interface between human and computer. Criteria for **loudspeakers** are *distortion factor, efficiency, strength of sound* and *endurance.*

Sensitivity is the most important characteristic of **microphones** and indicates which effective tension is yielded when it is exposed to a *sound pressure of 1 Pa.* A sensitivity of -60 dB corresponds 1 mV/Pa. At a distance of approximately 5m from an orchestra, an effective sound pressure of approximately 1 Pa can be measured. A typical sound card produces sounds with a *FM-synthesis* procedure. **Mixing consoles** are used for synchronizing the individual signal levels of various sources.

8 Module Supplement

8.1 Literature

8.1.1 Books in English

BUFORD-KOEGEL, JOHN F. (1994): *Multimedia Systems.* New York. Addison-Wesley.

COOKE, DERYCK (1962): *The Language of Music.* London: Oxford University Press.

CRITCHLEY, M.; HENSON, R. A., EDS (1977): *Music and the Brain.* London: Heinemann.

FISHER, LEONARD EVERETT (2001): *Alexander Graham Bell.* North Lebanon (TN): Greenleaf Press.

HEATH, STEVE (1999): *Multimedia and Communications Technology.* 2nd Ed. Oxford: Focal Press, Butterworth, Heinemann. 7-43.

MCLAUGHLIN, TERENCE (1970): *Music and Communication.* London: Faber and Faber.

PINKER, STEVEN (1994): *The Language Instinct.* New York: William Morrow.

RODMAN, ROBERT D. (1999): *Computer Speech Technology.* Artech House.

WATKINSON, JOHN (1994): *The art of digital audio.* Second edition. Woburn (MA): Focal Press.

WHITE, GLENN D. (1987): *The Audio Dictionary.* Second Edition. Seattle (WA): University of Washington Press.

WU, CHWAN-HWA; IRWIN, DAVID J. (1999): *Emerging Multimedia Computer Communication Technologies.* Upper Saddle River (NJ): Prentice Hall. 27.

8.1.2 Articles in English

BRENT, MICHAEL R. (1999): Speech segmentation and word discovery: a computational perspective. *Trends in Cognitive Sciences,*Vol. 3, Iss. 8, August 99, 294-301.

GRAPS, AMARA (1995): An Introduction to Wavelets. *IEEE Computational Sciences and Engineering,* Vol. 2, No. 2, 50-61.

HARRER, G.; HARRER, H. (1977): Music, emotion and autonomic function. In: Critchley, M.; Henson, R.A.: *Music and the Brain: Studies in the Neurology of Music.* London: Heinemann, 202-216.

HOOD, J. D. (1977): Psychological and Physiological Aspects of Hearing. In: Critchley, M.; Henson, R.A.: *Music and the Brain: Studies in the Neurology of Music.* London:

Heinemann, chapter 3.

KYRIAKAKIS, CHRIS; TSAKALIDES, PANAGIOTIS; HOLMAN, TOMLINSON (1999): Surrounded by sound. *IEEE Signal Processing Magazine,* Vol. 16, Iss. 1, January 99, 55-66.

LIBERMAN, A. M.; MATTINGLY, I. G. (1985): The motor theory of speech perception revised. *Cognition,* 21, 1-36.

OBAIDAT, M. S.; LEE, C.; SADOUN, B.; NELSON, D. (1999): Estimation of pitch period of speech signal using a new dyadic wavelet algorithm. *Information Sciences,* Vol. 119, Issue 1-2, 21-39. Elsevier.

SANDLER, MARK (2000): Digital music in the 21st century. Digest of Technical Papers. *IEEE International Conference on Consumer Electronics,* 412-413.

TREMAIN, THOMAS E. (1982): The Government Standard Linear Predictive Coding Algorithm: LPC-10. *Speech Technology Magazine,* April 1982, 40-49.

YEN, KUAN-CHIEH; ZHAO, YUNXIN (1999): Adaptive co-channel speech separation and recognition, *IEEE Transactions on Speech and Audio Processing,* Vol. 7, Iss. 2, March 99, 138-151.

8.1.3 Books in German

ALBRECHT, FRANK-WERNER; MAYER-FASOLD, C.; VEIT, IVAR (1995): *Beschallungstechnik.* 3. Auflage. Renningen: Expert Verlag.

BORUCKI, HANS (1993): *Einführung in die Akustik.* Mannheim: BI Wissenschaftsverlag.

DICKREITER, MICHAEL (1997): *Handbuch der Tonstudiotechnik.* 6. Auflage. München: K. G. Saur.

ENDERS, BERND (1997): *Lexikon Musikelektronik.* Mainz: Schott.

FREYER, U. G. P. (1997): *DAB-digitaler Hörfunk.* Berlin: Verlag Technik.

FROEBISCH, DIETER K.; LINDNER, HOLGER; STEFFEN, THOMAS (1997): *Multimedia Design: Handbuch zur Gestaltung interaktiver Medien.* München: Laterna Magica. 229-234.

HERKNER, WERNER (1992): *Psychologie.* 2. Auflage. Wien, New York: Springer. 61-78.

HOFMÜLLER, HELMUT; SEIWERT, MARTIN (1999): *Digital Audio/Video: Digitalisierung, Schnitt und Mastering unter Windows (Edition Screen Multimedia).* München: Addison-Wesley-Longman. 153-300.

JARZ, EWALD M.(1997): *Entwicklung multimedialer Systeme; Planung von Lern- und Masseninformationssystemen (Serie Gabler Edition Wissenschaft).* Wiesbaden: Gabler. 193-211.

MATHELITSCH, LEOPOLD; GERHARD FRIEDRICH (1995): *Die Stimme: Instrument für Sprache, Gesang und Gefühl.* Berlin et.al.: Springer.

PIERCE, JOHN R. (1989): *Klang, Musik mit den Ohren der Physik.* 2. Auflage. Heidelberg: Spektrum.

REIBOLD, HELMUT F. (1999): *Das Einsteigerseminar: Musik und PC.* Kaarst: bhv Verlag.

SILBERNAGL, STEFAN; DESPOPOULOS, AGAMEMNON (1983): *dtv-Atlas der Physiologie.* 2. Auflage. Stuttgart, New York: Thieme. München: Deutscher Taschenbuch-Verlag.

STEINMETZ, RALF (1998): *Multimedia-Technologie: Grundlagen, Komponenten und Systeme.* 2. Auflage. Berlin [et al.]: Springer. 23-46.

VEIT, IVAR (1996): *Technische Akustik: Grundlagen der phsyikalischen, physiologischen und Elektro-Akustik.* 5. Auflage. Würzburg: Vogel.

WEBERS, JOHANNES (1979): *Tonstudiotechnik: Handbuch der Schallaufnahme und -wiedergabe bei Rundfunk, Fernsehen, Film und Schallplatte.* 3. Auflage. München: Franzis.

ZANDER, HORST (1998): *Das PC-Tonstudio: von der Audioaufnahme und Verarbeitung mit dem PC bis zur Master-CD.* Poing: Franzis.

8.1.4 Articles in German

CARSTENS, MATTHIAS (1999): Musik kompakt: Audio-Kompression mit MPEG Layer-3. *c't: Magazin für Computer Technik,* 21/99, 242-250. Hannover: Heise.

MUSMANN, H.-G.; WERNER, O.; FUCHS, H. (1993): Kompressionsalgorithmen für interaktive Multimedia-Systeme. *it + ti 2/93, Informationstechnik und Technische Informatik,* 35 (2), Oldenbourg Verlag, 4-18.

STEINBRINK, BERND (1999): Die Zukunft der Audio-CD: Formatvielfalt oder Standardscheibe?. *c't: Magazin für Computer Technik,* 21/99, 252-253. Hannover: Heise.

8.1.5 Journals

Audio Electronics (ISSN: 0004-7546) | Audio Amateur Publications

AV Video and Multimedia Producer (ISSN: 1090-7459) | Knowledge Industry Publications Inc.

Computer Music Journal (ISSN: 0148-9267) | MIT Press

Computer Speech and Language (ISSN: 0885-2308) | Academic Press Inc.

Digital Signal Processing (ISSN: 1051-2004) | Academic Press Inc.

Journal of the Audio Engineering Society (ISSN: 0004-7554) | Audio Engineering Society

Journal of the Acoustical Society of America (ISSN: 0001-4966) | American Inst. of Physics

IEEE Signal Processing Magazine (ISSN: 1053-5888) | IEEE Institute of Electrical and Electronics Engineers

IEEE Transactions on Speech and Audio Processing (ISSN: 1063-6676 electronic:1063-6676) | IEEE Institute of Electrical and Electronics Engineers

IEEE MultiMedia Magazine (ISSN: 1070-986X) | IEEE Institute of Electrical and Electronics Engineers

Multimedia Systems (ISSN: 0942-4962; electronic: 1432-1882) | Springer Verlag KG

Multimedia Tools and Applications (ISSN: 1380-7501) | Kluwer Academic Publishers Group

New Review of Hypermedia and Multimedia – Applications and Research (ISSN: 1361-4568) | Taylor Graham Publishing – Journal Department

8.2 Internet Links

Up-to-date Internet Links for this module can be found on the homepage of this book **www.basiswissen-multimedia.at** (in English and German) under Volume 1: Technology, Module 3: Audio Technology Supplement.

8.3 Examination Questions

Question Type 1: Dichotomy Questions (answer yes or no)

01	Feelings emerge already in each of the specialized sense organs.	❒ Yes ❒ No	
02	According to the law of WEBER, a stimulus increase must be always one specific fraction of the initial stimulus.	❒ Yes ❒ No	
03	The middle ear with the tympanic membrane and oval window serves as a mechanical impedance transformer.	❒ Yes ❒ No	
04	With the aid of the tone quality (timbre) it is possible to localize acoustic sources within a room.	❒ Yes ❒ No	
05	With "morpheme" we mean the smallest importance supporting (bedeutungstragend) linguistic unit.	❒ Yes ❒ No	
06	When "streaming" the data are transmitted successive and played almost in real time.	❒ Yes ❒ No	
07	A WAV-file is a "digital copy" of the sound pressure at the microphone.	❒ Yes ❒ No	
08	A MIDI-file stores the "form process" (Formverlauf, see in MM dictionary) of a sound and can include every sound event.	❒ Yes ❒ No	
09	On a Soundcard the analogous signal sources of an ADC are changed into digital signals and conducted to the signal processor.	❒ Yes ❒ No	
10	A MIDI input-equipment produces a MIDI-In-Data stream which is stored directly as a digital signal.	❒ Yes ❒ No	

Question Type 2: Multiple Choice Questions

01	In psychophysics of the auditory perception it is valid that ... ❒ a) ... the sound intensity is proportional to the sound frequency. ❒ b) ... spatial hearing is allowed besides other by the reverberation. ❒ c) ... the character of a sound results from his overtone content. ❒ d) ... sensations arise not in the sense organs, but in the brain.
02	During voice output ... ❒ a) ... the reproducing voice rendition represents the simplest procedure. ❒ b) ... a great problem is the semantics. ❒ c) ... by formant synthesis ASR is mainly used. ❒ d) ... intelligibility is a basic requirement, naturalness wanted.
03	During the digitalization of audio-signals ... ❒ a) ... with a sampling rate of 88 kHz is worked mostly. ❒ b) ... the file size is always a problem. ❒ c) ... the file size is mainly determined by the sampling rate. ❒ d) ... is worked always with the WAV-Format.
04	A WAV-file ... ❒ a) ... is limited on music reproduction. ❒ b) ... is based on the RIFF-format. ❒ c) ... allows streaming. ❒ d) ... is small and platform-independent.
05	MIDI ... ❒ a) ... is a standardized data format especially for voice reproduction. ❒ b) ... is suitable for external control of music instruments. ❒ c) ... is platform independent. ❒ d) ... supply always the same reproduction result.
06	In order to reduce an audio file it is favourable ... ❒ a) ... to convert MIDI into WAV. ❒ b) ... to increase the sampling rate. ❒ c) ... to carry out data compression with ADPCM or MPEG. ❒ d) ... to abandon (freiwillig verzichten) on Stereo.
07	Audio-CDs ... ❒ a) ... are written (beschrieben) with signals at a sampling rate of 44,1 kHz. ❒ b) ... work with average file sizes of 650 kB/s. ❒ c) ... store audio files in 16 bit packets. ❒ d) ... employ MIDI for sound storage.
08	Criteria of a Soundcard are ... ❒ a) ... frequency response. ❒ b) ... harmonic distortion. ❒ c) ... signal-to-noise ratio. ❒ d) ... linearity.

8.4 Answers

Correct answers to Group „Question Type 1“: 01 no; 02 yes; 03 yes; 04 no; 05 yes; 06 yes; 07 yes; 08 no; 09 yes; 10 yes;

Correct answers to Group „Question Type 2“: 01 b) c) d); 02 a) b) d); 03 b) c); 04 b); 05 b) c) 06 c) d); 07 a) c); 08 a) b) c) d)

8.5 Exercises

- Calculate the required storage capacity for a music file with a length of three minutes and 46 seconds in CD quality. Which methods of compression are available?
- Listen to a MIDI file and a WAV file and compare the sound quality, as well as the advantages and disadvantages of both types of recording. How does an MP-3 file sound in comparison?
- Work with a Speech Recognition Program (see on the accompanying website) and investigate its strengths and weaknesses!

8.6 Themes for Debate

- Which advantages are attached to the implementation of dB? Why is the sound level measured in phon?
- In which areas can automated speech recognition be used most meaningfully?
- Where will the largest area of application be in the future? Do you think, that MP-3 files will replace audio CDs?

8.7 Timeline: Audio Technology

1400: Sound recording of tower chimes by means of revolving toothed cylinder.

1737: Mechanical flute players (automats) from J. DE VAUCANSON.

1809: Investigations onto acoustic vibrations and the discovery of the "sound figures" on oscillating surfaces by CHLADNI.

1843: MORSE establishes electric telegraphy.

1860: REIS designs a telephone.

1868: Punched tape control for a mechanical (autom.) organ from MACTAMMANY.

1877: BELL develops a usable phone. EDISON introduces his phonograph and CROS develops the wax disk for sound recording.

1881: First presentation of Stereo from ADER.

1887: US patent for BERLINER'S gramophone.

1888: Experiments with sound on a record: SMITH suggests a sound wire device.

1889: First coin-operated juke-box in the USA.

1895: Shellac record from BERLINER.

1896, 14th May: First wireless audio transference from MARCONI: Radio.

1898: Functioning magnetic sound recording equipment with wire from POULSEN.

1904: Electrical piano from WELTE.

1907: RAYLEIGH develops a theory of sound phases.

1912: Long-playing record from EDISON.

1915: Record player with electrical motor.

1921: Audio becomes a mass communication agent: Radio.

1925: Electrodynamic cone loudspeaker from KELLOG & RICE.

1926: First usable sound films.

1927: Fully electric Juke-Boxes.

1928: Magnetizable paper tapes from PFLEUMER.

1932: First stereo record from EMI. In Germany BASF develops the Acetylcellulose tapes for sound recording.

1935: Magnetophone K1 from AEG (Allgemeine Elektrizitäts Gesellschaft).

1943: First tape recorder with cassette from AEG.

1948: Long-playing record on vinyl basis. A micro-groove record with 45 revolutions per minute is introduced by RCA.

1950: Audio recording on magnetic tape becomes standard: Tape recorder.

1952: AEG introduces the magneto phone KL15.

1958: Stereo records are on the market.

1965: Compact tape recorder from Philips (still standard).

1966: Noise suppression from DOLBY.

1972: First optical storage media from Philips and MCA (Laserdisc).

1977: Radio Shack introduces the first personal computer: Audio on PC.

1979: Digital disk (CD) in contemporary form.

1982: Audio on Laserdisc commercial: CD-Player.

1983: MIDI as standard.

1987: DAT (Digital Audio Tape).

1988: The MPEG (Moving Picture Experts Group) as working group for ISO is set up, to define audio and video standards.

1989: Integrated copy protection for DAT Recorders. Release of MPEG-1.

1991: CD-ROM. Release of MPEG-2.

1992: GSM standard for digital car telephones.

1995: Release of MPEG-4.

1997, April: MPEG-2 Advanced Audio Coding (AAC) is released as an international standard.

2000: Wideband information networks: music in the internet via Satellite.

2010: DAB (Digital Audio Broadcasting) in CD quality is to replace the UKW radio in Europe.

8.8 Glossary

AAA Customary denotation for the entire recording procedure. The first alphabetic character indicates the recording mode, the second the mixing technology and the third is the master carrier. A stands for Analogue, D for digital (AAA is a pure analog, DDD a purely digital production).

ADPCM Adaptive Differential Pulse Code Modulation, used to compress of audio data, for example with CD-I in order to extend playing time.

AES Audio Engineering Society (New York).

AIFF Audio Interchange File Format, the sound file standard format for MacIntosh Apple Computers; it processes multi channel samples with different sampling and resolution.

Active Box is a Loudspeaker with integrated last stage amplifier.

Amplifier is an appliance or circuit which increases the strength of an electrical current, signal, etc.

Audio-Dub from "dubbing" Synchronisation or re-touching of sound files.

Balance is the ratio of volume strength between the left and right channels.

Binaural applied to a system of sound reproduction that uses two separated microphones and two transmission channels to achieve a stereophonic effect; particularly one in which the sound is delivered to each ear separately by earphones.

bpm abbreviation for beats per minute. Unit of measure for the musical tempo.

Humming is a low-frequency murmuring sound caused by an error in the mains power and/or missing mass.

Cardioid is a curve somewhat resembling a heart in shape. If straight lines are drawn through a fixed point in the circumference of a circle, intersecting the circle at different points, and such that the length of each line on each side of the point of intersection is equal to the diameter of the circle, the extremities of these lines will trace out a cardioid, having its cusp at the fixed point.

CD Quality Standard for recordings on audio CDs that are digitalized with a resolution of 16 bits and a sampling rate of 44.1 kHz.

CD-R Compact Disk Recordable (once only).

CD-RW Compact Disk Re-Writeable.

RCA Radio Corporation of America.

Cinch RCA Standard for a HiFi connection.

Clipping Distortion of an audio signal by the over-control of a preselector.

Cut-off Frequency is the frequency value at which there is a marked increase in the attenuation (or decrease in the amplification) of an oscillation, particularly of an ac or voltage by a filter.

Damping is the action of damping an oscillation or an oscillating body, the resistance to an oscillation; also, the amount of this, as measured by the rate at which the oscillation diminishes in amplitude (dB).

dB is the abbreviation for deci Bel (one-tenth of a Bel, after ALEXANDER GRAHAM BELL) used here to express a single power level or sound intensity relative to some reference level (stated or understood).

dBm is the basis measure in audio technology for voltage levels. 0 dBm = 0,775 volts at 0,1 mW at 600 ohms.

De-emphasise is the restoration of the initial frequency response; after digitalisation the higher audio signals raised for the purpose of static decrease (pre-emphasis): The de-emphasis lowers these back.

Detune means to alter or adjust an oscillatory system, so that its resonant frequency no longer coincides with the frequency of an other oscillation with which it interacts.

DFT Discreet Fourier Transform. After JOSEPH FOURIER (1768–1830), a French mathematician, Mathematical function that analyses a sampled audio signal in his overtone spectrum and determines the corresponding sinusoidal functions as coefficients. So the original signal can be set up later again. Also known: Fourier's coefficient, expansion, integral, transformation, analysis, series and law.

Dynamic measured in dB, indicates the ratio of the minimum and the maximum level of an audio device. Human hearing reaches pain level at a dynamic of 130 dB.

Equalizer is called a circuit or passive network designed to modify the frequency response of a circuit (as a transmission line or an amplifier), particularly in order to compensate for frequency-dependent attenuation or phase shifts. Usually every input port of a mixer is furnished with an equalizer so that the sound of the individual instruments can be optimised.

Fade-In/Fade-Out means the gradual increase and decrease in the loudness of a sound.

FM Synthesis Sound generation on the basis of the frequency modulation.

Gain Control at the entry of a mixer or device that adapts the input signal to the line level of the following stages (dampens or amplifies).

GND Ground (earth).

HiFi High Fidelity. Improvements in technology have meanwhile outdated the original DIN 45 500 standard.

Line Level and connection designations.

Master original CD from which copies are made.

Preselector A tuned circuit preceding the first mixer in a super heterodyne receiver or an analogous filter in a microwave receiver.

SNR Signal-to-Noise Ratio indicated in dB.

SPL Sound Pressure Level, sound intensity in dB.

Module 4: Graphics Technology

"Some people believe that the long era of "lingual culture" is at an end and is making room for a new "visual culture". If communication does actually shift from language to pictures, then the associated aesthetic criteria will gain importance over the currently prominent literary criteria.

Herbert W. Franke at the First European Software Festival 1991 in Munich

Learning Objectives

Sight

Video technology

Picture formats

Compression

To begin with, we will concentrate on the **psychophysics of sight**, with **colour**, the dimensions of colour perception and with the technical basics of **video technology** (such as depth of colour, different colour models etc.). This is followed by the different **picture formats** (Vector graphics, bitmaps and metafiles) and finally the important **concept of compression**, after acquiring some knowledge about file sizes..

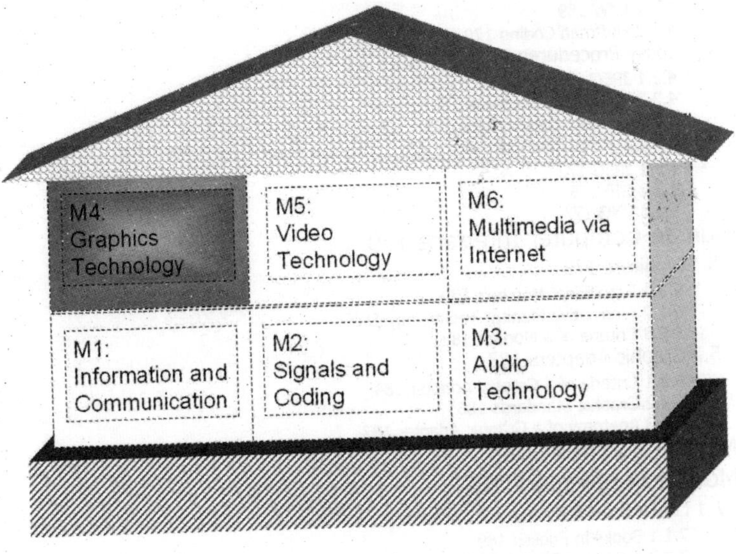

Images and **Graphics** are the backbone of every multimedia application and increase the attractiveness of the end users screen. Pictures can often illustrate complex contents. An old chinese proverb states that "one picture is worth a thousand words". After language and music, pictures are humanity's third greatest cultural achievement. Pictures have been used as a communication media since the stone age (cave paintings). Also, our writing consists basically of pictures.

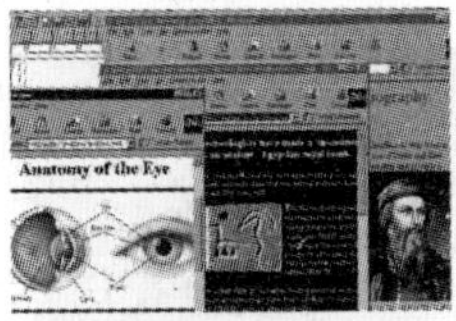

Fig. 4.1 Images are also the backbone and success of the WWW

In this Module we start with **non-moving pictures,** known as **stills** (black & white, grey tones and colour) and turn to moving pictures in the next module "Video Technology".

Building on the contents of the preceding modules 1 and 2: "Information and communication" and "Signals" we review the technological and psychophysical basics of the picture technology.

Psychology of Learning in Volume 2

In volume 2 Learning" we will deal with details of the psychology of learning.

Designing and Didactics in Volume 3

In volume 3 "Multimedia Design" this knowledge is expanded to cover psychological perception and didactic organization principles.

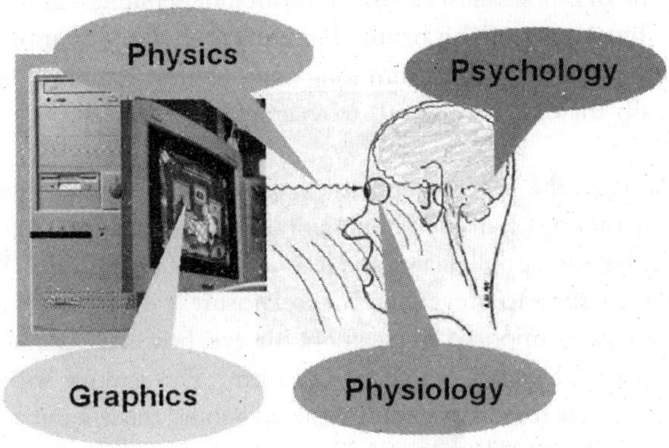

Fig. 4.2 Video technology is also a matter of the interplay between technology and psychophysics, combining the elements of physics, physiology and psychology

1 The eye as an Image Sensor

1.1 Eye and Vision

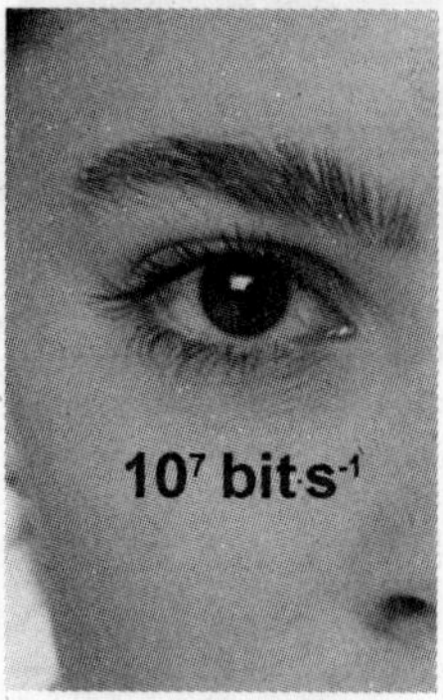

Fig. 4.3 Information absorption through the eye (bit.s^{-1} = bps)

The Eye (oculus) is the most important "sense-organ". 90% of all information reaching our (post-connected) brains is obtained via our eyes.

Only around 20 bit per seconds of information regarding smell can be assimilated by the nose whereas the enormously large information capacity of 10^7 bps can be assimilated optically.

The great significance of the sight is obvious, and explains why the visualization of contents is of central importance for multimedia-systems.

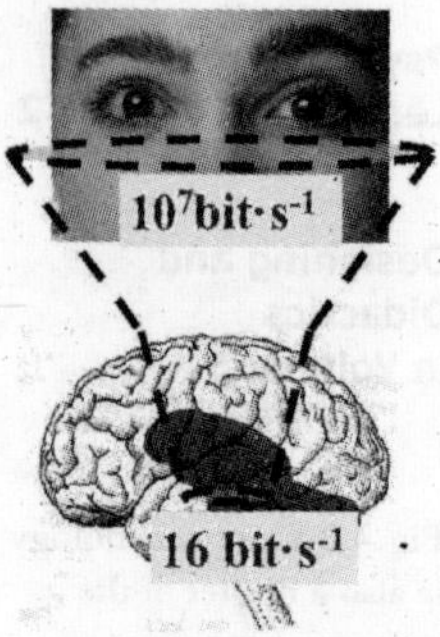

Fig. 4.4 Only approx. 16 bit per seconds can be stored in the Long Term Memory (LTM)

Actually, only approximately **16 bps** can enter the short-term memory via the sensory memory in order to be memorized into the long term memory (Figure 4.4).

This is dealt with in more detail in Volume 2 „Basics Multimedia: Learning"

The eye is one of our smallest organs. It is not independent – as for example the heart – but a **part of the brain**. The eyeball (bulbus) is approximately ball-shaped, on the average 24 mm long and only few grammes heavy (fig. 4.5). Physically the eye corresponds to a camera.

The light reaches the eye through the pupil (1). The size of the pupil is controlled by the iris (2) in the same manner as a camera lens (filter). With low intensity light the pupil dilates and lets more light into the eye. With very bright light it narrows to prevent an "overexposure". The lens (3) is used to focus the image. As opposed to a camera the eye, however, can not modify the position of the lens but can change its form. This is done with the help of the ciliary muscle (or ciliary circle), situated behind the iris and around the margin of the lens(4). When looking into the distance pressure applied by the ciliary muscle and reducing the curve of the lens. The actual sensory perception takes place in the **Retina (5).**

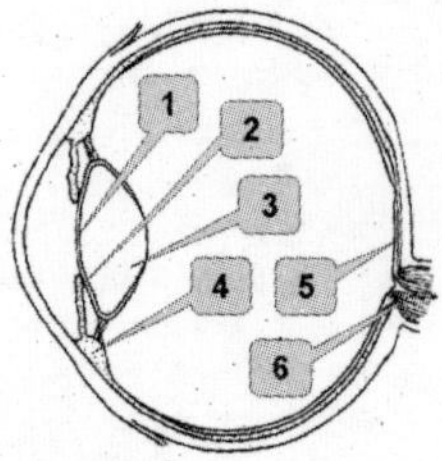

Fig. 4.5 Sectional drawing of a right eye

The **Optical Nerve** (nervus opticus, (6)) is a bundle of fibres reaching into the centre of the brain (Chiasma opticum, see fig. 4.8) and is histologically and evolutionary diverticulum of the brain and therefore, surrounded by cerebral membrane to the back of the eyeball. The optic nerve sends the information received to the brain. The visual stimulus information is processed by a very specific part of the brain, the **visual cortex**, situated in the **occipital** (fig. 4.8).

1.2 Image generation

Some 126 million *sense cells* clothe the inner eyeball. These, approx. 400,000 cells per square millimetre register the incoming light. Each second more than 16 pictures are transmitted to the brain via the optic nerve. A bundle of optical nerves (fasciculus) is made up of approx. one million single nerve fibres.

The light which reaches the eye is broken down when at the cornea, intersperses the front ventricle, the eye lens and the vitreum and hits the light sensitive **Retina,** which appears as a convex screen. The human retina, as by all vertebrates, is an inverse retina: The photosensitive layer is away from the light, so that the light entering the eye must first penetrate the *complete thickness of the retina* in order to reach the **photoreceptors** (fig. 4.6).

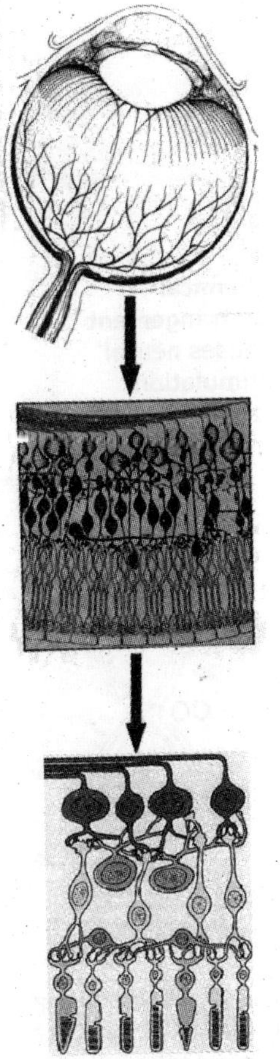

Fig. 4.6 The eyeball is coated by the retina, which is in turn made up of light sensitive rods and cones

The receptors are long (30 μm), highly differentiated cells which consist of a cell body with a cell nucleus and a synaptic end-bulb. Their longitudinal axes are oriented parallel to the direction of the incoming light incident, thereby standing vertically on the pigment epithelium. Morphology distinguishes between to types: **Rods** with cylindrical extremities and **Cones** with coned shaped extremities. It was early established that the rods can work by a low light intensity while the cones act as receptors for bright light and colour.

The **Duplication Theory** is based on the following: The cones are for daylight and colour vision, the rods for night-sight. This theory is supported by the fact that nocturnal animals frequently only have rod retina. The conversion of light energy into electronic impulses, takes place in the area of the extremities. The photons, which hit the *photo pigments,* cause structural changes in the stereo structure. This causes permeability alterations within the membranes with subsequent potential alteration of the photoreceptors.

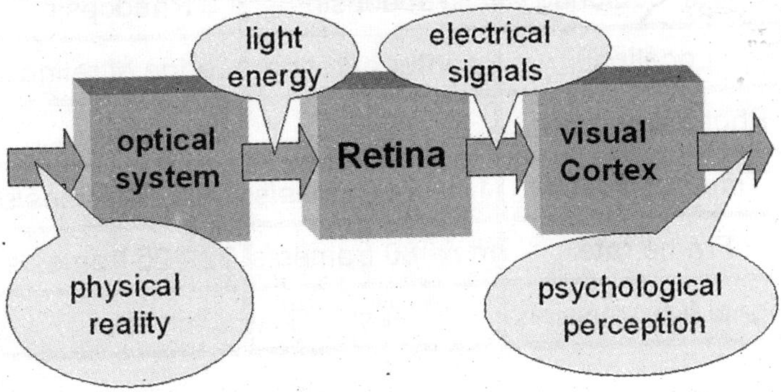

Fig. 4.7 Information arrives in the form of light through the eye lens onto the retina via the optical nerve into the optical centre at the rear of the head

The extremities of the photo-receptors are in direct contact with the pigment epithelium. The synaptic end-bulbs (end-buds) provide connection with the next neuron in the optic tract. Horizontal and amakrine cells serve as a cross-connection within the retina.

Chemical rearrangement causes neural stimulation

The light sensitive **vision colouring** are deposited (stored) in the membrane slice of the rod and cone extremities. These pigments are the means of transforming the light stimulus into an electrical stimulation of the receptors. The rods contain rhodopsin and the cones iodopsin. Within a reaction time of only 1 ms, incoming light impulses (stimuli) cause a **chemical** rearrangement, which in turn causes an **electrical** stimulation of the nerves.

1.3 Sight

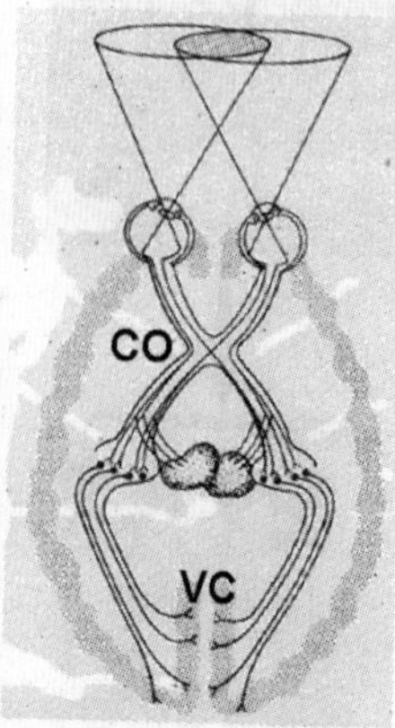

Fig. 4.8 The crossing of the optical nerves (CO = chiasma opticum) and the visual cortex (VC) is clearly recognisable in this sectional drawing of the brain (view from above)

The cones and rods convert optical impressions into **neural signals**, which are each guided, without interruption, via the respective optic nerve to a cell accumulation ("knee body") deep in the brain. The information about synapses to a neigh boring occipital cortex are transmitted from this field.

The primary field of vision in the occipital is not the end of the information processing route, the signals are also sent back.

Particularly interesting is the crossing over of the optic nerves (Fig. 4.8) whereby the right side of the field of view is transposed to the left visual field.

	cones	rods
Number:	6 Millions	120 Millions
Responsibility:	colour sight	B/W sight
Chem. couloring:	Jodopsin	Rhodopsin
Location:	center of retina	edge of retina
Photo sensitivity:	low	high
Time resolution:	18 – 24 frames/s	14 – 22 frames/s
Frame rate:	max. 80 frames/s	22 - 25 frames/s
Signal transmission:	fast	slow

Fig. 4.9 Comparison of the photo receptors

A break in the optic nerve means total blindness in that eye. However, if lesions occur further back a loss in the view field is caused. Destruction of both sides of the occipitalen Cortex leads to total blindness in humans (cortical blindness) whereas, by less developed mammals a relatively large vestigial sight remains.

The term "range of vision" generally refers to that section of the environment visible without moving the eyes. In theory, this field is purely circular, in fact it is individually limited by the nose and the eye sockets.

The senses and perceptions important to the design of Multimedia Products is dealt with in Volume 3

1.4 Colour Sight

1.4.1 The Term Colour

Up to now, the term "colour" has not been used explicitly, since electromagnetic radiation has no colour.

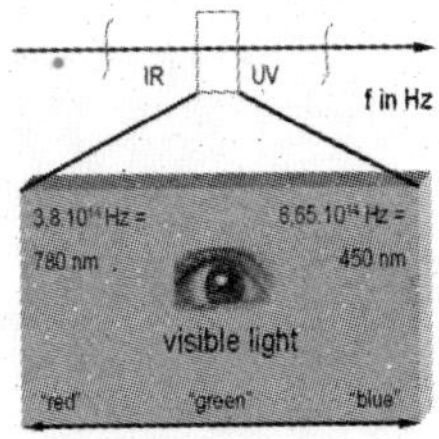

Fig. 4.10 Light is only a small part of the Electromagnetic Spectrum

---

The human eye converts electromagnetic radiation of a particular wave length into an information chain which can be understood by the human brain. The **brain** then sorts this information into an impression or *sense* of colour.

Objects, which are being illuminated by a source of light, reflect some parts of the light, while absorbing others. The light being *reflected* from the object (Physics) is seen by humans (Physiology) and interpreted as colour (Psychology). The perception described here covers the recognition of **dark** and **light** and also of **colour.**

Light is electromagnetic Radiation. The visible Spectrum for humans is a narrow wave band in the range between 400 nm (Violet) and 700 nm (Red).

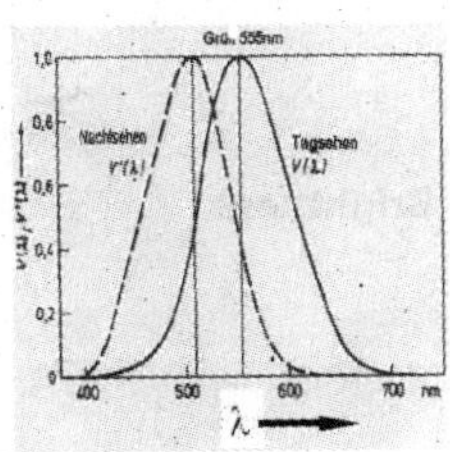

Fig. 4.11 The eyes greatest light sensitivity is by 555 nm; *V(λ)* = light sensitivity (day sight); V'(λ) = light sensitivity (night sight) cf. Holzinger (98), 53

There are three different types of cone in the retina, each connected to a different **light sensitive pigment**; red, green and blue. The *blue sensitive* cone only reacts to light at a wave length of 400 nm, while light at a wave length of 452 activates both the *blue sensitive* cone (strongly) and the *green sensitive* cone (weakly). Light at a wave length of 500 nm wave-length causes all three types of cone to react.

Therefore, the individual colour impressions are caused by the different *strengths* of reaction in the individual cones. When all react equally, the result is **white**.

When colours are considered only with regard to their tint and not to brightness and saturation, then the difference in wavelength of two, just distinguishable, colours lies between 2 nm and 10 nm – depending on which wave band the colours belong to.

Here, the greatest sensitivity of the different cone types is approx. 580 nm, 545 nm and/or 440 nm:

R
- The Sensory impression "red" is assigned to the cone type with the maximum sensitivity of approximately **580 nm.**

G
- The Sensory impression "green" is assigned to the cone type with the maximum sensitivity of approximately **545 nm.**

B
- The Sensory impression "blue" is assigned to the cone type with the maximum sensitivity of approximately **440 nm.**

24 bits are sufficient to code this "natural state" of colours in binary form with 256 different tints per colour.

24 bit

$3 \times 8 = 24$ bits (3 Bytes) are sufficient to code one colour.

1.4.2 Dimensions of Colour Perception

Three parameters are sufficient for the unique description of a colour:

- **Brightness,**
- **Tint and**
- **Colour saturation.**

However, the colours attributes are also described relative to their environment.

Brightness

Brightness is the attribute of a visual perception due to which a visual stimulus appears more or less intense and/or seems to radiate light within the area in which this stimulus is presented.

The variations in brightness extend from **"bright"** to **"dark"**.

The brightness can be determined both for stimuli within a context and also isolated (as against dark background) stimuli.

Relative Brightness (Lightness)

Relative brightness (or preferably, **Brightness contrast**) is the attribute of visual perception due to which the area on which the stimulus is presented appears to radiate more or less light relative to a similarly illuminated "white" reference area.

Due to this definition, this attribute can only be meaningfully gauged for colours on a presented **in front of a background**. Virtually a standardization of the light and the observation conditions takes place.

Hue

Hue is the attribute of colour perception which is known (through consensus) by **names** such as "red" , "green" etc.

Colourfulness

Colourfulness (also chromatic-ness) designates the attribute of a visual perception according to which a corresponding area is felt to be more or less colourful; it also describes **the intensity of the respective colour hue**.

An increase in the brightness of a stimulus with constant tristimulus values increases the "colourfulness" (except if the brightness is already very high).

Chroma

Chroma (Purity or intensity as a colour quality.) is the attribute of a visual perception, which makes it possible to judge how strongly one colour stimulus differs from another **of the same brightness.**

It is a matter of **relative colourfulness.** The stimulus must be presented in a context in order to judge this colour attribute.

Saturation

Saturation is the attribute of a visual perception, which makes it possible to judge how strongly one colour stimulus differs from another **independent of its brightness.** It describes the colourfulness of an area in relation to its brightness. The complementary attribute to this is termed as **White- concealment.**

Under normal observation conditions the saturation of a stimulus with given tristimulus values is constant by nearly all levels of brightness (except for very strong brightness).

Therefore, here it is a matter of the colourfulness of a stimulus in relation to its own brightness, whereas with the chroma, it is a matter of the colourfulness relative to an equally illuminated "white" reference area. Therefore, for the evaluation of the saturation of a stimulus this can be presented separately.

2 Images and Graphics

Digital computer images (graphics) differentiate between two completely difference categories: Vector Graphics and Bitmap images.

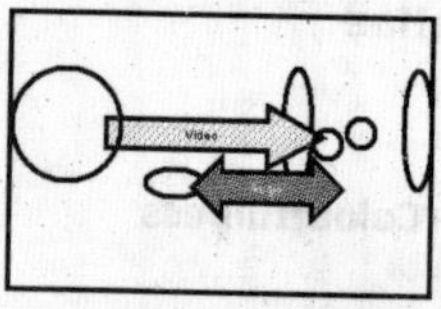

Fig. 4.12 Vector graphic

Before discussing individual details, a few simple definitions are needed:

A computer graphic, or more exactly a **vector graphic, ,** but abbreviated to graphic is build up of primitives and specified by attributes:

- **Graphical primitives** are simple shapes such as lines, squares, polygons, circles, ellipses etc.
- **Attributes** are, for example, line thickness, line colour, and line type (broken/unbroken).

Fig. 4.13 Bitmap Image

Some common **graphic formats** are, for instance, PostScript, EPS, CDR, DXF, ...

A digital image, more exactly a **bitmap image,** but abbreviated to image, is built up, per definition, of

Fig. 4.14 meta graphic

- *n* **lines** with
- *m* **pixels** (picture elements)
- in a **raster** (or grid).

Common **image formats** are, for instance, BMP (MS-Windows), MAC (Apple), RAS (Unix), TIFF, ...

A **meta graphic** contains both raster information *and* vector information. Common **meta formats** are, for instance, WMF, WPG, CGM and PICT. Images, irrespective of type, become very large very quickly. For this reason the **concept of compression** is extremely important. Widely used **compressed image formats** are, for instance, GIF and JPEG.

2.1 Image Types

Two factors play a central role in the employment of images in multimedia systems:

- **File size** and
- **Quality of representation.**

The Representation quality is, in turn, determined by two factors:

- **Colour depth** and
- **Resolution.**

The file size is critical in internet based Multimedia-Systems (see Module 6)

However, it is precisely with internet based multi medial systems that the online time increases proportionally with the increasing file size.

Whichever type of picture you use, it is important to consider carefully before deciding where to place them.

Basically, there are three different types of image:

- Black/white with 2 different possible values (**1 bit** information per pixel, either black or white, see Fig. 4.15),
- Grey scale or half-tone with 16 different possible values (**4 bits** of information per pixel) or with 256 different possible (**8 bits** of information per pixel, see Fig. 4.16)
- Colour with 16,7 Million possible values = True Colour, **24 bits** of information per pixel (8 bits each for red, green and blue).

Fig. 4.15 B/W picture with 1 bit of information per pixel (only black or white)

Fig. 4.16 Grey toned picture with 4 bits of information per pixel (2^4 = 16 shades of grey)

Basically three items of information are important with colour pictures:

- **Hue**, Wave length of the light, for example: green= 555 nm,
- **Brightness**, how close does it come to black or white. Black = 0%, White = 100%. The term luminance if also often used.
- **Chroma**, how intense is the light.

Warning: Scanners and colour monitors use a different colour map to define colours as table-printers and presses (see chapter 2.3). During the transmission from the screen to a printer the colours are converted from one colour map into another. This is the reason why it is not possible to achieve exactly the same colours in a print and the pictures look different.

Fig. 4.17 Grey tone picture with 8 bits of information per pixel (2^8 = 256 shades of grey)

2.2 Image Depth

Screens (VDUs) are important output devices for multimedia systems (see chapter 4). However, a screen can only display a limited number of colours at one time. This limit is called the **image depth**

$$C = 2^D$$

C Quantity of different colours (or shades of grey)

D Image depth in bits per Pixel (bit/px)

Example: An image depth of 4 bits per pixel results in 2^4 $(2 \cdot 2 \cdot 2 \cdot 2 = 16)$ *different colour variations.*

The most frequently used image depths (fig 4.18) are 8 Bit =256 colours, 16 Bit = 65 536 colours (High Colour) and 24 Bit = 16,7 million colours (True Colour).

Of course, 16,7 million colours is *only a theoretical basis.* In order to display this number of colours, a screen with 4096 x 4096 pixels would be necessary.

Fig. 4.18 The image depth indicates the corresponding number of colours

colour depth	number of colours
1 bit	2 (black and white)
2 bit	4
4 bit	16
8 bit	256
16 bit	32.768
24 bit	16,7 Millions
32 bit	16,7 Mill. + extra channels

In actual fact, a **16 Bit colour coding** already approaches the normal human subjective colour sense very closely and is completely sufficient for a realistic colour reproduction. One refers to this as "real colour" in the area of RGB colour.

2.3 Colour Patterns

It is so far clear that colour is *not* a quality of a object: Colour is a subjective sense impression.

Colour is a subjective sense impression

In order to be able to use colour in multimedia-systems, an unique value must be assigned to every colour.
Not until this is done can different colours be identified and differentiated from each other.

Since most people are able to differentiate a maximum of 350 000 nuances of colour (more typical is between 50 000 and 300 000), colour mapping had to be introduced. This made it possible to describe individual colours with numerical values. An individual nomenclature (light yellow, even lighter yellow etc.) for a palette of this size would be simply impossible.

We distinguish between:

- physical -technical and
- perception orientated colour mapping.

A colour map serves to describe colours by means of an explicit colour scale. This can not describe all visible colours, but only a subset of them.

2.3.1 Physical-Technical Colour Maps

The physical - technical colour maps describe a colour as a mixture of the **Primary Colours.**

Since the human eye contains three types of colour sensative cones, the triplex theory was developed fairly early. This theory has remained, to date, the basis for colour television, colour monitors, colour photography and colour printing.

Fig. 4.19 Additive Mixing of light colours: the sum results in "white"

According to the triplex theory, all visible colours can be mixed from exactly three primaries. The condition for the criterion "primary" is that no one of the primaries can be mixed from the other two

The difference between the individual maps, lies in the choice of primary colours, and the method of mixing them.

With an **additive colour mix** (fig. 4.19) three "light colours" (such as the light from a torch) are mixed additively – it becomes increasingly brighter.

With a **subtractive colour mix** (fig.4.20) the three "body colours" (such as pigments in paint and printer colours) are mixed subtractively – it becomes increasingly dark.

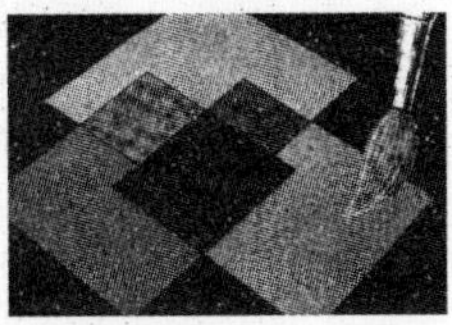

Fig. 4.20 Subtractive Mixing of body colours: the sum results in "black"

Belonging to the most important physical technical colour maps are:

- RGB Map: (additive colour mixing – computer screens, Television.),
- CMY Map: (subtractive colour mixing – printer output),
- YIQ Map: (USA television, is not really a separate map, but is derived from the RGB map).

Let us look now on this maps in more detail:

RGB Mapping

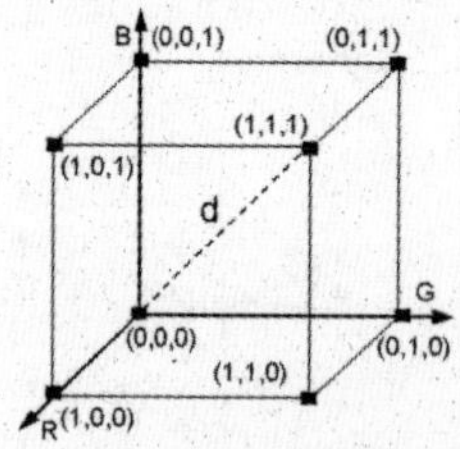

Fig. 4.21 In the RGB colour cube the grey tones are located on the main diagonal

The RGB Map is an **additive colour map.** If the three primary colours; red (610 nm), green (535 nm) and blue (470 nm) are mixed with specific intensity (0,3 R + 0,59 G + 0,11 B = 1), "colour" produced is White.

With the RGB Map, all displayable colours are expressed as points of a unified cube originating in a Cartesian coordinate system. The three primary colours; red , green and blue, are put on the positive axes of this coordinate system (fig 4.21).

The main diagonal of this cube stretches from the point (0,0,0) to the point (1,1,1) and contains colours with equals parts of all three primary colours. This represents all shades of grey; originating in black (0,0,0) and ending in white (1,1,1).

The respective colour is then calculated by the proportion of the three primary colours to be added to black.

Cartes, latinized form of the name of René Descartes, the famous French philosopher and mathematician (1596-1650)

> The RGB Map is implemented to display colour on screens (Monitors).

In Colour Visual Display Units three types of phosphor are applied to the Cathode Ray Tube (CRT). These triple colour can be accessed by three independent electron guns and a colour picture created from three monochrome (single colour) frames (RGB).

If two different screens use different kinds of phosphorus, different colours are produced. However, with a transformation computation, the colour specified on a cathode-ray tube can be synchronized with the tone scale of another CRT.

> The RGB Map is the most frequently employed map for the description of colours in computers and is based on computer hardware.

The HLS colour map is based on the intuitive method (see chapter 2.3.2) used, for instance, by painters.

Instead of declaring the proportions of Red, green and blue, a qualification of the colours is made via hue, luminance and saturation.

CMY-Colour-Model

In order to visualize the colours better: see Colour Tutorial [W5]

Basically, the CMY map (Cyan, Magenta, Yellow) uses the same subset of the Cartesian coordinate system as the RGB model, with the difference that "white" (brightest light) is now at the point of origin instead of "black" (no light). Colours are not specified by what is added to black but instead, by what is subtracted from white. The CMY Map is therefore referred to as a as **subtractive colour map.** The mixture of the colours Cyan, Magenta and yellow make black.

The CMY map is used for the colour-output on printers, it corresponds to the physical process of white light reflection.

The colour put onto the paper during this "three-colour print" guarantees that specific sections of the spectrum are filtered out and can no longer reflect.

For example, the cyan colour on the paper prevents red light being absorbed by the surface. Thus only the green and blue parts of the spectrum are reflected. The print colour Magenta absorbs green and the yellow print colour absorbs blue. If cyan and yellow are printed onto the paper, only the green part of the spectrum is reflected. When all three colours are used, all three colours are absorbed, resulting in black.

CMYK Colour Mapping

Cyan-Magenta-Yellow-Black

For professional colour printing, additional black ink is frequently used (K for black in CMYK), since it produces a darker black than the one achieved by the mixture of the three primary colours. The drying-time is also shortened with this "Four-colour" printing method by the reduced use of cyan, magenta and yellow ink. However, the storage demands increase by around a third since the information now has to cover four colours instead of the earlier three.

CMYK images are displayed on screen with the aid of the bright RGB mapped colours. Therefore CMYK images must be internally converted to RGB for the monitor. This is usually done by image editing programs, for example Photoshop.

YIQ Mapping and YUV Mapping

Y = Luminance signal
I/Q = Chrominance signals

The YIQ mapping is used in commercial colour television technology (NTSC standard, USA) and guarantees the downward compatibility of colour to black and white television.

Tristimulus: Each of three reference colours which can be combined additively in specified proportions (tristimulus values) to produce any given colour

The colours are expressed in the colour parameters **YIQ,** Y representing the brightness (Luminance) and IQ representing the colours (Chrominance). A black and white television receiver only displays the Y components.

Luminance-Plane (Y) Chrominance-Planes (U and V)

In application, it has been shown that the human eye observes tristimulus values at a lower resolution as brightness values. Therefore, some digital picture standards transform the RGB colour range into three "Planes", a luminance plane (gray shades, Y) and two chrominance planes (also referred to as U/V or Cr/Cb). The length of the edges of these planes of colour can then be halved, as we will see later by JPEG, which reduces the area, geometrically, to a quarter of its previous size. This reduces the amount of data enormously, however it also results in data loss.

This kind of a coding is is called the 4:1:1 **Colour space** (fig. 4.22).

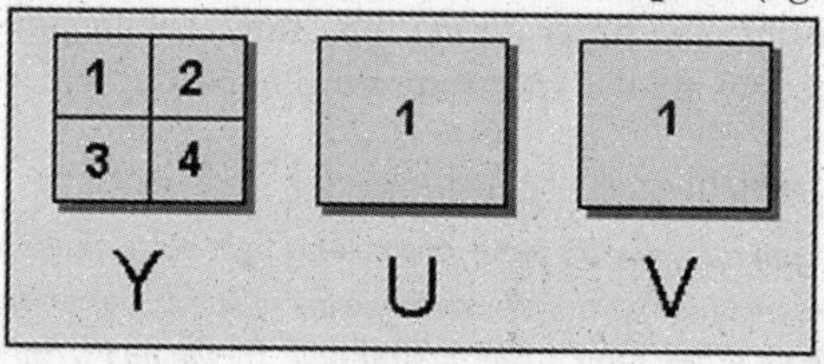

Fig. 4.22 The 4:1:1 colour space YUV mapping

Since the eye has far more receptor-cells for luminance than for colour changes, it is possible to transmit the colour information with narrower bandwidth without the (subjective) presentation deteriorating.

2.3.2 Sense orientated Colour Models

The perception oriented colour maps are aligned to human perception, which, in turn, is oriented to such parameters as:

- **Hue**,
- **Brightness, Lightness** and
- **Saturation**

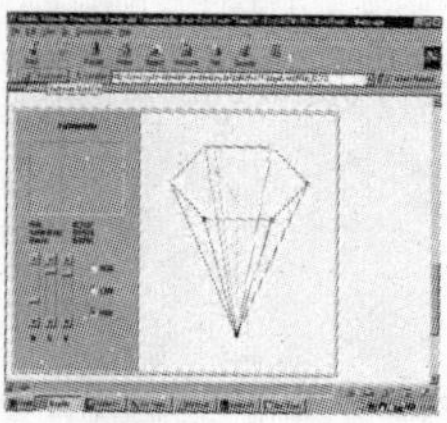

Fig. 4.23 The University Oldenburg has a very good colour mapping simulation online on the Web [06]

Included in the most important perception oriented colour maps are:

- **HSV Map** and the
- **CIE-XYZ Map.**

HSV Colour Mapping

As an user-oriented colour map, the HSV map has the advantage of corresponding more closely to the human notation of colour. This makes a purposeful colour selection simpler. This model is described by the following three parameters:

- **H**ue,
- **S**aturation,
- Brightness **V**alue.

With the HSV map the colour area is expressed by means of a hexagonal pyramid. The apex of the pyramid corresponds to a value V = 0 (Black), and the basis stands for V = 1 (White).

The tint (or hue) is obtained through the **H-value**, specified as a value between 0 and 360°, whereby the colours assigned to the six corners of the pyramids base receive the following values: Red 0°, yellow 60°, green 120°, cyan 180°, blue 240° and purple 300°.

The **S-value** lies between 0 and 1 and gives the distance of a colour at the axis going through the top of the pyramid and the centre of the base. The saturation describes the proportion of white light in the colour. The saturated colours at the sides of the pyramid do not contain any white light and therefore receive the value 1. White light and grey tones do not contain any colour of a dominating wavelength and receive the value of 0. Mixtures between saturated colours and white therefore have S-values between 0 and 1.

CIE Chromaticity Diagram

A colour stimulus causes an excitation of specific receptor-cells (R,G or B). This excitement can be expressed by **Standard Tristimulus Values**, whereby the relative proportions of the cone type stimulus can be represented by a chromaticity diagram. The extent (value) of the three primary colours which is necessary in order to cover all wavelengths of the visible spectrum is not, however, always positive. For instance, red is necessarily negative in order to obtain a 500 nm wave length. However, such a necessity of negative weighting is disadvantageous.

CIE not to be confused with CIX (Commercial Internet Exchange, which is, sometimes, also called CIE)

Therefore the CIE (Commission Internationale de l'Eclairage) defined, as early as 1931, **three standard primary colours** with the denotation **X, Y** and **Z** to replace the colours red, green and blue in the colour mixture. With these newly defined primary colours it is possible to create all colours in the spectrum with exclusively positive weighting. The three primaries X, Y and Z define a tridimensional colour area. All visible tristimulus values are defined in the layer X + Y + Z = 1. All perceptible colours of the same tint but different brightness are depicted by a point within the field.

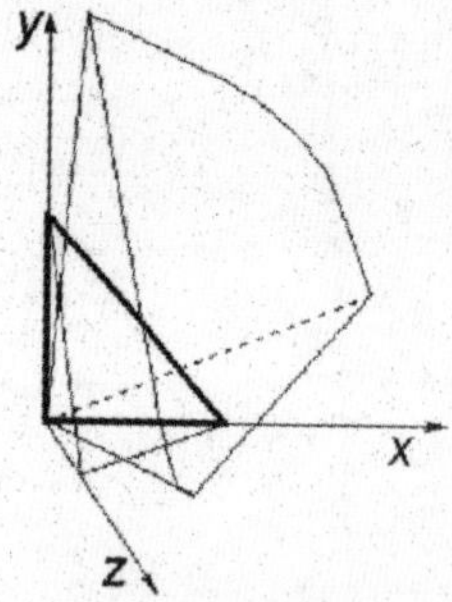

Fig. 4.24 The spatial CIE colour diagram

If the layer X + Y + Z = 1 is now projected on to the (X,Y) level, the result is the **CIE colour diagram** (also called chromatic diagram). The 100 pure colours of the spectrum now lie on the curved circumflex) edge. A standardized white.

With the CIE colour diagram, the dominant wavelength and purity of every colour can be measured. However no statement about luminance relative colour perception can be made. For instance, since the colour brown has an orange-red tristimulus value with a very low luminance relative to its surroundings it does not appear in the diagram. Therefore the CIE-diagram is certainly not a complete colour palette. There is an infinite number of levels in the (X,Y,Z) space, which are all projected onto the colour diagram. During this process information about the luminance always disappears. Each layer contains different colours.

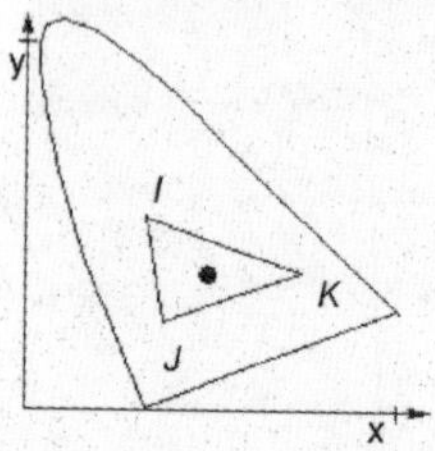

Fig. 4.25 The CIE colour triangle (gamut)

An important possible use of the CIE colour diagram is the definition of **colour palettes** (gamuts), which show the result of the sum of colours. If two arbitrary colours 'I' and 'J' are added, every colour along their interconnection line can be created by changing the relative proportions of the two colours. If a third colour 'K' is also used, a palette can be created with all colours within the triangle IJK, by mixing the colours 'I','J' and 'K' and varying the relative proportions of each colour. This principle also clarifies, why not all colours can be created by mixing the three visible colours red, green and blue; there is no triangle (gamut) which has corners located both within the visible field and also completely covering it.

2.4 Indexing and Dithering

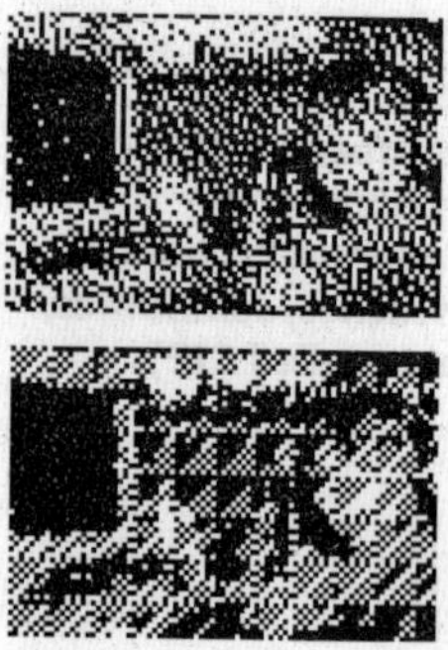

Fig. 4.26 Difference between Pattern Dithering (above) und Diffusion Dithering (below)

In order to display illustrations in a multimedia system without colour shifts in a determined colour depth, the plates must be adapted to the colour palette, in other words – **indexed**. A loss of quality inevitably occurs during the indexing. For instance, every one of the innumerable colour nuances of a 6,7 million colour image (Photographic quality) is assigned a colour tint from the 256 colour palette. This naturally leads to a corresponding coarsening of the image. The quality can be improved in this case by **Dithering** (Continuous tone procedure, continuous tone approximation). With the Dither process (literally "tremble") colours that are missing in the palette are simulated by the positioning of different coloured pixels (distribution raster). Our eyes register a colour impression approximate to the original. Dithering allows an acceptable picture quality even with a low colour depth. It can also be used for file size minimization. Dithering distinguishes between two types of grid (fig 4.26 shows a comparison):

- **Pattern Dithering** generates a **regular distribution raster**, and
- **Diffusion Dithering** utilizes a **random distribution.**

2.5 Resolution of Bitmap Images

The resolution specifies the number of the pixels that are available on a specific area for the display (presentation) of a character or graphics. On a computer screen (VDU) it is given in pixel per inch **(ppi),** on an output device (e.g. printer) as the number of printed dots per inch **(dpi)** and on a scanner, it is the number of pixels per inch of the picture being scanned, that can be recorded. The resolution of an output device influences both the accuracy of detail and the colour range achieved during the production of a bitmap picture.

A pixel is the smallest unit of a bitmap image.

Fig. 4.27 A picture with 72 dpi appears strongly "gritted" in print

A high-resolution bitmap image contains a great amount of data about the position and colour of every individual pixel in order to achieve a high accuracy of detail. Logically, a lower resolution bitmap image contains correspondingly less data and does not achieve the same accuracy of detail (fig 4.29).

Nevertheless one does not automatically achieve a better print result with a higher resolution bitmap image, it is possible that the output device is unable to process, or print, the large amount of data being transmitted. The resolution can be calculated with the following formular:

$$a = \frac{n_{px}}{l}$$

a Resolution in dpi
n_{px} Number of pixels per side
l Length of sides in inches

1 inch = 2,54 cm
1 cm = 0,394 inch

2.6 Image Size

Every single pixel of a 24 Bit True-Colour file needs 3 Bytes of working memory (RAM). Therefore, the memory required for an RGB picture is *n* pixels high times *m* pixels across times *three* bytes. (Vertical x Horizontal x 3)

An RGB image sized 9 x 13 cm (= 3.54" x 5.11") with a resolution of 300 dpi therefore needs 1062 x 1536 x 3 = 4,89 MB of storage space. The same picture in a 4 bit grey scale mode requires 1,6 MB. It is this very high memory requirement which makes the concept of compression so important.

3 Image File Formats

Our central question is: "Which picture is most optimal for which purpose"?

3.1 Vector graphics

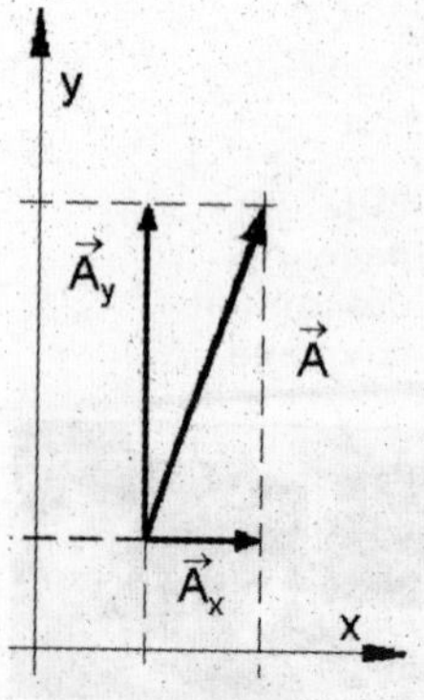

Fig. 4.28 A Vector is determined through starting point, direction and length (polar)

Vector graphics are also referred to as **object oriented graphics** and consist of mathematically exact defined curves (basic geometrical forms,: primitives) and lines that are designated as "vectors".

For example, in order to define a line, only three pieces of information are necessary:

- the coordinates of the starting point **(Origin),**
- the coordinates of the end point **(Vector top)** and
- the line width **(Attribute).**

Similarly, the centre coordinates (Origin), the radius (vector top) and the line width (attribute) suffice for a circle. Such graphics are **scalable**, this means that simply by modifying the measurements the object's size is arbitrarily vector graphics variable. Also vector graphics are resolution independent, they are displayed or printed according to the resolution settings of the respective printer or computer screen. Advantages of vector graphics:

- Vector graphics require less **memory space** than Bitmap images ,
- Vector graphics are **optionally exact**, the resolution is irrelevant,
- Vector graphics are **scalable without loss.**

Vector graphics are ideal for the storage of images containing line based information or elements, or images which can easily be converted into line based information (e.g. text).

Disadvantages of vector graphics:

- **Not optimal for complex images** with colours which change every pixel (e.g. Photographs),
- **Appearance is dependent** on the respective application program
- Identical data can not **always be identically** interpreted.

The output quality is naturally only optimum with vector output devices (Plotter).

Some examples of vector graphic formats include PostScript and DXF:

3.1.1 PostScript, Encapsulated PostScript

With appropriate Hardware (RIP) directly interpretable on laser printing devices

PostScript was developed in 1984 by Adobe and became known, as **laser printers** became widely spread, as a comprehensive printing format.

From a technical point of view, PostScript is a purely **page description language**.

PDL page description language

PostScript files are pure ASCII(Text) Files and can be created or modified at any time with an editor, although this is usually done by the respective graphics program.

PostScript details the complete construction of a print or screen page; text, vector graphics and embedded raster images. Raster images are expressed in hexadecimal numbers, as are the other image elements. However, the PostScript file format is not limited to page description but is actually a complete programming language..

File extension:	.ps .eps .epsf .epsi
Format:	Vector
Colours:	1/4/8/24 bit
Compression:	dependent on version
max. Size:	no limit

Fig. 4.29 The PostScript format at a glance

PostScript is continually being further developed. At the moment there are three variations:

- PostScript Level 1
- PostScript Level 2
- Display PostScript

Fonts

PostScript Level 1 is particularly for high-quality Fonts. It was released in 1990, after Microsoft and Apple disclosed their TrueType Format. A disadvantage of this variation is the limited colour support.

PostScript Level 2 also contains compression possibilities, for example JPEG. Level-2-Code is completely compatible to Level-1-Code with the great advantage of a complete colour concept with both device dependent and device independent colour schemes.

Display PostScript is a binary format (therefore no text) for a screen output of PostScript. Only few systems (e.g. Next-Computers) work with PostScript display.

RIP Raster Image Processor

PostScript printer's contain a (in system/printer) built-in processor that directly interprets the post-script code (RIP). Here, the PostScript text codes vector information is converted directly to individual pixels for the output device.

Since the Vector Information Data Interpretation takes place in the output device, PostScript is **hardware independent.**

Apart from PostScript printers, many graphic output devices, for example photo units and compositors use this graphic format.

EPS (or EPSF) stands for „Encapsulated PostScript File". In this version, the initial PostScript code is enclosed in a series of additional DSC comments (Document Structuring Conventions), which make it possible to mix the output (or the content respectively) with any other PostScript texts or graphics.

```
%!PS-Adobe-3.0 EPSF-3.0
%%BoundingBox: llx lly urx ury
```

Fig. 4.30 Document Structuring Conventions (DCS) in PostScript

It consists of at least two lines (fig 4.30): Adobe 3.0 identifies the current DSC Version and EPSF 3.0 identifies the current EPS Version.

The "Bounding Box" set the **boundaries** with the horizontal (x) and vertical (y) graphic corners coordinates (ll= lower left and ur = upper right).

Measurement units: 1/72" = 0,353mm

This boundary describes the rectangular area within which the graphic fits.. However, many PostScript Printers (for example, with MS-Windows) declare the boundaries of the whole pages, rather than just the area actually required for the graphics.

Export functions within the application program are mostly better (here the printer driver is not used). Some PostScript files can be converted into an EPS-file by inserting these two lines.

EPS is, however, only a subset of PostScript, which does not contain all commands.

In particular, an EPS file may only contain a single graphics page, whereas a PostScript file can contain as many as necessary.

PostScript or EPS files can be printed by post-script printers, however, only a few programs are actually able to import PostScript files, or to display them directly onto a screen. Usually an **empty frame** is displayed as "place holder" for the graphic.

Ghostscript [W-09]

> In order to display PS/EPS files on the screen before printing, a special PostScript Previewer is necessary. **GhostScript**. is a PS-Previewer program which is available for almost every platform.

With Display PostScript Systems, no extra Software is necessary, the files can be displayed directly onto the screen.

3.1.2 DXF

DXF is a format for vector oriented programs (for example in the fields of CAD/CAM/CIM).

It was developed by the company Autodesk, manufacturer of the well-known CAD program:

AutoCAD

AutoCAD. DXF is a pure ASCII format, it can therefore be read and modified by a normal editor. DXB is the binary version of a DXF-file.

File extension:	.dxf
Format:	Vector
Colours:	max. 8 bit
Compression:	none
max. Size:	no limit

Fig. 4.31 The DXF Format at a glance

Unlike many other vector formats DXF also stores tridimensional objects. The number of colours is limited to 256, which is however completely sufficient for CAD applications. Data compression does not occur.

This would not noticeably reduce the file size anyway, since a vector format has considerably less redundancy than a schedule bitmap file.

A DXF file has the following construction (fig. 4.32):

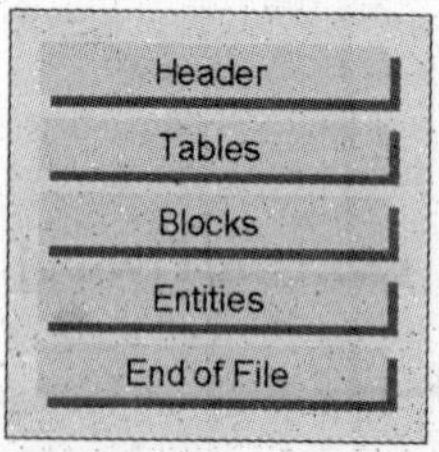

Fig. 4.32 The Architecture of a DXF File

In the **Header Section**, all variables, which will be discarded ("prepared") during the drawing, are set.

In addition, the current colours and the screen section to be used are defined. The **Tables Section** contains the definitions of the character dependent entries in tables.

In the **Blocks Section** the graphic elements that were defined as *blocks* during the character setting are stored.

The actual definitions of the character elements are stored in the **Entities Section**. This is the only Section which absolutely must exist in the DXF File.

3.2 Bitmap Images

Bitmap images (Bitmap = Pixel area) are made up of very small squares **(Pixels)** in a right-angled **raster** (a grid, see fig. 4.33).

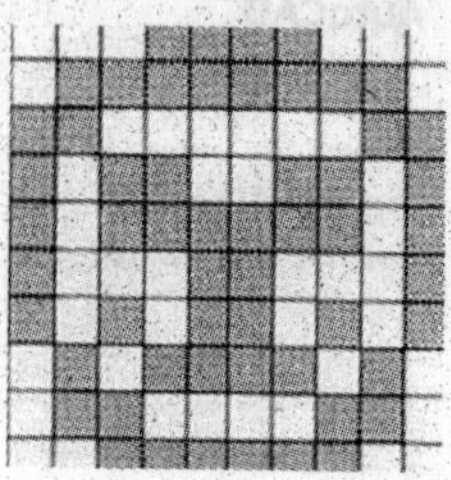

Fig. 4.33 Principle Architecture of a Bitmap image

Every single pixel contains the information as to its colour and weight, whether it is to be displayed as black, white, coloured or a shade of grey.

The size of a bitmap file is dependent on the amount of colour information contained in it.

Unlike vector graphics, which are manipulated by changing the lines and curves, bitmap images are altered by manipulating the **pixel groups**, thereby making bitmap images dependant on the image resolution.

When bitmap images are constructed with a low resolution, and subsequently enlarged or printed with a higher resolution, they frequently appear fuzzy or loose exactitude of detail. (fig 4.34).

Fig. 4.34 Using a resolution of only 72 dpi the raster of a bitmap image comes out strongly: The human eye recognizes the "rastering"

Advantages of bitmap images:

- **Manipulation of the pixels is very simple,** singularly or in groups (for example partial colour changes etc.).
- When the output device works directly with pixels, the bitmap image **can be optimal constructed** (printer).
- Particularly extensive output medium, for the **realistic representation** of objects (in contrast to vector graphics).

Disadvantages of bitmap images:

- **Differentiated representation** of the pixels.
- Smooth curves are represented through approximation of pixels on the raster grid: "indents" and "steps": **aliasing.**
- **Large files,** especially when colours are used.

Bitmaps are not easily reduced or enlarged: The individual pixels are simply duplicated by enlargement, changing the picture or the proportions; while reducing the image merely deletes individual pixels. This can best be seen by reducing and re-enlarging an image to its original size, then comparing the result with the original image.

Basically, Bitmaps can be printed satisfactorily using the resolution with which they were constructed.

There are hundreds of different bitmap formats.

However, only a few have actually been accepted and are now used in the field of multimedia. We will first review some basic formats, then the compression concept and finally common packed file formats.

3.2.1 BMP

Note: Bitmap has two *different meanings* in Multimedia Technology:

- Bitmap (Pixel array) generally as (any) halftone image and
- Bitmap with the file extension BMP as a file format (only) with MS-Windows and OS/2 Systems.

The BMP format definition is independent of the output device used (device independent).

It can be output to different screens or printers and meanwhile is also supported by many of the programs on other operating systems.

This format is based on the RGB colour model. However, through suitable construction of colour maps, it is also possible to code monochrome and grey scale images

Fig. 4.35 The BMP file format at a glance

File extension:	.bmp .dib
Format:	Raster
Colours:	1/4/8/24 bit
Compression:	none (or RLE)
max. Size:	65.536 x 65.536 px

The format defines a header area and a data area (fig 4.36). The header is called "BITMAP INFORMATION" and contains the information about size, colour depth, colour map and the type of compression. The data area *contains sequentially* the tristimulus values of every point of a line. Lines are extended into a value divisible by 32, justified and padded with zeros. Authorized values for colour depth are 1, 4, 8 and 24.

Word – a computer storage area consisting of 16 bits

The **Run Length Encoding Algorithm** (see compression concept; chapter 4) is offered for pictures with a colour depth of 4 or 8 bits per pixel, whereby any one unit of information consists of 2 bytes (called: word).

If the first byte value (word) is zero and the second value is larger than three, then this second value is the number of bytes containing the colour information for the next pixel as a reference of the colour map (no compression).

Otherwise, the second byte contains the colour information, as a reference to the colour map, and the first byte the number of following pixels affected. If the picture is coded with 4 bits per pixel then only four bits are used for these information. This means there is room for 2 values per byte. BMP still defines the possibility of a mandatory colour map being included in the header.

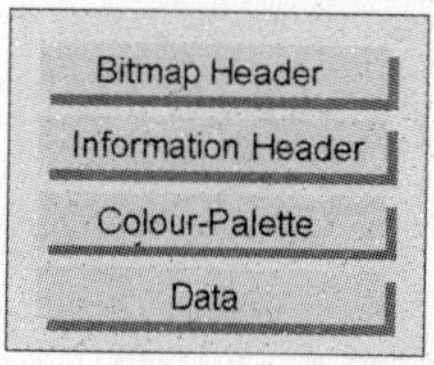

Fig. 4.36 Architecture of a .BMP File

Thus, a BMP file is made up of four sections: (fig 4.36): The Bitmap Header contains the file signature „BM“, the file length in bytes and the offset (difference) between the file begin and the file begin in bytes.

Information on the pictures found in the information header (height, width, horizontal and vertical resolution, number of colours used, if necessary the compression type).

The Colour Palette defines every colour by their proportions of red, green and blue. The data contains the line-by-line raster information of the image, starting at the bottom left corner.

In images with 1, 4 or 8 Bit colour information, the pixel value does not directly contain the colour information, but a pointer or index reference to the colour palette

In 24 bit images, the pixel value corresponds to the tristimulus value so no colour palette is needed.

3.2.2 MAC

MacIntosh Paint is the standard graphic format on Apple-MacIntosh Computers. On Apple computers the files are stored (saved) as file type PNTG, on PCs with the extention .MAC.

MacIntosh has been on the market since 1984 and is the proprietary computer family of the Apple Company. It has been suitable for multi media from the beginning.

MAC graphics always.have a fixed size of 576 x 720 pixels. The colour depth is 1 bit, this means that only B/W pictures can be stored. The resolution is a constant 72 dpi, which corresponds exactly to the screen resolution of MacIntosh computers (For comparison: Screen resolution of an IBM personal computer: variable from 70 to 120 dpi).

There are two versions of the MAC format:

- MacBinary,
- MacBinary II.

File extension:	.pntg .mac
Format:	Raster
Colours:	1 bit (b/w)
Compression:	none (or RLE)
Size:	always 720 x 576 px

Fig. 4.37 The MAC format at a glance

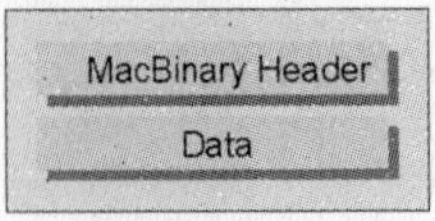

Fig. 4.38 Structure of a MAC file

A Mac-file has following construction (fig 4.38): The **header** always begins with a zero byte. This is followed by; the length of the file name, file, the file name itself, the file type (PNTG or MAC), a four-digit identification of the program that created the file (e.g.MPNT for MacPaint) and the status information. A MacBinary II header is somewhat longer than MacBinary header.

The **data** always begins with the byte sequence 00 00 00 02 (hexadecimal). It is followed by 304 bytes of pattern data. These data are not needed for the display of the image file. Before the actual display data, which can be packed to RLE, are another 204 zero bytes.

On a Macintosh computer every file is stored in the form of two files, the **data fork** u and the **resource fork**. In a MacPaint image the display data is only stored in the data fork, while the resource fork remains empty. When a MacPaint file is transferred onto another computer environment in binary form (for example a personal computer), the two forks are combined into a single file, and reconstructed at a re-transfer back to a Macintosh platform.

A Macintosh computer creates black points on a white background whereas PCs and other systems create white points on a black background.

3.2.3 RAS

UNIX is a multiuser operating system, developed by Bell Labs (AT & T), which is mainly employed in main-frame computers.

RAS is the graphic format of UNIX Workstations, especially Sun microsystems.

Most other UNIX platforms programs also support this format. RAS supports an arbitrary bit quantity per pixel.

File extension:	.ras
Format:	Raster
Colours:	variable
Compression:	RLE
Size:	variable

Fig. 4.39 The RAS format at a glance

A RAS file has the following architecture (fig 4.40): The header begins with the character string 59a66a95 (hexadecimal). This is followed by the width and height of the image in pixels, the number of bits per pixel, the size of the image data in bytes, a version number, the colour map (variant palette) and the size of the colour map in bytes.

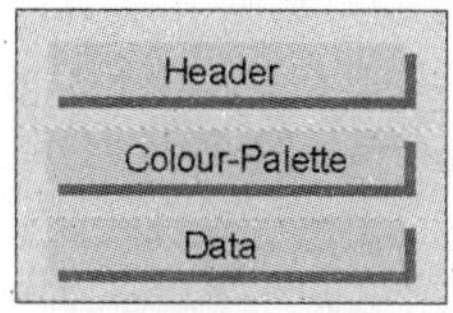

Fig. 4.40 Architecture of a RAS file

The colour map can have the following variations:

- 0000 No Map
- 0001 RGB Map
- 0002 another Map, not defined by RAS

Racing-files with a colour depth of 8, 24 or 32 bit do not usually contain a colour map since the colour data are contained in thc display data. Die RGB data can be stored as RLE compression data.

3.2.4 TIFF

Tagged Image File Format

The TIFF format was developed in 1986 by the Aldus Corporation (taken over in 1990 by Adobe). The goal was **portability** and **hardware independence**, which caused it to develop into one of the most important formats for bitmaps. From the beginning it was so extensively designed that it offers a large number of saving possibilities and apart from the actual graphic data, information about the graphics software used or scanner models can also be included.

File extension:	.tif
Format:	Raster
Colours:	1 bit to 24 bit
Compression:	none (or various)
Size:	max. $4 \cdot 10^9$ lines

Fig. 4.41 The TIFF Format at a glance

From the beginning, TIFF has been able to store images in black and white, grey shades and colour, including information regarding the colour model used. Even though these possibilities make the format more complicated, they also make it **universally** applicable. Not only the majority of scanners but also many graphic programs use the TIFF format.

The input of TIFF images can cause problems with some programs. Due to variants, as for example different compression methods, many programs only read a small part of all TIFF-Variants.

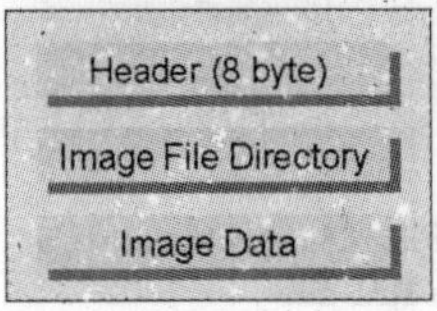

Fig. 4.42 The architecture of a TIFF File

The cause of the error in most programs can is to be found in the fact that the TIFF format is extremely precisely defined.

Problem solving by import difficulties: First save the file in uncompressed format and *then* import it.

"Little Endian" (The little end comes first.) the low-order byte is stored in memory at the lowest address

"Big Endian" (The big end comes first.) the high-order byte is stored in the memory at the lowest address

A TIFF-file consists of three sections which are separated by **tags** (Markers). (fig 4.42): The **header** contains the information about the file storage type (II for Intel little-endian, MM for Motorola big-endian) as well as the version number and the address of the first image file directory (IFD).

An **Image File Directory** (IFD) also consists of three sections: The **number of tags**, the **tags** themselves and the **address of the next IFD** (fig 4.43). Each tag contains information about the corresponding image (width, height, compression, X and Y offset etc.).

There are more than 90 different Tags, therefore the length of the IFD is not constant.

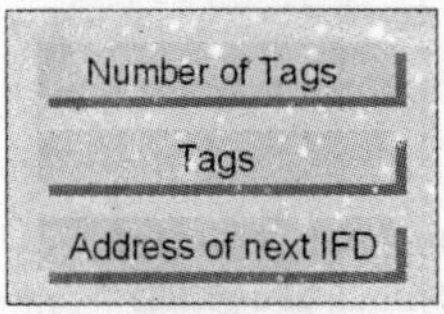

Fig. 4.43 The structure of a Image File Directory

An IFD can be placed anywhere in a TIFF-file, after the header. If a file contains several pictures then several arrangements of IFD and display data are possible. If no further picture follows, the address of the next IFD is 00 (hexadecimal). For storage, the pictures are divided into fixed length. The storage order of the **image data** is optional.

A determining difference to other picture formats lies in the generic approach. Generally one can code the graphic contents within a TIFF formates in different ways.

For example, a Preview picture can be coded in a simplified line oriented and uncompressed format in addition to a subsequent, essentially more complex picture, making a fast search within picture archives possible.

3.3 Metafiles

Meta formats combine the advantages of bitmap and vector formats. They can be used with almost all applications.

3.3.1 WMF

Windows Meta File

WMF is closely associated to MS Windows. It is employed, for example, for the exchange of graphics using a clipboard. Some graphic programs under Windows are also able to create this format.

File extension:	.wmf
Format:	Meta
Colours:	up to 24 bit
Compression:	none (or various)
Size:	no limit

Fig. 4.44 The Format WMF at a glance

WMF stores graphics from design statements with their corresponding parameters. The statements are designated as function calls under Windows. These interface with the **„Graphic Device Interface“ (GDI)** in order to output onto the corresponding hardware. The GDI contains libraries of graphic objects (Rings, oblongs, ellipses etc.).

The WMF object's unit of measure is a **twip.**

---

1 twip = 1 twentieth of a point = 1/1440 "

A WMF file has the following architecture (fig 4.45): The information regarding the storage area, the length of the header in words (1 word=2 bytes), the Windows Version being used, the complete length of the WMF file in words, the number of objects stored in the file and the length of the longest object is stored in the **Header**.

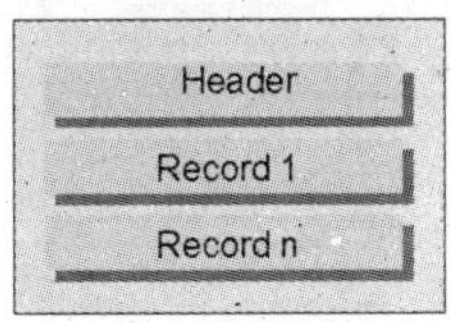

Fig. 4.45 The architecture of a WMF file

The last 2 bytes are always 0. An arbitrary number of records follow subsequently, each on embodying a GDI function with its corresponding parameters. Every record contains the length of the record in words, the number of the GDI function (defined in windows) as well as the parameters of the function.

Note: Some windows applications put an extra 22 Byte header in front of the WMF header. This starts with the character string 9ac6cdd7 (hexadecimal) and contains information needed in order to interchange the WMF file between different applications.

3.3.2 CGM format

Computer Graphics Meta file

The format CGM originates from the standardization of the graphic core system GKS. .

It is especially designed for the exchange of pictures between different systems and contains all commands and parameters necessary for determination standardization.

Fig. 4.46 The CGM format at a glance

File extension:	.cgm
Format:	Meta
Colours:	unlimited
Compression:	RLE, CCITT 3 and 4
Size:	no limit

The narrower format descriptions make the CGM format a genuine transfer format for vector data.

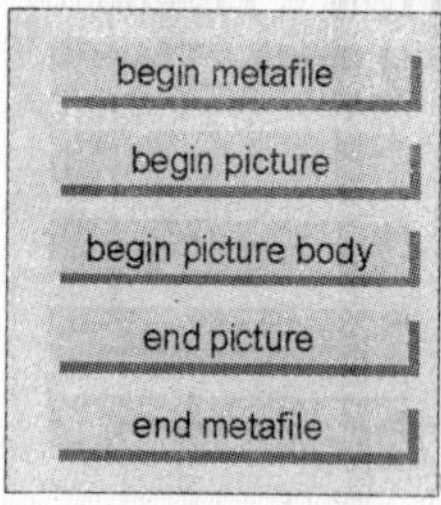

Fig. 4.47 Boundary elements in CGM format

A CGM file has the following construction (fig 4.47):

Boundary elements divide the individual **image description elements.** Beginning with the file identification, the font definitions, date accuracy conventions etc.

After the "begin picture", all picture description elements are combined and a processing and representation mode determined. In addition, coordinates area, line thicknesses and flag sizes are defined.

The " picture body" consists of three sections: **Control elements** determine the accuracy of the data and the "clipping area". In the **display elements** class, the various elements containing graphic information (for example line, tag, text, filling area and cell array elements) are collected.

The display of the graphical elements is controlled by the **attribute elements.**

Fundamentally three coding possibilities exist with CGM-files:

- **Character coding** (very short files, suitable for Network transfer),
- **Binary coding** (Storage in binary coded integer values) and
- **Plain text coding** (readable ASCII files, disadvantage: very long).

3.3.3 PICT

PICT files are Apple-MacIntosh specific and are based on the MacIntosh internal graphic protocol QuickDraw. Therefore PICT basically contains QuickDraw function calls.

File extension:	.pict
Format:	Meta
Colours:	up to 24 bit
Compression:	PackBits, JPEG
Size:	variable

Fig. 4.48 The PICT format at a glance

As already mentioned, every file on a MacIntosh Computer is stored in the form of two physical files, the data fork and the resource fork (cf. chapter 3.2.2).

With a PICT image only the data fork contains the display data while the resource fork (if existent) remains empty. The data are stored in binary format.

Now we have become acquainted with various vector formats, bitmap formates and metafiles, which partially permit a possible compression. Now we turn to the compression concept and review a few "genuine" packed file formats. The use of image formats in the internet will be covered in module 6.

To be exact it is called data compression (due to it is not possible with analog signals)

4 Compression concept

In multimedia systems, uncompressed pictures rapidly require a considerable storage capacity (cf. chapter 2.6). Primarily with raster displays it is necessary to reduce the volume of picture information.

Bandwidth problems see Module 6 chapter 2.1

In particular with multimedia communication over networks (e.g. the Internet) a data transfer of uncompressed pictures requires extremely high bandwidths. Thus, data compression is indispensable. However, data can also go lost through this compression, which is sometimes unwanted (although many times a loss of data is insignificant – otherwise no compression concept would work).

The key concepts of compression can be divided, first of all, into three main categories:

Entropy Coding

- Statistical approach (Entropy Coding): **statistical distributions** are searched for in the input datum stream. These are used for the reduction of the data. With this method, the input is considered as a pure bit stream without considering inherent semantics. Statistical procedures, also known as entropy coding, do not code the data to be transmitted, but only the source symbols.

Source Coding

- Semantic approach (Source Coding): It is assumed that the input data stream possesses a **semantic structure,** whereby the following approaches are of importance:
  a) Coding of **differences** (Prediction): it is assumed that, two successive blocks are not independent of each other. Therefore, *only the differences* are coded.
  b) **Reduction**: Here, an attempt is made to find frequency components, for example through a Fourier transformation (FT), with an amplitude too small to be important for the output signal. These are **specifically left out.** In the image area the **Discrete Cosine Transformation** (DCT) is used in place of the Fourier analysis.
  c) A further possibility consists of choosing a suitable procedure during the coding of the input stream. In this manor for example, the resolution chosen for coding the brightness is double that of the colour information in YUV Coding (cf. fig 4.22).

Hybrid Coding

- Hybrid Coding: (composite processes): These combine the advantages of the statistical and the semantic procedures. In this case a **Transformation** (Picture Processing) follows the **picture preprocessing** (A/D transformation and the choice of a suitable coding), in general a DCT. The result is subjected to one of the normal statistical procedures after specific frequency components have been removed by quantization.

With compression procedures we differentiate between:

- unaffected by loss (non lossy)
- and affected by loss (lossy) compression procedures.

Commonly **non lossy** compression procedures are:

- **RLE** (Run Length Encoding),
- **LZW** (Lempel-Ziv-Welch) and
- **Huffman** (CCITT) Encoding.

The best known **lossy** Compression procedures are:

- **JPEG** (Joint Photographic Experts Group),
- **Fractal Compression** according to BARNSLEY and SLOAN, and
- **Wavelet-Compression.**

4.1 Lossless Procedures

4.1.1 RLE

Run Length Encoding belongs to the statistical coding procedures (Entropy coding). It is one of the simplest procedures and it takes advantage of the characteristic that many data consist of series of identical bytes (fig 4.49). These series of same bytes can be represented by **data pairs** – consisting of a **character** and a **number.**

Fig. 4.49 series of identical bytes are reduced by using data

In the example in fig 4.49 a data reduction of 50 % is achieved (16:8 byte).

Run Length Encoding is particularly suitable for files with **long series of identical symbols,** as for example black and white images. Whereas, files with frequently changing bytes are not very suitable. In a worst case situation the new file could even be twice as big as the original.

This procedure is therefore frequently employed for facsimile (Fax) formats, in which very large areas of white are only occasionally interrupted black alphabetic characters.

4.1.2 LZW

The LZW procedure is named after the developers; LEMPEL, ZIV and WELCH and is used by a number of graphic formats (e.g. GIF). This procedure is based on the search for identical character strings and their replacement by references to previous identical strings. For this purpose an **assignment**

LZ78 process

table is created, in which the references' to the individual character strings are stored.

The assignment table is not stored in the actual file, but it must be recreated by every compression and decompression.

Example: The character string „whoiswho"is divided into the sub-strings „who" and „is". In the assignment table the word „who" receives the index "1" and the word „is" receives the index 0. The Codeword is then 101. Contrary to the Huffman Procedure, in which every source is coded, by the LZW procedure *only complete symbol series* are combined to a new Symbol.

4.1.3 Huffman Coding

short name: huff; also named squeezing

The idea of the Huffman Coding belongs to the statistical coding procedures and originates from the principal of MORSE (refer to Module 2, chapter 2).

Shorter codes are assigned to the **more frequently occurring symbols** (in this case alphabetical characters) than to those occurring more rarely. For example the code for an "e" only consists of an single Morse signal (dot), for the transfer of the seldom occurring "z" 4 morse signals are necessary (dash-dash-dot-dot).

4.2 Lossy Procedures

4.2.1 JPEG

JPEG is also the name of a

- Standardisation organisation, a
- Graphic format and an
- Image compression procedure.

This last is a standard, that of the Joint Photographic Experts Group which was developed in 1982. The "Joint" set up on the combined activity of ISO and CCITT. JPEG is an ISO standard since 1992.

The compression of the graphic data occurs in four steps (fig 4.50):

1st. Step **Data Reduction**: The eye s not able to distinguish as many colour details as differences in brightness. Therefore the colour information is reduced by **omitting individual points.** This procedure is called usually **sampling** (or more precisely colour-sub-sampling).

The reduction is carried out in horizontal and vertical directions separately. Thus it is also possible to tune different reduction steps for the different directions.

The most frequent reduction steps are:

- 1:1:1 (a value for the colour information is stored for every value for brightness),
- 2:1:1 (a value for the colour information is stored for every two values for brightness),
- 4:1:1 (a value for the colour information is stored for every four values for brightness (compare YUV colour map in chapter 2.3.1).

2nd. Step **Discrete Cosine Transformation** (DCT)

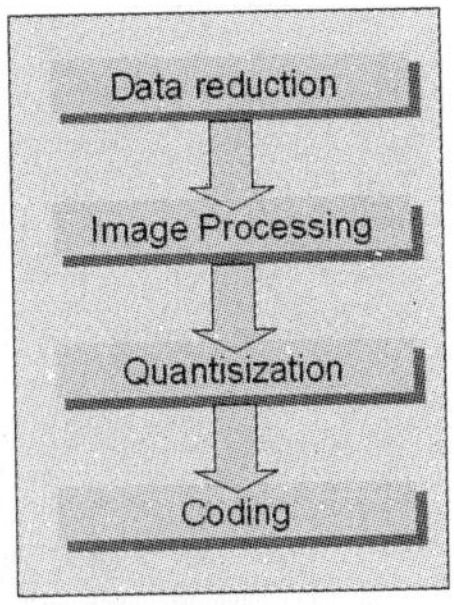

Fig. 4.50 The process of compression after the JPEG algorithm

DCT is based on the **Fourier transformation**, which represents the arbitrary signals as a superposition of sinusoidal waves of different frequencies and amplitudes (see module 2 signals).

A frequency and amplitude distribution is created from the local distribution of pixel values in a picture after the Fourier transformation. A frequency and amplitude distribution is created from the local distribution of pixel values in a picture after the Fourier transformation. Large, regular areas appropriate, in this case, the low frequency components, fine details the high ones. The predominant part of the visual information of an image with continuously distributed values is in the field of low frequencies.

Compression occurs through lower weighting and setting the amplitudes of the higher frequenced image sections to zero.

3rd. Step **Quantization**

The Quantization is in fact the step most affected by loss. From the linear process of the values the formation of a step like order occurs.

The quantization factor is, in this case, optional and determines the future file size and the quality of the reclaimable picture.

4th. Step **Entropy Coding**

The determined values are ordered in a zigzag sequence and are summarized by running length coding and/or Huffman Coding.

Fractal: A mathematically conceived curve such that any small part of it, enlarged, has the same statistical character as the original

4.2.2 Fractal Compression

Fractal image compression is based on fractal geometry. In 1988 MICHAEL BARNSLEY and ALAN SLOAN verified the possibility of such an image compression method.

self-affinity

The foundation of this was the observation, that natural objects frequently do not have the straight lines and smooth surfaces with which classical geometry works. Many natural forms obey the fractal geometry. Your jagged, apparently accidental shapes occur in large and small sizes.

Example: Near the edge of a cloud the same forms (rotated, reflected) appear again and again in increasing size.

Fractal compression attempts to find similarities in digital images and to use them for data reduction.

By a compression rate of up to 1:25, this procedure supplies as good a result as JPEG. With higher rates JPEG result in coarse shading (gritting). Strong contrast problems, caused by the omission of whole frequency ranges of the initial image through the DCT, are avoided. The compression is relatively time-consuming, however the decompression of a fractal packed picture is very fast.

At the moment, no standard image format exists which uses this compression procedure.

4.2.3 Wavelet Compression

With the aid of the JPEG, it is possible to achieve compression rates of up to 1:35 in acceptable picture quality. The wavelet compression procedure allows rates of approximately 1:65. Of the compression procedures discussed here this is certainly the most mathematically sophisticated. The strategy is comparable to JPEG. It is attempted to remove imperceptible details from the image. However, it is not completely disassembled into frequency components, but rather (little by little) increasingly coarser picture structures are filtered out.

A Wavelet Transformation transformation converts the Original image into Wavelet coefficients which basically describe reduced copies of the initial image.

Additionally, these coefficients still contain high and low-pass filtered versions of these pictures. The actual compression occurs in the so-called quantization interval.

With the aid of different strategies unimportant image details are combined. Subsequently, the result is subjected to an entropy codifying (for example the Huffman Procedure).

4.3 Compressed File Formats

4.3.1 JPEG

The JPEG File Interchange Format (JFIF) is a development of the C-cube Microsystems company for storing JPEG packed data. It can reduce image data by almost any factor (20, 50, in 150 ...), deletes however a relatively large amount of information, which must be recalculated later. .

File extension:	.jpg .jpeg .jfi .jfif
Format:	Raster
Colours:	up to 24 bit
Compression:	JPEG
Size:	65536 × 65536 px

Fig. 4.51 The File format JPG at a glance

Next to GIF, JPEG is the most important image file format for Internet based multimedia systems.

Warning: We are referring here to the file format JPEG. There are also other document types which carry out *data compression according to the JPEG procedure* (cf. chapter 4.2.1), for example PDF, EPS and PICT on MacIntosh. TIFF formats with JPEG compression also exist.

A JFIF-file has the following architecture (fig 4.55):

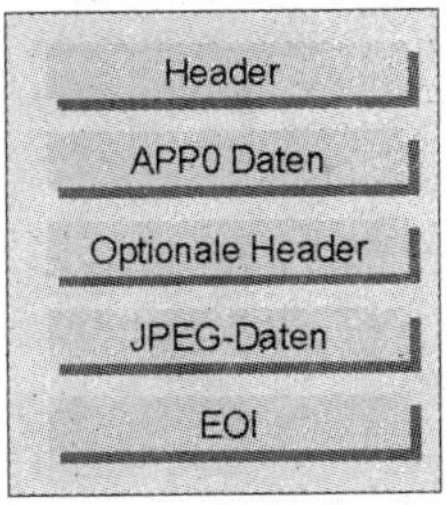

Fig. 4.52 The architecture of a JFIF file

The header contains the Start of Image (SOI) flag (FF D8 hexadecimal), the application flag (FF E0 hexadecimal), the size of the APP0 data (see below), the character string JFIF, the version number of the JFIF specification, the unit of measure (dots by inch, dots by centimetres or none), the resolution of the picture in the defined unit of measure and the resolution of the optional preview image in the APP0 data.

he APP0 data contain, if available, 24 red-green-blue data bits of a smaller version of the picture. This **preview image** is supposed to provide an first impression of the complete picture and is not packed. Optional headers (from version 1.02) make other variants of preview pictures possible, for example also those which are JPEG packed. Version 1.02 recommends only using these newer headers in order to store information about preview pictures. The actual image data consist of blocks of JPEG packed data. EOI ends the file.

The international standard of the Joint Picture Experts Group (JPEG) (ISO/IEC SC29/WG10 ISO 10918) is a standard for the coding of photographic stills.

The basis algorithm describes a transformation coding, based on the discrete cosine transformation (DCT) in the YUV colour-space (Chapter 2.3.1).

From the available transformations the DCT (derived from the discrete Fourier transformation) has proved to be particularly efficient.

A DCT applied onto a 8 x 8 pixelblock results, in turn, in a 8 x 8 pixelblock. The coefficients of the DCT permit themselves to be interpreted as a spectrum of the 8 x 8 input area.

While the energy of the video signal can be randomly distributed, the energy of the corresponding DCT block preferably concentrates on low frequencies coefficients. When the coefficients are numbered in zigzag the resulting values to be stored are; a DC coefficient, a few low AC coefficients and many AC coefficients close to zero.

The DCT is a loss-free procedure, since the codification is completely reversible. These values are now optimal suitable for coding with the Huffman procedure (or Shannon Fano coding - frequent byte values are replaced by short bit sequences) and subsequently with the RLE procedure.

A JPEG picture is composed of different picture components, such as the picture header, quantization tables and Huffman tables, frame header, scan header (for the distribution of the picture into different fields) and the actual display data.

The compression rate of the picture to be stored is freely adjustable. our different compression modes are possible within the JPEG procedure :

- Basis Procedure (based on the application of DCT as described here),

- Extended DCT Procedure (with higher, optionally progressive bit accuracy),
- Loss-free Procedure (not based on DCT), and
- Hierarchy Procedure (Combination of several pictures).

The YUV tristimulus values are coded in one of the comparable MPEG procedures (Record blocking, DCT, Entropy Coding and Huffman Coding).

The Procedure allows an efficient compression of images with a "natural" content. It is not however particularly suitable for the storage of computer generated pictures or graphics, since the coding of the colours of objects with sharp object edges are insufficiently accurate.

When JPEG-pictures are arranged sequentially, one refers to Motion-JPEG (M-JPEG). The audio is then separated into individual sections (samples) and inserted between these JPEG pictures (interleaved).

M-JPEG, see Module 5 Video Technology

This procedure is not internationally standardized, it is however frequently used by video digitalization in order to reduce the amounts of data emerging at the beginning. Since M-JPEG does not use any temporary redundancy, the compression is not sufficient for use in transmission in local area networks.

4.3.2 GIF

Graphics Interchange Format

GIF was developed in 1987 by the on-line service CompuServe. Their goal was a minimum file size for a platform independent exchange of graphic via mailboxes. Since there are programs able to incorporate GIF graphics for virtually for all usual hardware (Amiga, Atari, IBM-compatible, MacIntosh), it is as a **transfer format** across hardware boundaries where it is of particular importance .

Fig. 4.53 The GIF format at a glance

File extension:	.gif
Format:	Raster
Colours:	max. 8 bit only
Compression:	LZW
Size:	65536 × 65536 px

Next to JPEG, GIF is the only image format able to display typical Web browsers without further ado, and therefore of utmost importance for Internet based multimedia systems.

Currently there are existing two versions of the GIF-format:

- GIF87a
- GIF89a

A GIF-file is limited to a colour depth of 256 colours, it can however, contain several images. Also interlacing and transparency are possible..

Interlaced-Modus

The GIF format also has its own method of **interlacing**. In the **"Interlaced"** mode the file is built up on the screen step-by-step: First a rough overall picture can be seen which becomes progressively more detailed. Without interlacing, the files are built up line for line.

Motifs in the GIF format can also be optionally displayed (without the oblong box). If a colour in a GIF image is stored as transparency value, the background appears in a browser with exactly this colour.

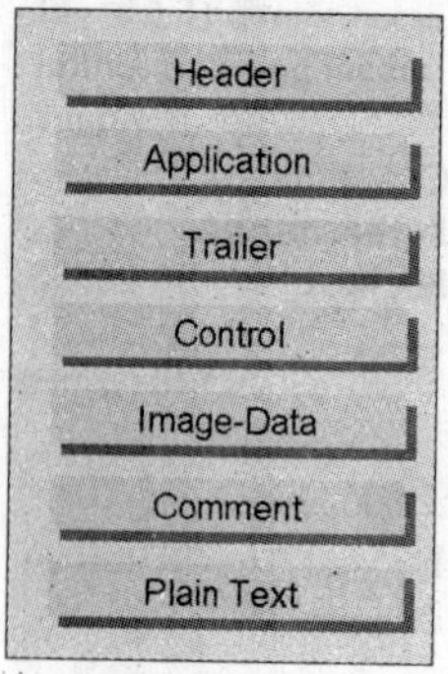

Fig. 4.54 The architecture of a GIF-file

Basically, a GIF file has the following architecture (fig. 4.54): The header contains the signature. The signature contains the alphabetic characters GIF and a version number (87a or 89a). The end of the header marks the beginning of the data area.

The **application section** allows the coding of information about the program created by the GIF file. The trailer marks the end of the data stream.

The **section control** navigates the display of each subsequent image data block. Information regarding delay and translucency are also possible.

The **image data section** consists of an image header, an optional colour map and the actual pixel data. A screen definition determines the following data: Height and width of the screen in pixels, The resolution flag, the background colour of the graphics as well as the aspect ratio. The resolution flag contains information about the number of bits per pixel and the number of colours used in the bits. In addition a flag exists, which shows the optional global tone scale's presence. The aspect ratio is computed from the ratio of pixel width and pixel height.

The **global colour tone scale** is responsible for a precise colour rendering of images that were designed for display on different hardware. Every colour is defined by the proportion of red, green and blue it contains: 0 (none) to 255 (100%). By means of this colour definition it is then possible to find the most appropriate colour for each pixel available on the respective hardware ..

The **image definition** block begins with a image separator (2C hexadecimal) and contains information about the position of the left upper corner of the image on the screen in pixels, about the width and height of the image in pixel (may not be larger than the previously defined screen) as well as various flags. These flags indicate whether a local colour tone scale exists, whether the image is to be output sequentially or in interlaced mode and how many bits are used to describe a colour of the local tone scale. An available local colour tone scale for an individual image has priority over the global colour tone scale.

In sequential mode the image is coded line by line from to top left to bottom right and displayed , whereas, the interlaced mode is used to obtain an image with maximum speed. For this purpose, the image buildup is divided into 4 steps:

- In the first transition every eighth line is output, starting at line 0; 0, 8, 16 ... etc.
- In the second transition every eighth line is output, starting at line 4; 4, 12, 20... etc.
- In the third transition every fourth line is output, starting at line 2; 6, 10, 14... etc.
- Transition four finishes the image, starting at line 1 and out putting every second line; 1, 3, 5... etc.

This procedure makes it possible to "visualize" the screen content clearly enough after the first 50 percent of the image has been built up.

The actual raster data are LZW packed in both the sequential mode and interlaced mode. The GIF end flag is always 3B hexadecimal.

Finally, the section plain text makes an ASCII based text coding possible, for example; composition, colour, size, position, extension or direction.

animated gifs
animated icons

GIF distinguishes itself through its loss-free, but nevertheless efficient compression rates and through the possibility of nesting several pictures within a file. It is also ideal for the preparation of simple **animations**.

4.3.3 PNG

PNG (pronounced: "ping"`) stands for Portable Network Graphics and is a new file format for image data. It was developed at the beginning of 1995 especially for the World Wide Web (WWW) is supposed to replace the Graphics Interchange File (GIF) format, which was the standard format for loss-less picture storage up to now.

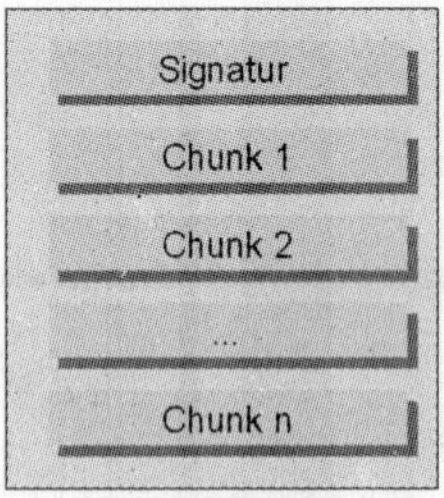

Fig. 4.55 The architecture of a PNG-file

PNG is supposed to unite the advantages of GIF and JPEG.

A PNG-file has the following architecture (fig 4.56):

The data stored in a PNG file are organized in blocks of different lengths. Every block contains a specific kind of information, as for example the actual image elements, textual comments, colour maps etc.

Every PNG file consists of a signature and a series of as many blocks as desired, the chunks. The signature is only used to identifying a PNG file as such, while the actual picture information is stored in the chunks.

Chunks contain all the information which can be stored in a PNG file. Thereby, different types of information are stored in different chunks with different models. Each chunk consists of four components: Length, type, data and CRC (Cyclic Redundancy Check).

Fig. 4.56 The Format PNG at a glance

File extension:	.png
Format:	Raster
Colours:	up to 48 bit
Compression:	lossless
Size:	unlimited

5 Human-Computer Interface

The System Graphic Card Monitor is virtually the most important interface between computers and human beings (Eyes). Therefore, the human aspect must particularly be taken into account in the technical parameters.

Psychology of perception Volume 3

Since the graphic card and the monitor form a unit, the quality of the overall system depends on the least effective of the two components. Even when the technical components of these systems are continuously being further developed, an outlasting basic principle exists, which we will review later.

5.1 Monitors

Output device monitors for image display are known by many different names, „Monitor", „Screen", „Display" abbreviations such as VDT (Video Display Terminal) or VDU (Visual Display Unit) are common. For image display, multimedia systems increasingly employ traditional cathode ray tube (CRT) and also alternative monitor technology. The most important criteria for the appraisal of a monitor are resolution, colour reproduction and image quality. In the meantime, there are various technological variations of monitor.

5.1.1 Traditional Monitors

Traditional monitors basically work as television receivers (without the receiver section).

The screen consists of small dots (pixels) which are arranged in an oblong raster. Most frequently, the principle of the CRT is involved. During the build-up of the image the electron beam samples every point line by line and illuminates a corresponding phosphorus particle. Colour monitors require three electron beams, that sample the screen simultaneously and cause three phosphorus particles in the primary colours red, green and blue (RGB) to luminate.

monochrome (one colour), polychrome (many colours)

Through the combination of the three colours, and by varying the intensity, many different colours can be created. A hole or slot mask (trinitron) guarantees that every electron beam hits the correct phosphor field.

The image is buffered in the graphic card before it is displayed. The larger the space on the graphic card, the faster the image can be built up.

5.1.2 Alternative Monitor Technology

Plasma Monitors

Plasma displays (monitors) consist of two glass sheets between which there is a *Mosaic* consisting of tiny gas-filled cells. An electrical transmission grid holds the entire area under electrical voltage. Through electrical discharges into single, separately addressable cells, the gas emits ultra-violet rays that stimulate the phosphorus deposition of the cells to luminescence.

Liquid Crystal Display

The liquid crystal display, (LCD) employs organic substances enclosed in sheets of glass, known as liquid crystals, whose molecular qualities resemble firm crystals. On the application of a current/voltage/ the liquid crystals align themselves along the direction of the electrical field there acquiring different optical characteristics.

TFT
Thin film transistor

DSTN
Double Super Twisted Nematics

The **TFT-Display** is currently the best screen for Notebooks. The individual image elements are controlled by steamed, translucent, horizontal and vertical conducting paths. At every crossover a thin film transistor (TFT) turns the electrical fields for the polarization of the liquid crystals on and off. Luminosity, colour and focus are therefore considerably better than with the, more easily produce, DSTN monitors.

Electro Luminescence Displays

ELD
Electric Luminescence Display

Electro luminescence Displays (ELD) employ a substrate for the display, on the area of which a series of ultra-thin semiconductor circuits are placed using the photograph-lithographic method.

The coating consists of substances which yield light when subjected to sufficient electric voltage. The image elements' selection is controlled by transistor circuits.

LED Monitors

LED = Light Emitting Diode

The pixels of LED screens each consist of three coloured LED (RGB) and one white LED for brightness control. These light-emitting diodes form the active colour matrix.

For a VGA resolution, a minimum of 1,2 million transistor functions are necessary.

Touch Screens

Fig. 4.57 Finger instead of mouse: intuitive Interaction via Touch-Screens

The most natural form of interactivity (see volume 3, module 5) can be achieved by a use of systems with touch-sensitive display surfaces. Principally, four Touch Screen technologies are differentiated (fig 4.57):

1. Resistive: A mechanical pressure on that a resistive touch screen closes an *electrical contact* between two conductive layers (fig 4.58). Since the pressure only sets up a connection between the two layers, the resistive touch screen can be activated by any solid object (a gloved finger, a pencil). This technology is used in, for example, Personal Digital Assistants (PDAs) e.g. the Psion and Palm.

Fig. 4.58 The Principle of the resistive Touch-Screen, cf. [W7]

- Advantages: no alignment (justifying) is necessary, exact positioning, mainly in the Medical field (use with gloves is possible);
- Disadvantages: unfocused, low brightness, the monitor is less durable.

This technology, determined by the number of layers applied, has less brightness and less focus. If for example a normal LCD monitor has a brightness of 200 cd/m², then the LCD monitor with surface wave technology lies at 185 cd/m² and a five wire resistance monitor has 170 cd/m². Since the brightness must be fully turned on, the durability of the monitor is less.

2. Capacitive: A pane of glass coated with ultra-thin metal lies over the actual screen of a capacitive touch screen. From the corners of the display, a low voltage of alternating current, which creates a weak electrical field, is applied to the electrode grid of the conducting layer. When the user touches the screen they represents as it were a condenser electrode and "grounds" the area (field). From the (low) electricity which is diverted around the users finger the **touch controller** determines the respective *coordinates* of the contact point. Correspondingly, capacitive touch screens only respond to the touch with a conductive object (special metal pen, finger etc.).

- Advantages: higher resolution, higher light efficiency, not influenced by surrounding light;
- Disadvantages: *Calibration* necessary, sensitive to errors from exterior influences.

3. Acoustic: Surface acoustic wave technology. This technology is based on audible waves. The edges of the screen are equipped with ultra audio transmitters with reflectors at each opposite edge and a piezoelectric receiver in one corner. ultra acoustic waves are continuously be sent across this reflector system. As long as this field is undisturbed, the waves arrive without obstruction at the receiver. If the field is disturbed however, (through a finger, pen or similar), then the position of this object is determined from the missing wave course within this field. This technology also makes it possible to determine the pressure applied by means of the amount of energy absorbed.

- Advantages: still higher resolution, definition of the applied pressure, no light reduction on the screen;
- Disadvantage: Positioning necessary (Maintenance requirement !).

4. Light: Infra-red. touch screens with infra-red technology work, on principle, as light barriers. The infra-red senders and infra-red receivers in the screen frame build up an (invisible to our eyes) "Light grid".

If this grid is disturbed by a finger or other object, the sensor electronics detect the appropriate x and y coordinates of the contact point by means of the missing rays.

- Advantages: no light reduction of the screen, no wear;
- Disadvantages: interference sensitive (reacts on approach), resolution is low, position errors with convex screens.

5.1.3 Criteria of a Monitor

Resolution

The resolution is an important factor for image quality (cf. chapter 2.5). The specification takes place through the following combination:

$$a = m \cdot n$$

m maximum number of displayable pixels in a line (Width)
n number of possible lines
a number of dots (Pixels) that are displayable

The maximum resolution is the total number of pixels that the monitor is able to display.

Refresh Frequency

Vertical frequency

The best known value is the vertical refresh frequency. This indicates how often the image is built up in one second.

The higher the refresh frequency, the calmer the image appears. It should be at least 72 Hz, but should not exceed 110 Hz (typical value: 90 Hz).

It is important that this information refers to the "non-interlaced mode" (ni). Interlaced means that the odd and even line numbers are alternately refreshed (Line interlacing), and should be avoided if possible.

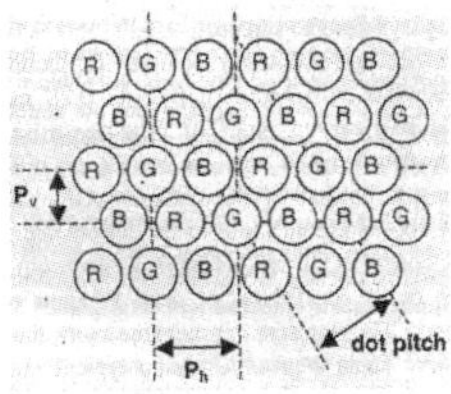

Bild 1.59 DOT-Pitch on a standard CRT

Line frequency

Line frequency, also often referred to as horizontal frequency, indicates how many lines the electron beam can write per second.

This value gives information about the image repetition rate at a specific resolution and determines the quality of the image display. The lower limit of a monitor should ba at least 70 kHz (see chapter 5.2.1.4).

Pixel frequency

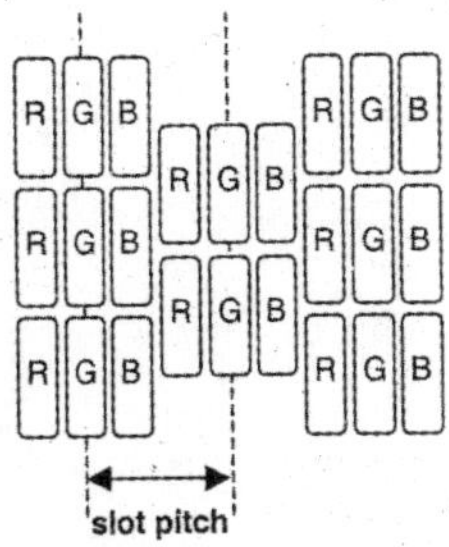

Fig. 4.60 Slot-Pitch on a slit mask CRT

This indicates how many dots the electron beam can control (select) per second; it is the result of line frequency x horizontal resolution.

Band width

This refers to the frequency limit of the video amplifier in the monitor and is a measure of the quality of the image. A bandwidth of 1.5 to 2.0 times the pixel frequency is necessary for a maximal sharp image with good contrast.

Shadow Mask Distance

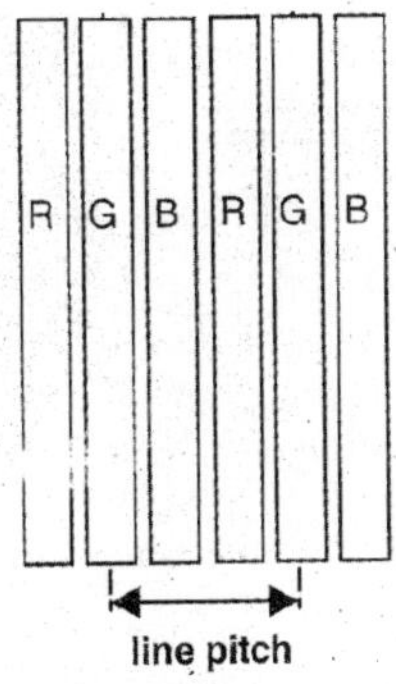

Fig. 4.61 Line Pitch on a Trinitron CRT

The Shadow Mask Distance is the distance between two apertures of the shadow mask. The **DOT pitch** (fig 4.59) rather than the vertical (P_v) or horizontal (P_h) shadow mask distance is decisive by shadow mask tubes (Delta tube). The smaller this is the higher the resolution.

Typical values lie by 0.25 to 0.31 mm. With the aperture grille thermionic valve (fig 4.60) we refer to **slot pitch** and with a trinitron tube of **line pitch** (fig 4.61).

5.2 Graphic Cards

The Graphic Card delivers the computer signals to the monitor. The quality of a monitor can only be exploited when the graphic card actuates this correctly. Conversely, a graphic card can also overtax a monitor. Newer monitors fade out, very old monitors can become defective.

The progress of hardware technology is particularly noticeable during the execution of graphic cards. An important criterion is compatibility: New programs should be displayable on older systems.

This demand is achieved by hardware methods when the newest graphic cards are also compatible with older graphic standards. However, also higher programming languages support this compatibility by supplying suitable routines, which adapt the respective program to fit the hardware.

Since the development of the graphic standard VGA (in 1987) the monitor is controlled in **analog** mode because with today's usual resolutions and colour depths the data transfer would no longer be feasible.

Newer **flat screens** (Liquid crystal screens, see chapter 5.1.2.2), on the other hand, are accessed directly in **digital** form. A graphic card with a direct digital outlet is needed.

We review, first of all, the criteria for a graphic card, sum up some graphic standards and then look at the design (anatomy) of a graphic card.

5.2.1 Criteria of a Graphic Card

The most important criteria for the evaluation of a graphic card are colour depth, resolution, refresh frequency, line frequency and video band width.

Colour Depth

The colour depth (cf. chapter 2.2) states how many different colours the graphic card can supply to the monitor simultaneously. 16 bit (64 000 displayable colours = HICOLOUR) are sufficient for multimedia, however, for the preliminary printing stage at least 24 bit (16,7 million displayable colours = TRUECOLOUR) are necessary.

Resolution

On the condition that the selected monitor can display the corresponding resolution, the achievable resolution depends primarily on the amount of the fonts overlay buffer and the employed colour depth.

By a resolution of 1024 px horizontally times 768 px vertically times 24 bit colour depth, a theoretical memory requirement of bit is calculated. In practice this means a theoretical 4MB buffer.

In practice the performance of a graphic card depends particularly on the graphic processor on the graphic card and from the respective software driver.

Refresh frequency

This is also the best known value of a graphic card and indicates how often the image is rebuilt up per second.

Refresh frequencies from 75 (hertz) Hz are pleasing to the eye, 90 Hz are optimal, 120 Hz should not be exceeded.

Since the refresh frequency strongly depends on the resolution employed, it is better to use the line frequency for the evaluation.

Horizontal Frequency

The line frequency of a graphic card confers information about the image repetition rate at specific resolution and is therefore an important criterion with regard to the quality of the image display.

Valid:

$$f_V = \frac{f_H}{a_V + a_{VR}}$$

f_V vertical refresh rate in Hz
f_H horizontal frequency in Hz
a_V vertical resolution in px
a_{VR} resolution reserve of 5 % from a_V

Example: A graphic card has a line frequency of 69 kHz at a resolution of 1024 x 768 dots (768 dots vertically):

$$\frac{69kHz}{768Hz + 38Hz} = 85Hz$$

Video Band Width

A Graphic Card can also be judged by the video band width.
Valid:

$$b = f_H \cdot (a_H + a_{HR})$$

b Video Band Width in Hz
f_H Horizontal frequency in Hz
a_H Horizontal resolution in px
a_{HR} resolution reserve of 10% from a_H

Example: A graphic card achieves a video band width of 77 MHz and on this a resolution of 1024 × 768 should be run, the formula is resolved according to f_H, which gives a value of approximately 69 kHz, which, in turn, gives the pleasing-to-the-eye refresh rate of 85 Hz.

5.2.2 Graphic Standards

It is important to consider that, unlike workstations, PCs were originally designed (in 1981) to work exclusively with ASCII-characters ... still far from multimedia.

The oldest graphics adapter was the MDA (Monochrome Adapter Display) from IBM (in 1981) and was regarded for several years as the standard for monochrome graphic cards.

Modern graphic cards are equipped with their own processors. The following table should provide a rough view of the development of the different graphic standards in the PC field:

Fig. 4.62 Various Graphic Standards

Standard	Description	Resolution	f_H	f_V	VRAM	b
MDA	Monochrom Display Adapter	only Text Matrix 9 x 14	18, 432 kHz	50 Hz	4 KB	16,257 MHz
CGA	Colour Graphics Adapter	640 x 200	15,75 kHz	60 Hz	16 KB	14,3 MHz
HGC	Hercules Graphic Card	720 x 348	21,8 kHz	50 Hz	32 KB	16,257 MHz
EGA	Enhanced Graphics Adapter	640 x 350	21,8 kHz	60 Hz	64 KB	16,3 MHz
VGA	Video Graphics Array	640 x 480	31,5 kHz	70 Hz	256 KB	28 MHz
SVGA	Super VGA	1280 x 1024	90 kHz	90 Hz	512 KB	100 MHz
8514/A		1024 x 768	31,4 kHz	70 Hz	1024 KB	

5.2.3 Anatomy of a Graphic Card

The CRT controller (CRTC) which controls the intern running is the core of a graphic card. This CRTC can be removed, then the personal computer takes over the control.

The electron beam runs from to the left to right and from top to bottom, whereby the image is successively built up. The period which the electron beam requires for the return run is, however, shorter than the CRTC needs to collect new information about the construction of the coming line from the Memory Array. This causes a short pause and, since the electron beam can not be stopped, a so-called **Overscan** arises. This effect is by the (black) edge next to the actual screen content .

The **pixel dot clock** element acts as a central clock pulse generator and synchronises the CRTC and the **timing controller** (Synchronisation Element).

The palette receives the data streams from the CRTC and guides the *palettisierten* data to the three **digital analog converters** (DAC) separately. These convert the *palettisierte* pixel information into three RGB analog signals. Finally, the analog signals for the actuation of the monitor and the respective synchronisation impulse are provided (fig 4.61) in the **analog interface** (fig 4.61).

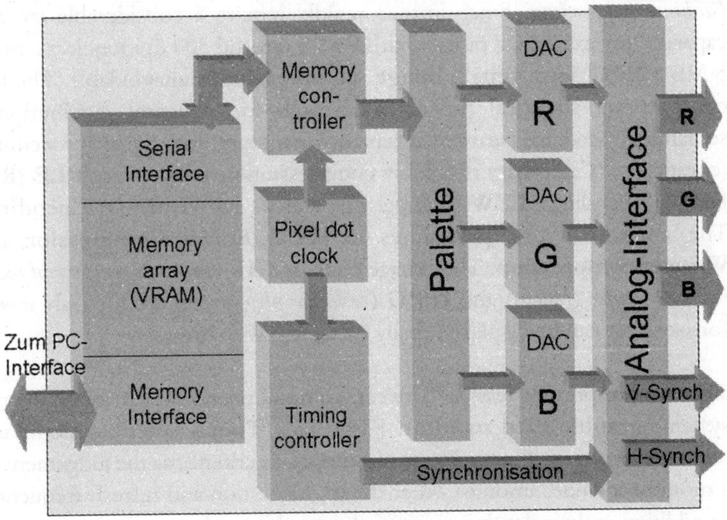

Fig. 4.63 The architecture of a typical PC Graphic card

If the graphic processor, on the on the graphic card, also relieves the computer's main processor (CPU) during the calculation of the display data, we refer to an accelerator.

6 Module Summary

The eye is our most important sense organ. It converts light; *electro-magnetic radiation* in the wave band of 400 nm (Violet) to 700 nm (Red), into information readily comprehensible to the brain. Our perception includes "brightness-darkness" and "colour". Three pieces of information are sufficient to describe a colour: Brightness, tint and colour saturation.

A **vector graphic** (post-script, EPS, CDR, DXF usw.) is built up of graphic **primitives** (Lines, oblongs, polygons usw.) and specified by their **attributes** (line width, line colour usw.), while a **bitmap image** consists of a *raster* of *n lines* with *m pixels*. A **meta-graphic** contains both bitmap and vector graphic information.

Colour maps permit the *description of individual colours* through numerical values. Physical technical colour models describe a colour as a *mixture of primaries*: The sum of the additive mixture of spectrum colours (RGB) results in "white" and the sum of the subtractive mixture of surface colours (CMY) results in "black". The mixture of surface colours (CMY) results in "black". Perception oriented colour models (HSV, CIE-XYZ) are aligned to the *response* from human senses and are orientated to such parameters as tint, brightness and saturation.

In printing the **TIFF** format is important, characterized by *portability* and *hardware independence*. Since images rapidly require a considerable storage capacity (for example a picture with 9 x 13 cm and 300 dpi requires almost 5 MB without formatting), **image compression** is unavoidable. The key concepts are statistical procedures (search for statistical distributions), semantic procedures (search for semantic structure) and hybrid procedures (composite). Customary non-lossy compression procedures are **RLE** (Run Length Encoding), **LZW** (Lempel-Ziv-Welch) and **Huffman-Encoding.** The best known lossy procedures are **JPEG**, **Fractal Compression** and **Wavelet compression**. The image formats **GIF** (*256 colours, optional mode, better for simple graphics*) and **JPEG** (*better for photographs*) are the only image formats that can be displayed easily by typical Web browsers.

The most important *interface* between computers and human beings is the systems **graphic card monitor**. Particularly **Touch Screen** systems use natural interactivity forms. The most important criteria for the judgement of a monitor include, amongst other things, resolution and refresh frequency. In addition, colour depth is a criteria by graphic cards.

7 Module Supplement

7.1 Literature

7.1.1 Books in English

FOLEY, J.; VAN DAM, A.; FEINER, S.; HUGHES, J. (1990): *Computer Graphics: Principles and Practice.* 2nd Ed. New York: Addison-Wesley.

GOLDSTEIN, E. B. (1999): *Sensation and Perception.* 5th Ed. Belmont (CA): Wadsworth.

GONZALEZ, RAFAEL C.; WOODS, RICHARD E. (1992): *Digital Image Processing.* Reading (MA): Addison-Wesley.

HEATH, STEVE (1999): *Multimedia and Communications Technology.* 2nd Ed. Oxford: Focal Press, Butterworth, Heinemann, 44-78.

MURRAY, J.O. ; VAN RYPER, W. (1994): *Encyclopedia of Graphics File Formats.* Sebastopol (CA): O Reilly.

WU, CHWAN-HWA; IRWIN, DAVID J. (1999): *Emerging Multimedia Computer Communication Technologies.* Upper Saddle River (NJ): Prentice Hall, 23-125.

7.1.2 Articles in English

AMER, PAUL D.; IREN, SAMI; SEZEN, GUL E.; CONRAD, PHILLIP T.; TAUBE, MASON; CARO, ARMANDO (1999): Network-conscious GIF image transmission over the Internet. *Computer Networks,* Vol. 31, Iss. 7, April 99, 693-708.

EICKELER, S.; MÜLLER, S.; RIGOLL, G. (2000): Recognition of JPEG compressed face images based on statistical methods. *Image and Vision Computing,* Vol. 18, Iss. 4, March 2000, 279-287.

SPEKOWIUS, GERHARD (1999): Characterization of Color CRT Display Systems for Monochrome Applications. *Journal of Digital Imaging,* Vol. 12, No. 3, 102-113.

7.1.3 Books in German

ABMAYR, WOLFGANG (1994): *Einführung in die digitale Bildverarbeitung.* Stuttgart: Teubner.

BESTENREINER, FRIEDRICH (1988): *Vom Punkt zum Bild. Entwicklung, Stand und Zukunftsaspekte der Bildtechnik.* Karlsruhe: Wichmann.

BORN, GÜNTER (1996): *Referenzhandbuch Dateiformate.* 4. Auflage. Bonn: Addison-Wesley.

CAMPENHAUSEN, CH. V. (1993): *Die Sinne des Menschen: Einführung in die Psychophysik der Wahrnehmung.* 2. Auflage. Stuttgart: Georg Thieme.

FELLNER, WOLF-DIETRICH (1988): *Computer Grafik.* Mannheim, Wien, Zürich: BI-Wiss.-Verlag.

GIBSON, J. J. (1973): *Die Wahrnehmung der visuellen Welt.* Weinheim: Beltz.

HOLZINGER, ANDREAS (1998): *Von der Wachskerze zur Glühlampe: Fächerübergreifende Einführung und historische Entwicklung der Lichttechnik.* Thun, Frankfurt/Main: Deutsch.

JARZ, EWALD M. (1997): *Entwicklung multimedialer Systeme; Planung von Lern- und Masseninformationssystemen (Serie Gabler Edition Wissenschaft).* Wiesbaden: Gabler, 230-238.

KNODEL, H.; BAYERHUBER H. (1993): *Linder Biologie.* Stuttgart: Metzler.

KRAUS, HELMUT (1997): *Digitales Fotografieren: mit Digitalkameras zum perfekten Bild.* Bonn et.al.: Addison-Wesley.

STEINMETZ, RALF (1999): *Multimedia-Technologie: Grundlagen, Komponenten und Systeme.* 2. Auflage. Berlin (et.al.): Springer, 23-46.

WILTGEN, MARCO (1999): *Digitale Bildverarbeitung in der Medizin.* Aachen: Shaker.

7.1.4 Articles in German

BERGHORN, WILHELM; BOSKAMP, TOBIAS; JUNG, KLAUS (1999): Schlanke Bilder: Der zukünftige Bildkompressionsstandard JPEG 2000. *c't: Magazin für Computer Technik.* 26/99, 184-185. Hannover: Heise.

BERGHORN, WILHELM; BOSKAMP, TOBIAS; SCHÖNFELD, STEVEN; STARK, HANS-GEORG (1999): Winzig mit Wavelets: Aktuelle Verfahren zur Bilddatenkompression. *c't: Magazin für Computer Technik.* 26/99, 186-197. Hannover: Heise.

KUHLMANN, ULRIKE (2000): Finger statt Maus: Touchscreen-Techniken im Vergleich. *c't: Magazin für Computer Technik.* 15/00, 116-118. Hannover: Heise.

KUHLMANN, ULRIKE; LABUSGA, STEFAN (1999): Digital zum Bild: Sechs Grafikkarten mit digitalem Ausgang. *c't: Magazin für Computer Technik.* 24/99, 132-135. Hannover: Heise.

7.1.5 Journals

Computer Graphics Forum (ISSN: 0167-7055) | Blackwell Publishers

Computer Vision and Image Understanding (ISSN: 1077-3142; electronic:1090-235X) | Academic Press Inc.

IEEE MultiMedia Magazine (ISSN: 1070-986X) | IEEE

IEEE Transactions on Medical Imaging (ISSN:0278-0062) | IEEE Institute of Electrical and Electronics Engineers

Image and Vision Computing (ISSN: 0262-8856) | Elsevier

International Journal of Computer Vision (ISSN: 0920-5691 | Kluwer

Journal of Digital Imaging (ISSN: 0897-1889) | Society for Computer Applications in Radiology

Multimedia Systems (ISSN: 0942-4962; electronic: 1432-1882) | Springer Verlag KG

Multimedia Tools and Applications (ISSN: 1380-7501) | Kluwer

New Review of Hypermedia and Multimedia - Applications and Research (ISSN: 1361-4568) | Taylor Graham Publishing - Journal Department

Videre – a Journal of Computer Vision Research (ISSN: 1089-2788; electronic:1089-2788) | MIT Press

7.2 Internet-Links

Up-to-date Internet links to this module are on the book home page **www.basiswissen-multimedia.at** under Volume 1: Technology – Module 4: Image technology available (in English and German).

7.3 Exam-Questions

Question-Type 1: Yes/No (Dichotomy):

01	Up to 10^7bps can penetrate into our long-term memory over our optical channel.	❒ Yes ❒ No	
02	The presentation quality of pictures is determined mainly by two factors: Colour depth and resolution.	❒ Yes ❒ No	
03	A bitmap picture consists of graphic primitives, for example lines, squares, polygons and so forth.	❒ Yes ❒ No	
04	Within the additive colour mixture three light colours (for example the light of shining phosphor) are mixed additively, the sum gives white.	❒ Yes ❒ No	
05	The resolution of a bitmap picture indicates the number of the pixels that are available on a specific area for the representation.	❒ Yes ❒ No	
06	DXF is a vector format for CAD-programmes and stores also tri-dimensional objects.	❒ Yes ❒ No	
07	TIFF is one of the most important formats for raster images and is universally usable.	❒ Yes ❒ No	
08	RLE is a lossy procedure and is suitable for files with long series of same characters.	❒ Yes ❒ No	
09	With the aid of the JPEG compressing procedure compression rates of up to 1:35 are possible.	❒ Yes ❒ No	
10	GIF is suitable rather for line based graphics and JPEG rather for colour pictures. Both are most important for the WWW.	❒ Yes ❒ No	

Question-Type 2: Multiple Choice:

01	Our eye ... ❒ a) ... is not a separate organ, but part of the brain. ❒ b) ... corresponds physically to a camera. ❒ c) ... absorbs approximately 90 % of all information of our environment. ❒ d) ... converts electro-magnetic light radiation into nerve signals.
02	Appertaining to the most important dimensions of the colour perception are ... ❒ a) ... saturation. ❒ b) ... solution. ❒ c) ... Dithering. ❒ d) ... brightness.
03	Vector graphics ... ❒ a) ... are scalable, but need, however, more storage space than bitmap pictures. ❒ b) ... are ideally for the storage of text. ❒ c) ... can be made infinitely exact. ❒ d) ... consist of tiniest squares in a grating (or latice?).
04	Bitmap-pictures ... ❒ a) ... it results in jags and stairs (aliasing) with smooth curves easily. ❒ b) ... are very simply to handle (manipulierbar?). ❒ c) ... can be printed in every arbitrary solution satisfactorily. ❒ d) ... on principle are very small files.
05	Appertaining to the customary lossy compression means ... ❒ a) ... RLE (Run Length Encoding). ❒ b) ... JPEG (Joint Photographic Experts group). ❒ c) ... Wavelet compression. ❒ d) ... LZW (Lempel-Ziv-Welch).
06	The Graphics Interchange (GIF) format... ❒ a) ... is over all of great importance as a transfer format. ❒ b) ... is next to JPEG displayable by all Web browsers. ❒ c) ... allows the "exempting" (freistellen im Graph. Sinne?) of motives. ❒ d) ... allows no preparation of animations.
07	The most important criteria for the judgement of a monitor includes ... ❒ a) ... refresh frequency. ❒ b) ... resolution. ❒ c) ... shadow mask distance. ❒ d) ... screen diagonale.
08	For a graphic card ... ❒ a) ... a colour depth of 8 is bit sufficient. ❒ b) ... the quality depends on the graphics processor and the software driver. ❒ c) ... a refresh frequency from 70 hertz is eye-pleasing. ❒ d) ... the information line frequency gives insights into the repetition rate.

7.4 Answers

Correct answers to Group „Question Type 1“:
01 Nein; 02 Ja; 03 Nein; 04 Ja; 05 Ja; 06 Ja; 07 Ja; 08 Nein; 09 Nein; 10 Ja;

Correct answers to Group „Question Type 2“:
01 a) b) c) d); 02 a) d); 03 b) c); 04 a) b); 05 b) c) 06 a) b) c); 07 a) b) c); 08 b) d)

7.5 Hands-On: Exercises

- You have a 640 × 480 pixel, uncompressed, colour image. How much memory does your image need? How can you decrease the storage requirement? Which disadvantages result from that?
- Scan in a picture. To what must you pay attention with the setting? With which resolution must the picture be scanned in order to a) be shown on the Internet b) embedded in a book or other document? Which format is better for which purpose?
- Experiment with this picture in an image-processing program (for example Photoshop). Store the image in different formats and resolutions. Compare them!

7.6 Themes for Debate

- Why is the eye our most important sense organ? Discuss the function of sight and its importance for information gathering.
- Why are vector graphics usually far smaller than comparable bitmap-pictures? Discuss the advantages and disadvantages of both formats..
- Why is the concept of compression of such basic importance? Discuss the advantages and disadvantages of different compression procedures.

7.7 Timeline: Graphics Technology

3500 B.C.: earliest (known) example of a combination of picture and text from Mesopotamian (Blausch Stone).

3000 B.C.: earliest document of Egyptian hieroglyphics of Pharaoh ZER.

2450 B.C.: Agalmatolite (Architrave) of rose granite.

800 B.C.: Legend of stone skirting with Phoenician text.

550 B.C.: PYTHAGORAS OF SAMOS sets up a first (false, but interesting) theory of sight: The eyes emit "vision-rays".

400 B.C.: PLATO is also of the opinion that the eyes send out rays of light in order to see pictures.

250 B.C.: ARCHIMEDES Principle of the "camera obscura".

1450: GUTENBERG develops the letterpress with movable letters.

1551: CARDANO'S camera obscura with optical lens.

1824: First metal picture (asphalt process) from NIEPCE.

1826: First picture of nature through the action of light onto a chemical layer from JOSEPH NICEPHORE NIEPCE.

1839: Photograph from DAGUERRE.

1841: TALBOT applied for a patent for Talbotypie, as the first photographic negative-positive process.

1842: Basic principles of the facsimile (FAX) from ALEXANDER BAIN.

1851: ARCHER'S wet printing plate process.

1855: MAXWELL'S additive colour mixing procedure.

1862: DUCOS DU HAURON'S theory of colour photography.

1871: MADDOX'S gelation dry printing plate.

1888: EASTMAN'S Kodak camera.

1907: The beginning of colour photography.

1911: Colour printing plate from Agfa.

1913: Miniature camera "Leica" from BARNACK.

1924: Facsimile with Kerr cell (KAROLUS).

1930: Subtractive three colour technology from Technicolor (USA).

1937: Negative-positive picture process from Agfa.

1942: Coloured infrared film from Kodak.

1951: "Graphics display" with a vector scope on the "Whirlwind" computer.

1958: Computer TX-1 at MIT uses a "graphics console".

1959: First pictures of the back of the moon by radio transmission from Lunik 3

1965: The birth hour of computer art: Presentations of computer graphics in public.

1968: DEC 338 intelligent graphics terminal.

1969: Graphical User Interface (GUI) developed by Xerox (ALAN KAY).

1977: Apple II released.

1978: JACOB ZIV and ABRAHAM LEMPEL publish a new "Lossless data-compression algorithm" – root for the PNG image format.

1980: PCX picture ratio for the first PCs.

1981: Shock for the photograph industry: The first electronic camera with a magnetic tape cassette. The (non-moving) pictures can be transmitted directly on a television receiver. The digital photograph begins.

1981: Graphics adapter MDA from IBM.

1982: Disc-camera of Kodak. Beginning of the evolution of the JPEG picture ratio. AutoDesk Company founded; AutoCAD released. Adobe founded by JOHN WARNOCK. ACM begins publication of TOG (Transactions on Graphics). JIM CLARK founds Silicon Graphics (SGI).

1983: AutoDesk introduces to first PC based CAD-software. SGI IRIS 1000 graphics workstation.

1984: Canon develops a computer-controlled camera with monitor. Minolta introduced a "speaking" camera. Thomson Digital Image founded (TDI).

1985: Post-script from Adobe (JOHN WARNOCK).

1986: TIFF format from Aldus.

1987: CompuServe (BOB BERRY) develops a portable, packed picture ratio: GIF; TIFF is developed by Aldus and Microsoft in order to provide portability and hardware independence with the coding of an image.

1988: PICT format of Apple released.

1990: Kodak photograph CD. The JPEG image format becomes the ISO 10918 Standard.

1993: Through application of the WWW, the (text based) Internet becomes 'illustrated'.

1995: Development of the PNG Image Format begins.

1997: PNG 1.0 released as RFC 2083

2001: Sandia National Labs develop a 3 × 4 meter screen with 20 million pixels.

7.8 Glossary

Animated GIF is a graphic image (on a Web page) that moves. In particular, an animated GIF is a file in the Graphics Interchange Format specified as GIF89a that contains within the single file a set of images that are presented in a specified order. An animated GIF can loop endlessly (e.g. Java, Flash etc. can be used to achieve the same effects, but animated GIFs are usually easier to create and much smaller in size thus faster to display.

Bitmap defines a display space and the color for each pixel or "bit" in a display space (matrix). The image cannot be immediately rescaled without losing definition.

BMP graphics file format, most known .

bpi short for „bits per inch" (1 Inch = 2,54 cm).

CMYK Cyan Magenta Yellow blacK, Colour-System.

CRT Cathode Ray Tube, part of the visual display unit (VDU).

GIF Graphics Interchange Format. Besides JPEG a „Quasi-Standard" in the Web.

JPEG Joint Photographic Experts Group, developed a graphics format (file extension: JPG).

JPG an image in the so called JPEG format.

Morphing is a kind of "animated transformation" of one image into another by gradually distorting the first image.

PNG Portable Network Graphics, especially developed for the Web.

Polygon smallest closed unit, in which a vector graphic can be dismantled.

Raytracing is a technique to create realistic images by calculating the paths taken by rays of light entering the observer's eye at different angles. The paths are traced backwards from the viewpoint, through a point (a pixel) in the image plane until they hit some object in the scene or go off to infinity.

Rendering is the conversion of a high-level object-based description into a graphical image for display (creation of visual information out of e.g. textual information).

Shading is a technique for the shading of curved areas, to make them appear more realistic.

True Colour graphic modus with 16,7 Mio. Farben (24 bit per pixel).

VDT video (or visual) display terminal is a term used, especially in ergonomic studies, for the computer display. A display is the visual interface to the computer user, using e.g. a cathode ray tube (CRT), liquid crystal display (LCD), etc. Major issues include the readability of content; the effect of prolonged visual interaction with the display content in terms of eye and other muscular fatigue and deterioration; proper viewing distances; and the amount and effect of exposure on users to the extremely low-frequency (ELF) radiation that emanates from VDTs.

VDU video display unit, see VDT.

Vector has two independent properties: magnitude and direction. The term also denotes the mathematical or geometrical representation of such a quantity. Examples of vectors in nature are velocity, momentum, force etc. A quantity that exhibits magnitude only, with no specific direction, is called a scalar (e.g. speed, mass, etc.). Vectors can be depicted graphically in two or three dimensions. Magnitude is shown as the length of a line segment. Direction is shown by the orientation of the line segment, and by an arrow at one end.

VRAM Video RAM, means all forms of random access memory (RAM) used to store image data for a computer display. All types of video RAM are special arrangements of dynamic RAM (DRAM). Video RAM is really a buffer between the computer processor and the display and is often called the frame buffer. When images are to be sent to the display, they are first read by the processor as data from some form of main (non-video) RAM and then written to video RAM. From video RAM (the frame buffer), the data is converted by a RAM digital-to-analog converter (RAMDAC) into analog signals that are sent to the display presentation mechanism such as a cathode ray tube (CRT).

Module 5: Video Technology

„Televison has been around for fewer than sixty years, but in that time it has become a major influence in the life of almost everyone in the developed nations. In some ways, though, television was just an enhancement of commercial radio, which had been bringing electronic entertainment into homes for twenty years. But no broadcast medium we have right now is comparable to the communications media we'll have once the Internet evolves to the point at which it has the broadband capacity necessary to carry hig-quality video."

Bill Gates in the "The Road Ahead" Page 72

Learning objectives

Analogue Video

Digital Video

Video-File-Formats

Now we have a basic knowledge of audio and still images, we turn to **„moving pictures"**. Without any doubt this is the most fascinating, and in combination with audio also the most technically sophisticated method of providing information. We will first discuss the basics of analogue and digital video technology and then concentrate on the current video file formats.

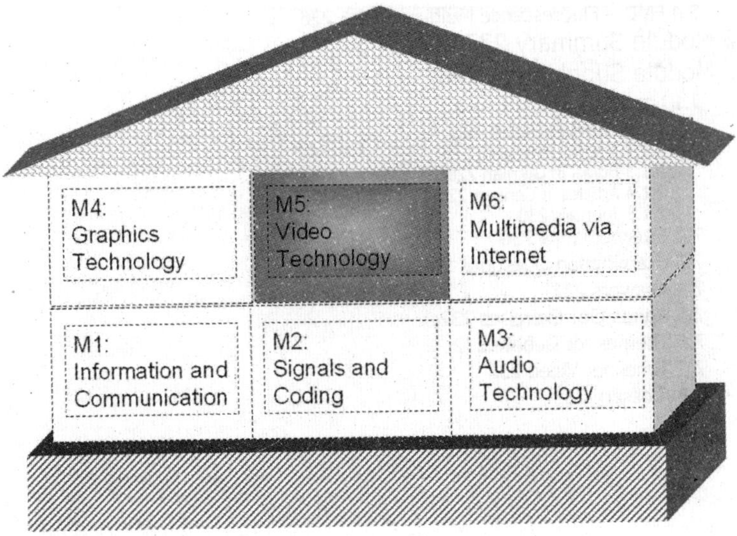

The term **Video** is understood to mean every type of moving images. The term **Video Technology** is understood to refer to the general procedures and equipment necessary for the creating, storage and reproduction of audio and video information (sound and pictures).

Unlike traditional analogue video technology, **digital video technology** digitizes the signals from an analogue video camera and stores them in digital form. With **Digital Video (DV)** a digital video camera is employed and the, already digitized, signals are stored directly onto magnetic tape –similar to that used with a DAT-Recorder.

Fig. 5.1 DV Cameras record the video signal directly in digital form [W4]

Together with the Digital Audio Technology (DAT), Digital Video Technology forms the basis for processing and presentation of continuous data in Multi Media Systems.

Nowadays DV is celebrating success almost everywhere but the difficulties of reproduction of digital video sequences on a PC can be shown by the following example: For a single, full colour, frame with a resolution of 1024 × 768 pixel (0,8 megapixel), 2.4 MB is needed.

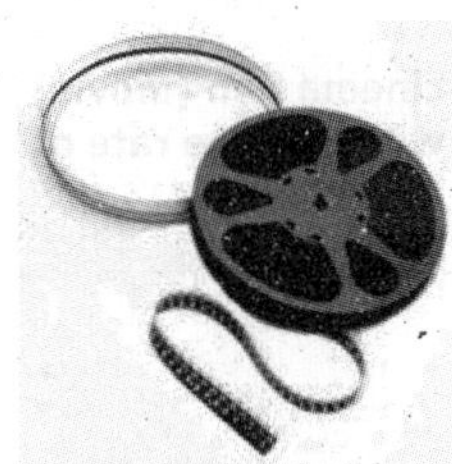

Fig. 5.2 A digital video is nothing more than the sequential viewing of individual pictures

In order to receive a realistic moving images , 25 to 30 picture per second are necessary. This leads to a data stream of approx. 60 MB/s on the data bus.

A one minute video would therefore require 3.6 GB of storage capacity. A standard CD has a storage space of 0.7 GB.

Facing the problems caused by sending these huge amounts of data across the Internet is the subject of Module 6. The example also amplifies once again the importance of "Compression", one of the subjects of Module 4.

Fig. 5.3 The future of storage media is in the silver disk - the *far* future is FMD

For this reason the video medium of the future is Digital Versatile Disk (DVD), which can store almost 30 times as much as a standard CD-Rom. However, the real breakthrough for the DVD format will not take place until it is as easy for consumers to record onto DVD as it is to use a video (band) recorder today.

In view of the continuously increasing storage requirements new developments are, of course, to be expected. One approach n this direction is the Disk Fluorescent Multilayer (DFM) which has up to 1 TB Storage space (1 TB = 1000 GB). This is equivalent to 1,000,000,000,000 printed characters!

1 Video Fundamentals

Refer to Psychophysics of the eye in Module 4

The human eye is also the receptor organ for registering moving pictures, therefore its psycho-physical qualities define the limiting conditions for our conception of „video".

Starting point is the **relatively slow visual perception:** Fast consecutive stimuli *can not easily be distinguished from each other,* thus the projection of rapidly successive individual images gives the appearance of „moving" pictures.

The onset of this „pseudo-movement" lies at a speed between 16 and 24 frames per second.

---

cinema film (movie) with a frame rate of 24 pictures/s

The traditional motion picture film (movie) was based on a frame frequency of 24 frames per s (fps), at which a strong flickering was noticeable. Therefore each frame was interrupted by an aperture at a rate of one or two times – to increase the frame frequency to 48 or 72 stimuli per second.

1 meter (m) = 39,37 inches;
1 centimeter = 0,39 inches;

For a traditional television broadcast (fig. 5.5), the optical („analogue") picture is broken down into a **raster** (grid) the dimensions of which are determined by the *resolution capability of the human eye* (fig. 5.4)

For economical reasons the luminosity of the individual pixels are not transmitted simultaneously (parallel) but sequentially (one after the other).

With a viewing distance of *5 times the diagonal width of the screen* (approximately 2,5 m for a 51 cm screen) and given the human eye to have a resolution capability of 50 to 90 arc seconds it is necessary for the picture to be displayed with a minimum of **480 lines** in order for the raster to remain invisible.

CCIR = Comité Consultatif International de Radiodiffusion
625 lines vertical, 833 pixels horizontal, 50 fields/s

The 625 line CCIR Standard has been in effect since 1952. With a ratio of 4 : 3 (width to height) this means 833 pixels per line (fig. 5.4).

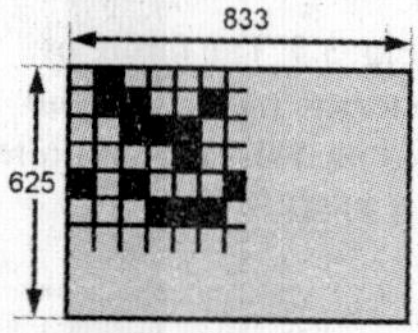

Fig. 5.4 The geometry of the TV picture size is dependent on the ratio of the width (W) to the hight (H)

To produce the effect of moving pictures by displaying individual images, a minimum field frequency (frame rate) of 25 frames per second is necessary, to give the human eye the appearance of a continuous movement.

For bright pictures, a frequency of 25 pictures per second is unsatisfactory since *the flickering produced by the sudden darkening of each pixel* is still too noticeable, which produces a phenomenon known as „large area flickering".

Flickering is the name we give to periodical fluctuation in the perception of brightness (luminosity). This effect can be reduced technically by so called „frame refreshers".

The developers of television were faced with a problem: the planned transmission channel could only transit a certain quantity of information – sufficient for only 25 pictures per second.

interlacing

A partial solution was achieved by the application of **„interlacing"**: The pictures were not reproduced in their natural sequential order, instead, during the first 1/50th. of a second the odd-numbered lines and in the next 1/50th. of a second the even-numbered lines were displayed.

In this manner 50 pictures per second were displayed, each with only half the number of interlaceable lines, reducing the flickering below the awareness threshold of the viewers.

Actually a picture only becomes truly free of flickering at a frame rate in excess of 75 frames per seconds (=75 Hz).

This value differs from person to person individually within a range between 72 Hz and 80 Hz. See Module 3, Chapter: Visual Display Units (VDUs).

In a television camera the conversion of the **luminance** (brightness value) of the picture into corresponding electric signals occurs through special **image converters.** Through a optical lens system the picture is displayed on a photocathode of the pick-up tube (photo valve) and is scanned, **line for line,** by an electronic beam (fig. 5.5).

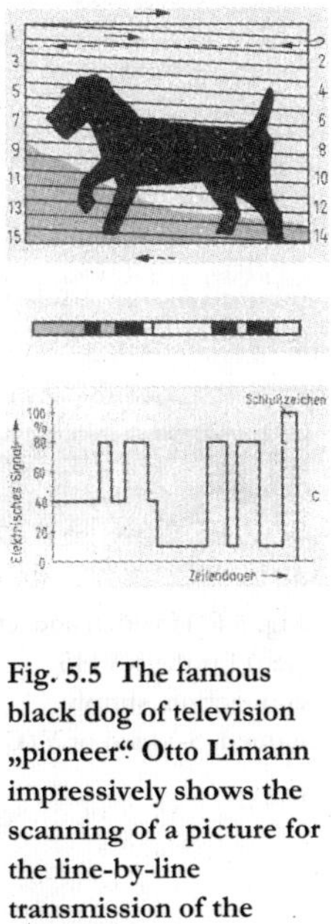

Fig. 5.5 The famous black dog of television „pioneer" Otto Limann impressively shows the scanning of a picture for the line-by-line transmission of the luminocity.
Master (top),
b/w variation in line 12 (middle),
electrical luminance signal (below)
from Limann (1979), 23

For a television picture $25 \times 625 \times 833 = 13\,015\,625$ pixels per second must be transmitted. That can be achieved with a bandwidth of **5 MHz** (1 MHz = 1 Million Hz). The television broadcast stations work in a frequency range between 48,25 and 788,75 MHz, therefore at wavelengths of about 6 metres (1 metre m = 1,094 yards) to 0,4 centimetres (one transmitter each for video and audio signals). The video signal is amplitude modulated (AM) and the audio signal is frequency modulated (FM).

In the receiver, the image is recovered by demodulating the video signal. Both signals are *separated,* the amplified **audio signal** is feeded to the loudspeaker while the **video signal** is feeded to the control electrode of the cathode-ray tube (CRT).

The video signal influences the brightness of every pixel of the electron beam, which is gliding, line for line, across the screen, *synchronized* by the camera.

In this way a **„dot picture"** is built up, *pixel-for-pixel,* which, if the sequence is *rapid enough* for the related viewing distance, produces a picture with an (for the human eye) invisible raster (graticule).

In order to guarantee an exact synchronisation of the electron beam in the television camera and the beam in the cathode ray tube, the recording station marks the beginning of every line with a unique **line synchronizing signal** and the beginning of every half-frame (interlacing) is marked with a unique **frame synchronizing signal.**

1.1 Analogue Recording Formats

Analogue video has matured somewhat but still has a vital disadvantage:

Fault Cascading

With several copies the faults accumulate to that the quality of each copy is worse than the one before.

Meanwhile this form of video presentation has reached it's physical boundaries so that improvements are hardly possible.

Video signals can be recorded in different analogue formats. The most common formats are (in order of decreasing quality):

- **Betacam** (SP), used in professional studios,
- **U-matic**, virtually replaced by Betacam,
- **S-VHS**, improved version of the widespread VHS,
- **Hi-8**, improved variant of the Video 8 system, and
- **VHS** (Video Home System), the most popular video system.

Fig. 5.6 Hosiden socket (left) for the S-VHS connection, simply named S-Video or Y/C

These standards differ considerably in the number of lines per frame and in the type of signal recording.

1.2 Video signals

We can differentiate between video signals by their quality:

1.2.1 FBAS (Composite Video)

At the lower end of the high-quality scale systems which transmit an „signal only" as it were stand includes U-matic, the widespread **VHS** and the classical television signal of an aerial (antenna).

The FBAS signal is a complement of the (black and white) video signal.

Since the complete television picture cannot, of course, be represented by one single electric signal, every individual pixel must be described by individual voltage ratings. For this purpose the FBAS-signal was developed and is widely known as the Composite-Signal.

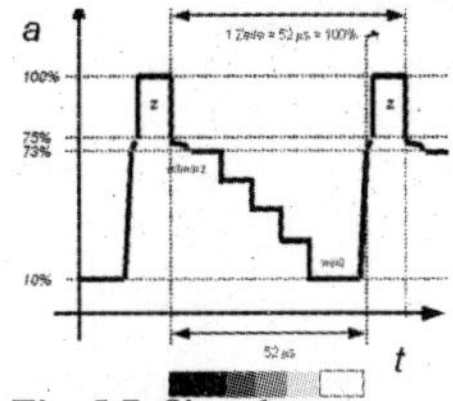

Fig. 5.7 Signal response of a composite video signal (Grey steps); a = amplitude

Each letter stands for a specific feature of the signal:

F Chrominance signal: The three colours red (R), green (G) and blue (B) are summarized in the chrominance signal.

B Video signal: The brightness and darkness tint of every point is determined through an electric voltage value (for example white = 10 %, black = 75 % of a defined threshold).

A Blanking signal: So that the cathode ray tube becomes blankedly („blanked“) during the beam flyback .

S Synchronization signal: guarantees the synchronisation of the beam deflection between sender (pick-up-tube) and receiver (cathode ray tube).

Home computer (for example the historical Commodore C64), used a FBAS signal in order to represent the video signal produced in the computer on a „usual“ television set. The FBAS signal is transmitted over one single cable, while with the RGB signal the chrominance signals are splitted into three separate cables. The picture of a FBAS-signal is not qualitatively as valuable as that of a RGB-signal.

1.2.2 Separated Video (Y/C, S-Video)

A grade higher in the quality scale, there are systems which use *separate signals* for *luminosity* **(Y)** and *colour* information **(C).** *Chrominance* means colorimetric difference, these signals, when added to the luminance signals, provide the hue and saturation components of the colour image. The bandwidth of the chrominance signal may be reduced to less than one half that of the luminance signal *before the deficiency is noted at normal viewing distances.* **S-VHS** and **Hi-8** use these types of signals and are also referred to as **S-Video.**

1.2.3 Component Video

Even higher quality systems use **three separate signals.** Depending on the colour model (refer to module 4) the following signals can be employed:

- **RGB** (Red, green, blue). This signal type is of high quality, but inefficient for analogue video and therefore rarely used by this equipment;
- **YUV** (Luminance, hue (tone-colour), saturation);
- **YIQ** (Luminance; I = R-Y the difference from Red to total Luminance; Q = B-Y the difference from Blue to total Luminance;

Betacam SP, the widespread Broadcasting Standard (SP stands for „superior performance"), has been a byword for professional video production for 20 years and is an analogue component format using YIQ.

1.3 Digital Recording Modes

A digital camera digitizes, compresses and records the picture with the helical scan method onto magnetic tape, while the image is being made. At the same time the sound is digitally recorded, in CD quality, onto the tape.

The following procedures prevail (quality increases from top to bottom):

- **DV** (Digital Video), a manufacturer independent standard; the signals can be transmitted, for example with the interface „Fire Wire" IEEE 1394, to a PC without any loss of data.
- **DVCAM,** Sony's advanced version of the DV standard with increased track width (15 μm instead of 10 μm) and fully compatible with DV.
- **DVCPRO,** Panasonic's advanced version of the DV standard but incompatible with DV,
- **Betacam-SX,** uses the MPEG-2 compression algorithm with 4:2:2 for professional use, but is fairly rare.
- **Digital Betacam,** portable via PC-SDI or other SDI components, higher quality than television.

SDI = Serial Digital Interface, determined in SMPTE (Society of Motion Pictures and Television Engineers) Standard 259M

In the broadcasting industry the **SDI**-interface is standard in digital signal transmission. Digital video signals and audio signals with a total bandwidth of **270 Mbps** are transmitted over SDI.

Fig. 5.8 The IEEE 1394 „Fire Wire" [W6]

A frequently used interface for transferring digital signals from recorders (Camcorder) to PC (video editing) is the **IEEE 1394**„ from Apple called the „Fire Wire" and from Sony called „iLink". On most appliances it is marked with DV out/in.

The interface IEEE 1394 is a serial bus system that connects up to 63 appliances. For the data transfer, four-pole wires (with a maximum of 4,5 m) are sufficient, plus two for an electrical current supply. The transmission rate is up to 50 MByte/s (for comparison: Ultra-SCSI has 20 MByte/s and Wide-U3-SCSI 160 MByte/s).

Fig. 5.9 The Universal Serial Bus (USB) is very practicle (ex: for digital photography)

Particularly by digital cameras (fig 5.9) able to record short sequences (30 to 90 seconds), frequently use the **USB-Bus** (Universal Serial Bus) originally developed by Intel (1995). The data is transmitted **serially** via a **twisted-pair wire** at a rate of 12 Mbit/s. Two other wires carry the operating voltage (5 volt) and the earth (0 volt, ground terminal). This has the advantage that some USB equipment does not require any (other) electrical current.

Up to 127 items of equipment can be run on one USB and the maximum transfer distance from the hub (or PC) to the instrument (for example Camera) is 5 meters (approximately 16 feet). By connection different equipment this distance can be increased. USB equipment has the advantage that new equipment can be added and removed while in operation, the integration of the drivers occurs automatically. There are two types of plugs: USB A (for example video camera, mouse, keyboard) and USB B (for example scanner, modem, hub), making it virtually impossible to connect them wrongly ((fig 5.10).

Fig. 5.10 The USB connection is extremely practical

1.4 Transmission Standards

Different transfer standards determine how a video signal is transmitted to a receiver (for example a television receiver):

- PAL (Phase Alternation by Line) in Europe, South America etc.,
- SECAM (Systeme Electronic Pour Couleur Avec Memoire) in France, Russia, and
- NTSC (National Television Standard Committee) in USA and Japan.

The difference between the norms can be seen in the following table:

System	frames/s	lines/frame	line frequency	resolution in px	aspect ratio
PAL	25	625	15 625 Hz	425 × 290	4 : 3
SECAM	25	625	15 625 Hz	465 × 290	4 : 3
NTSC	30	525	15 734 Hz	330 × 242	4 : 3
HDTV	50	1250	-	700 × 700	16 : 9

Fig. 5.11 The various standards at a glance Caution: HDTV serves here as a comprehensive term only, different arrangement formats exist

Digitized, a PAL frame has 768 × 576 pixels.

... only 576 instead of theoretically possible 625 – because not all lines contain image information

The number of transmitted lines does not correspond with the number of recorded lines. The output device, for example a video player, must convert the line number.

HDTV (High definition Television), a comprehensive term for different formats, forms the basis for the development of future television technology. The innovations comprise of, among other things:

HDTV has an aspect ratio of 16 : 9 – this is better adapted to the human visual field

- Viewing distance: 2 to 3 m
- horizontal angle of camera coverage: 45 degrees /field of vision/
- width/height ratio 6 : 9

1.5 Digital Video

Digital video has basic advantages over analogue video:

- Quality is independent of the transmission channel characteristics
- reproduction without loss of quality,
- virtually unrestricted life span,
- Error correction is considerably more diversely possible,
- precise digital filters can be used, which means
- Image manipulations and effects at a lower cost and higher quality than analogue video.

Compression (Module 4, chapter 4) is essential!

Digital video also has enormous disadvantages: The bandwidth is more than 200-times that of analogue video signals, causing an extreme increase in frame rate, memory requirement and baud rate. Compression is indispensable.

Fundamentally, a digital video consists of a sequential (one after the other) string of individual video frames:

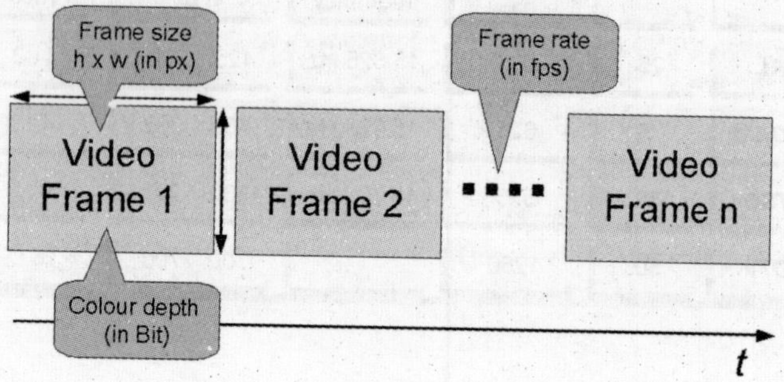

Fig. 5.12 A digital video consists of a number of frames per time unit (Frame rate) in a particular dimension (Frame size) and with particular colour depth

The physical size of video files depends on several factors:

- **Frame size:** the smaller the frame measurement, the less storage space necessary (240 × 180 px, 160 × 120 px or the even smaller „stamp format").
- **Frame rate:** the number of frames per unit of time (usually counted in seconds = fps), the lower the frame rate the smaller the file. Nonetheless, as the frame rate goes down the movements become more „jerky". The lowest limit is 15 fps.
- **Colour depth:** the less colours used, the smaller the file.

- **Audio-Soundtrack** – the narrower the „sound depth" the smaller the file. Stereo needs twice the file size of mono;
- **Codec** – (compression/decompression algorithm – see next chapter) some are more suitable than others for specific purposes. For example, for videos where the background does not change considerably, codecs with frame-difference algorithms are more suitable. Most video processing programs allow the use of different codecs and key-frames.

The following formula can be used to calculate the approximate (rough, unprocessed) video file size:

$$Fs = (f \times r \times c \times t) + As$$

f Frame size (width × height) in px
r Frame rate in fps
c colour depth in bit,
t time in s
A_s size of soundtrack

Example:

One minute of analogue video is to be converted into a digital video in a quarter of VGA size (320 × 240), with 30 fps, 24 bit colour depth with stereo sound (11 kHz, 8 bit).

hint: bit/8 = bytes divide the colour depth by 8 to get the result in bytes

F_s = ((320 × 240 px) × 30 fps × 3 Bytes × 60 s) + 1,2 MB = 416 MB

In digital video one generally differentiates between :

- **Architectures,** e.g.: Video for Windows, DirectMedia, DirectShow, Windows Media, Real, Quicktime,
- **Codecs,** e.g.: MPEG-1, JPEG, Indeo, Cinepak, wma, wmv, RealAudio/ Video, DV
- **File formats,** e.g.: MPEG, MHEG, AVI
- **Streaming**, e.g.: Real, ASF, Quicktime (particularly important for Internet, see module 6).

Architectures

Codecs

File-Formats

Streaming-Formats

Streaming-Video in Module 6, chapter 2.6

Some manufacturers frequently offer a number of things together, for example a whole multimedia architecture (with extras), Codècs and the ability to process various file formats.

2 Multimedia-Architectures

Architectures, supply the applications (Programs such as Video Player, Editor and Presentation Tools etc.) with simple call up functions in order to record, to play and to process videos. Codecs are embedded in this architecture and various file formats can be used.

The Multimedia architecture defines the frame for the respective software components for the production, presentation and storage of multimedia data, thereby defining interfaces to codecs and file formats.

Currently some multimedia-architectures are more commonly implemented:

- DirectShow
- Windows media
- Real (see module 6, chapter 2.6)
- Quicktime

2.1 DirectShow

API Application Programming Interface

The *DirectX-API* for image data processing has been available under Windows systems since 1996. DirectX builds on characteristics of the available hardware and attempts put these to optimal use. The technical performance and the functional scope of modern graphic adapters naturally improves with every new graphic adapters generation. In order to make this expanding service available for video processing, Microsoft developed DirectShow-API, building directly onto DirectX.

DirectShow offers the possibility of component based software development by means of the COM-standard. These components can be combined and transfer the video data stream through all successively controlled components (so-called DirectShow Filters).

For the video recording all frame grabbers (image digitizers), which have VfW- (Video for Windows) or WDM-(Windows Model) drivers available, are supported, making the frame grabber exchangeable. The so-called Video Renderer, a DirectShow component that exploits the abilities of the built-in graphic adapter, takes over the representation of the picture on the monitor enabling the justification or scaling of a picture with degradation.

Any number of transformation filters to process the data stream can be placed between the capture filter and the renderer filter. In this case, the control of the individual components and the entire data stream is taken over by a main application, which, according to need, can combine, separate start and stop the components.

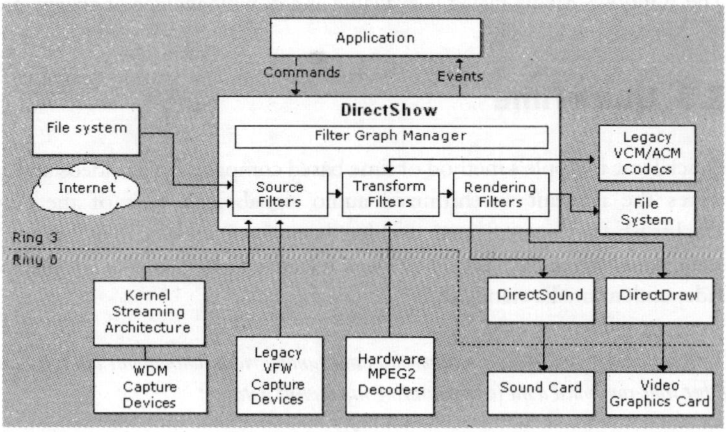

Fig. 5.13 DirectShow from Microsoft [W19]

2.2 Windows Media

Microsoft introduced the Net Show module, which offers streaming functionality, at the same time as the Internet Explorer 4.0. Meanwhile Net Show has been renamed **Windows-Media-Technology** and consists, as does real Media, of:

- a client (Windows Media Player),
- various development tools and
- two media servers.

On the server side, the Windows Media Services Servers or the Theatre Server can be employed. Both servers differ by the bandwidth of the transmitted streams, whereby the Theatre Server can transfer a full motion MPEG video, in full screen width, with a guaranteed performance over a high speed net.

The **Windows Media Player** is a front-end application for viewing multimedia contents. It supports the formats MPEG-1, MPEG-2, MP-3, WAV, MIDI, MOV, VOD, GOLD, AVI, Quicktime, RealAudio and RealVideo and the Net Show ASF.

ASF = Advanced Streaming Format

The ASF does not replace any one file format, but combines files of different formats into one package.

The Media Player can be run on a PC as an off-line application or be integrated into a Web Site as an online component.

The Windows Media Player is available as a download, free of charge, from the Microsoft web page.

2.3 QuickTime

QuickTime is Apple's method of time based compression of videos and also stores the relevant synchronized audio signal. It is part of the Apple MacIntosh Computer System and has been compatible with Windows for some time. Since the version 3.0 was released, it has become an platform independent media standard.

Time based data are mainly multimedia data (audio, video, animation) but can also be other time-controlled data (e.g. measuring instrument data).

The data records are called **"Movies"** (.mov). QuickTime places a great number of functions at the programmer's disposal with which to develop individual multimedia applications without having to program such basic functions as the fabrication of a film or the plotting of an animation.

Although QuickTime offers very complex functions which facilitate the job of programming, the resulting applications tend toward a similar appearance (look-and-feel).

Personal new developments, such as new compression algorithms or drivers for a new video digitizer, can be linked in and then be used from all applications in the same way as the standard routines.

Unfortunately, the fact that the technical details are concealed by QuickTime from the user and programmer precludes any precise statements about the mode of operation and details of the implementation. Particularly the image compressors, which would be of special interest here, were almost all developed by Apple, and the technical details not generally known.

Many digital camera manufacturers integrated the QuickTime technology into their models, thereby making it an industrial standard format for digital contents. As general platform standard QuickTime allows both Macintosh and Windows customers to exchange photographs and "Movies".

With QuickTime, relatively high quality web based television is possible.

3 Codecs

Since pure digital video files are extremely large (a few seconds can require megabytes of disk storage), **compression** is a very important topic (cf. Module 4, Chapter 4: Compression concept).

Video data can be compressed in a number of different ways. Basically, each compression procedure requires a corresponding de-compression procedure, to make it possible to view the packed video.

Software and/or Hardware for the compression/decompression of multimedia data (videos in particular) is named Codec (**CO**mpression/**DEC**ompression).

Codec = Coder/Decoder

Among CODECs we can distinguish between

- Hardware Codecs (for example Video Editing System) and
- Software Codecs (also known as Soft Codecs).

Do *not* confuse file formats with codecs, for instance AVI (Chapter 2.3) says nothing about the compression employed.

With hardware CODECs „jerky" pictures are virtually impossible, but Software Codecs can easily overload the computer processor (CPU).

All codecs in common use are strongly **asymmetric:** The unique compression process lasts an extremely long time, on the other hand the decompression for viewing is very fast.

Customary hardware and/or software dependent codecs are:

- Cinepak (24 bit colour depth, compression factor 7 : 1),
- Indeo (Intel),
- Microsoft RLE (Random Length Encoding, only for Windows),
- Video 1 (Video and/or Microsoft Video 1),
- MPEG-1,
- Motion JPEG,
- H.261,
- H.263.

Cinepak, originally developed by SuperMac Technology for Apple, now is more or less a de-facto-Standard

As described in chapter 2, **Video for Windows** and **QuickTime** are Multimedia architectures which allow the integration of digital video into a graphic user interface. They were primarily developed in order to play video only with software programs. The corresponding files have a standardized construction, with Video for Windows, for example, these are **AVI-files** (Audio/Video Interleaved).

Different codecs can be used within the framework of each architecture. With Video for Windows these are:

- Cinepak,
- Indeo,
- RLE,
- Video 1;

and with QuickTime correspondingly

- Cinepak,
- Indeo,
- MPEG-1 (with additional hardware).

Every codec has specific advantages and disadvantages which are of importance in determining the purpose and quality:

Fig. 5.14 An overview about common Codecs which has established meanwhile by using digital videos

Codec	format	pros	cons
Cinepak	mov, avi	good quality, good colour reproduction	slow calculation
Indeo	mov, avi	excellent by motifs with little movement	slow calculation, unsteady over large areas
RLE	avi	lossless, relatively fast	restricted to 8 bit colour depth
Video 1	mov, avi	good quality, fast calculation	high data rate, restricted to 16 bit colour depth
MPEG-1	mpeg	Television quality	slow calculation

A codec is not automatically determined by the file format of the video (as for example AVI, Quicktime etc. but through the configuration at the production of the video clip.

If a video cannot be viewed with the usual players, the cause could lie in the use of exotic code. There are numerous web pages where codecs can be downloaded (for example [W10]).

4 Video file formats

A substantial difficulty in the use of digital videos consists of the gigantic amount of data required. Compression is therefore essential. The most important video formats are MPEG, MHEG, AVI and Quicktime. The „simplest" choice is the M-JPEG procedure, which is no longer commonly used. We will deal with the uses in the Internet more particularly in the next module.

4.1 M-JPEG

The M-JPEG (Motion JPEG procedure) is based on a **serialization** of individual images packed in the JPEG-format. Every individual image is individually packed in JPEG. These video files are almost always stored in AVI format under Windows and as Quicktime files by Apple.

The quality of the lossy JPEG compression (see module 3) is, in wide boundaries, configurable. Compression rates up to a factor of 25, while retaining good quality, are possible, however, the integration of audio data is not defined in M-JPEG.

Actually, M-JPEG is hardly ever used. The reason for this is, although the procedure for the individual image compression is standardised up to „quantization table", that there are no standards for the composition of packed JPEG individual images and corresponding audio. The file format for M-JPEG and the sequence of audio and video components in a M-JPEG file are proprietary. This means that each manufacturer defines their own M-JPEG file format at the cost of inter-operability. This has caused a a trend towards DV or MPEG file formats to be seen in the last few years.

4.2 MPEG

MPEG stands for **Motion Picture Experts Group** (see module 2 „Signals and Coding"). Founded in January 1988, it is an alliance of experts with the goal of developing standards for the encoded representation of moving images and audio data, separately and combined.

The official name is: **ISO/IEC JTC1 SC29 WG11,** from:

- ISO – International Organization for Standardization
- IEC – International Electrotechnical Commission
- JTC1 – Joint Technical Committee 1
- SC29 – Sub-Comittee 29
- WG11 – Work Group 1 (Moving Pictures Experts Group)

Fig. 5.15 The MPEG-Logo: (analogue) Video and Audio into – digital Output out [W14]

Since MPEG began, ,with the first meeting in May 1988 (with 25 participants), it has grown and advanced to the worldwide significant committee which it is today.

Today approximately 350 experts from 200 firms and organizations from more than 20 countries participate in the MPEG meetings. The MPEG assembles three times a year (March, July, November) for meetings lasting 5 days. At these meetings the standard MPEG are defined and developed.

The following MPEG-standards are being or have been developed:

- MPEG-1 = ISO 11172 (Coding of moving pictures and audio up to 1,5 Mbps); 320 × 240 px, 30 fps, Software-Decoder, low quality;
- MPEG-2 = ISO 13818 (Generic coding of moving pictures and associated audio); 720 × 480 px, 1280 × 720 px, 60 fps, Audio in CD-Quality, Hardware and Software, for NTSC, HDTV, DVD;
- MPEG-3 (originally intended for HDTV, 1920 × 1080 px, Interlace-Technique, 30 fps, 20 to 40 Mbps, since MPEG-2 is sufficient, work on the MPEG-3 was stopped.);
- MPEG-4 = ISO 14496 (Coding of audio-visual objects) Standard for Multimedia-Applications (first introduced in 1998, released in 2000, however, with parts still being worked on);
- MPEG-7 = ISO 15938 (Multimedia Content Description Interface), standard for content representation and multimedia search (work still in progress);
- MPEG-21 = ISO Draft (Multimedia-Framework), in development.

Mainly MPEG-1 and MPEG-2 are still being used for digital video in near television quality. MPEG-1 is employed in the semi-professional field. MPEG-2 was defined with digital television in view and supports line interlacing.

4.2.1 MPEG-1

MPEG 1 was introduced in 1992 and works with a bandwidth of approximately 1,5 MBit/s. Approximately 1,25 Mbps are allotted to video, the rest is shared by two audio channels. The resolution at 25 frame/s is 360 × 288 px (Europe CIF) and 352 × 240 × 30 (CIF USA). Although interlacing is not supported, VHS recording is possible.

In order to keep the files as small as possible, the the so-called **„interframe compression“** is applied in the MPEG-1 process. Only the *differences* from the previous frame are stored.

Movement Compensation is the integral part of the MPEG coding algorithm: Two consecutive pictures of the same scene hardly differ. Instead of coding two full frames, using large memory storage, only the details which have altered are stored.

The attempt is made to describe as many frames as possible only by the **differences** in their content to that of the previous coded frame.

Unlike the AVI-format, this is done with the motion compensation function. This function determines sections of display shift, such as when objects move or by camera pan shots. The movements in these display sections can be expressed in the form of two-dimensional shift vectors. In practice, a slow camera pan shot can be achieved with almost no coding of direct picture information.

The standard resolution of 352 × 288 px (at 50 Hz) corresponds to half of the PAL resolution (768 × 576). The data rate for audio is determined at a maximum of 112 kbps and for video at approx. 1100 kbps. This makes a total data rate of about 1200 kbps.

74 minutes of MPEG-1-Video fit onto a CD (650 MB).

An MPEG video data stream consists of the following 6 „layers" (fig. 5.16)

- Video Sequence,
- Group of Pictures,
- Picture,
- Slice,
- Macroblock,
- Block (8 × 8 px).

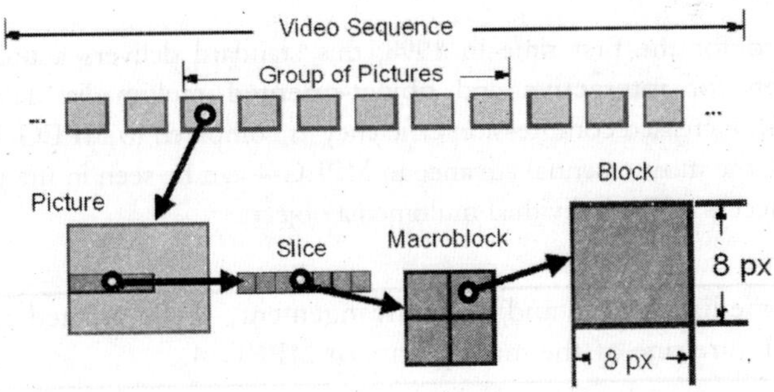

Fig. 5.16 The „layers" of MPEG-1

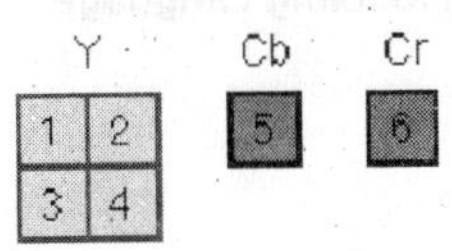

Fig. 5.17 YUV-Blocks within the Macroblock

Six blocks, each 8 × 8 px are sequenced within a macroblock: first, four luminance blocks, then two chrominance blocks (fig. 5.17). A number of macroblocks form one „Slice Layer".

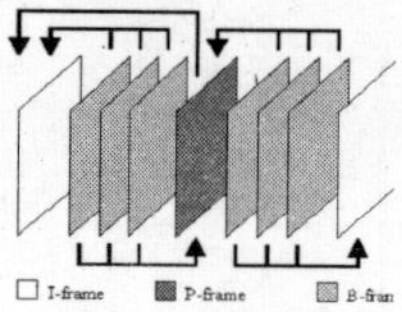

Fig. 5.18 The order and relationship of the individual frames in a MPEG-compression.

Within a **GOP** (Group of Pictures), consisting of 9 or 15 pictures, three different image types (Frames) are used:

- I-Frames (Intra Frames) contain the **complete image information,**
- B-Frames (Bi-directional Predicted Frames) contain only the **difference** to the previous picture and
- P-Frames (Predicted frames) contain only the **algorithm** which which the screen content can be computed on the basis of preceding pictures.

4.2.2 MPEG-2

Structured on MPEG-1, MPEG-2 takes the characteristics of video signals particularly into account. MPEG-2 is therefore intended as the foundation/ basis/ of future standards for data reduction in the transmission of digital television signals.

The operating principle of MPEG-2 is comparable to that of MPEG-1, covers, however, the characteristics of interlaced-pictures better. This is a decisive advantage of full format videos (720 × 576 px). The most important differences to MPEG-1 are:

Scalability= a choice of various quality levels in one video data stream

- Scalability (see profiles and levels in [W20])
- Interlacing and
- Optional sampling rates of colour components (4:2:0, 4:2:2 and 4:4:4)

Approximately 6 Mbps is sufficient for MPEG-2 to supply the required quality on DVD and for digital television. Audio data are recorded directly with the video signal.

Interlacing = Coding half pictures is also possible

4.2.3 MPEG-4

Introduced for the first time in 1998, this standard delivers a uniform description for **interactive** and **object-oriented** multimedia data. In addition to increased compression efficiency as compared to MPEG-1 and MPEG-2, the most essential advance in MPEG-4 can be seen in the user's random access of the individual multimedia objects.

Virtual Reality Modeling Language

Multimedia objects and their arrangement, scene-plotted in VRML, are one of the main points of MPEG-4.

The individual objects can be constructed with different coding procedures. (for example: Stills with JPEG, video with H.261/H.263, audio with G.723, AC-3, etc.). The high flexibility of MPEG-4 permits the integration of numerous **interactive elements**. These can be most often found in self-developed tools (also with proprietary solutions).

The decisive innovation in MPEG-4 is then internationally regulated behaviour of objects and the representation in a standard description form thereby enabling interoperability: manufacturer independence. (Hardware, operating systems etc.).

In conclusion, it can be stated that MPEG-4 is not a fixed standard, but a framework with the following main aims:

- Object-oriented VRML by means of **Media Objects,**
- **Interaction** between users and the multi media world,
- Extendability, **Inter-operability** and Flexibility,
- **Integration Capability** for nonspecific media objects (AVO, e.g. text objects, audio objects, 2D and 3D objects etc.)

MPEG-4 integrates these objects and organizes them into a **tree structure**, whereby compression is always applied to the objects individually. MPEG-4 is also used in Virtual Reality (see module 6). **Media-objects** are separated into

- **Natural media objects** (a) visual objects, e.g. text, graphics and animation and b) auditory objects e.g. speech, sound, music and
- **Synthetic media objects** (a) visual objects, e.g. synthetic grid objects with texts and b) auditory objects, e.g. synthetic speech.

MPEG-4 also makes various tools and algorithms available for specific applications, such as the compression of frames, videos and 2D or 3D surface pictures; content-related coding of pictures and video, and an improved error-resistance by error sensitive applications. This is of extreme importance in **Mobile Computing,** particularly with faulty transmission channels .

For authors, MPEG-4 offers improved reusability and the possibility of protecting copyrights.

4.2.4 MPEG-7

Unlike texts, it is still not possible to create automatic catalogues from the contents of audio and video files.

For example, internet Search tools find large numbers of texts which describe film scenes but only very rarely do these include a link to a corresponding multimedia file.

To date, there is still no general description format for this type of multimedia contents. The "Multimedia Content Description Interface", developed in 1996 and named MPEG-7, was designed to close this gap.

MPEG-7 is a standardized description of different types of multimedia information. This description is associated with the content itself in order to guarantee a rapid and efficient search (and result) for the users.

The launching of MPEG-7 as an ISO standard is scheduled for the end of 2001.

MPEG-7 can be used completely independently of the previous MPEG standards (1, 2, 4): It is not a compression procedure for audio-visual data. For this reason the jump to the number 7 was made. There is no MPEG 3 (recalled), MPEG-5 and MPEG-6 were never even planned.

4.2.5 MPEG-21

The work on this standard was first started in the middle of the year 2000.

MPEG-21 attempts the description of a multi medial framework and to anticipate future trends for an environment in which a large number of contents are supported. First results are not expected until 2002.

4.3 MHEG

Since multimedia presentations continue to gain importance it is obvious that a *standard* **transfer format** should be developed which will enable a playback of videos on as many systems as possible.

MHEG Multimedia and Hypermedia Information coding expert Group

MHEG, a team of the subcommittee SC29 of ISO, has developed just such a transfer format - the MHEG standard

Further teams of the SC29 are JPEG (joint photographic expert group), MPEG (motion pictures expert group) and JBIG (joint bi-level expert group).

MHEG describes Multimedia Presentations on the object level in its final form. Editing is unnecessary.

ASN.1 Abstract Syntax Notation One (ISO 8824) as basis for the description of the packets employed in the OSI Protocols

Necessary for the execution of MHEG Presentations are:

- **Formatter** and
- **Syntax analyst**, the
- **MHEG Engine** and a
- Unit for the **decoding of ASN.1 Data Structures.**

The formatter sends and stores, the syntax analyst reads the data. Due to these two units a data exchange between heterogeneous platforms is possible.

A presentation in the MHEG-format remains compatible because it has already been analysed syntactically and semantically. The MHEG Engine adjusts the MHEG presentation to the runtime environment during playback (at viewing time).

The respective presentation programme is responsible for the presentation of the objects in the presentation programme, not the MHEG standard.

MHEG only provides control mechanisms and determines the structure information of a hypermedia document.

Interactive television makes a spectator response to the sender possible, per Set Top Box, telephone line etc.

In this way **"Interactive Television"** can be implemented, for example.

In order to illustrate the demands on such a format clearly, the individual elements of a multimedia presentation could be represented in the form of atiming analysis.

Example: A presentation begins with music. As soon as the voice of a speaker is heard in the audio sequence, a graphic is flashed onto the screen, followed by a text. When the text disappears, the viewer can use a stop button to interrupt the audio sequence. Now, the title of a desired video sequence, to be displayed at the end of the modification, can be entered into the input area (fig. 5.19).

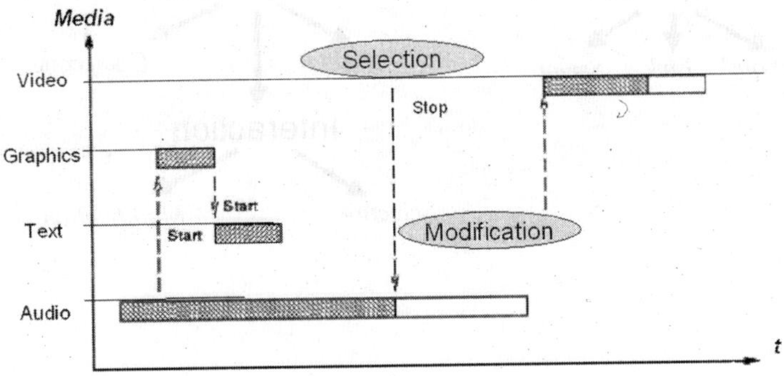

Fig. 5.19 Time diagram of an interactive multi media presentation (modification according to Meyer-Boudnik (in 1994))

A multimedia transfer format must take the following elements into account:

Die **Content Data,** consisting of several individual pieces of information, which are coded in various different media formats. Each of these pieces is handled as an individual **Content Object** in MHEG.

The term **Behaviour** covers all actions that refer to the state of the existing content components (for example start and stop).

The actions in MHEG are represented by **Action Objects.** It is a matter of conditional, spatial and chronological connections between the content objects.

An alteration in the state of a **Content Object** can act as a trigger for other objects actions. This is implemented in MHEG by a **Link Object.**

User Interaction takes place via **Selection Objects.** MHEG also offers **Modification Objects** for more complex modifications of the operating sequence.

Container (Composite Objects) make it possible to transmit a presentation written in MHEG in one piece. For this purpose, individual objects are integrated in Container Objects.

All these considerations lead to the following class hierarchy (fig. 5.20):

Fig. 5.20
The class hierarchy of the MHEG Object.

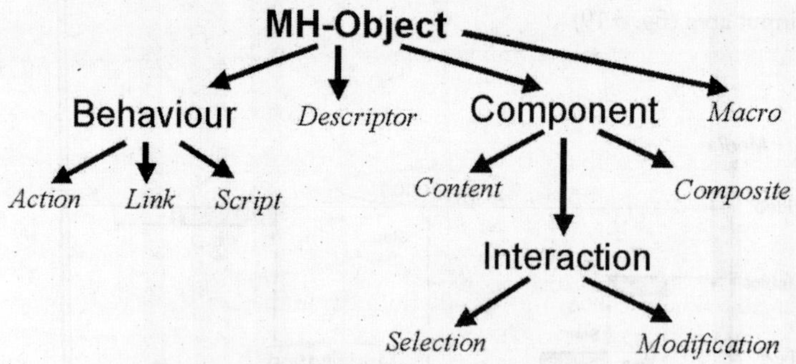

4.4 AVI

AVI is the abbreviation for **Audio Video Interleaved,** it was introduced with Microsoft Windows 3.1 as a multimedia upgrade and is based on the **RIFF** (Resource Interchange File Format).

„Interleaved" means that Audio and Video are woven in each other. Audio and video information are stored together, and can be reconstructed together.

interleave = To insert or introduce something at regular intervals between things or between the parts of a thing

The first specification of AVI is almost as old as Multimedia-PCs itself. The format was created by Microsoft as a uniform solution to video-clip playbacks. The original specifications for the years 1992/1993 demonstrate just how far we have come: 15 pictures per second, at a maximum resolution of 160 × 120 px.

As a rule, AVI File are packed. The most frequently used compression codecs are **Cinepak** and **Indeo** (Chapter 1.5).

packed = compressed

Basically, the AVI File resolution can be in full PAL Format (768 × 576 px), however typical values lie around 320 × 240px with 25 to 30 fps (frames/second).

An AVI file in Cinepak Codec has a size of about 60 MB/min at a resolution of 384 ×288 px and 25 fps. An AVI-file in Indeo 5.10 Codec has a size of about 40 MB/min at a resolution of 384 ×288 pixels and 25 fps.

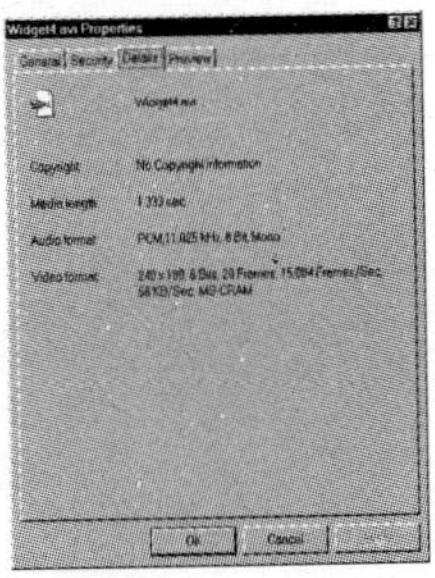

Fig. 5.21
The properties of an AVI File

Software which converts AVI into MPEG-1 requires approx. 10 to 20 minutes to compute the compression of one minute of film.

With a Windows operating system the data rate of an AVI file can easily be found out. Click with the right mouse button on the **file name** (in explorer), with the left mouse button on **properties** and again on **details** (fig. 5.19).

An AVI-file consists of different, interlaced, data structures, so-called **Chunks**. These can in turn be partitioned, individually, into further sub-chunks.

The chunks start with an ID (Identifier), specified as FOURCC (Four Character Code), the byte(s) of which is/are interpreted as ASCII Code.

The ID is followed by a length specification which refers to the succeeding data.

5 Video Storage Media

5.1 Classical Magnetic Tape Storage

Video films are generally archived onto magnetic tapes. The fear that the band might be destroyed (band spill, magnetism) always exists. Copying the film onto a new band is involves loss of quality.

Magnetic tapes consist of *plastic film* (PET) with a magnetizable vapour-deposited layer, on which the data are stored. In Information Technology (IT) magnetic tape cassettes are called streamers and/or **DAT (Digital Audio Tape)**. These tapes have a *high storage capacity* in the gigabytes range.

The DAT-Technology is being replaced (by Sony) through so-called „Advanced Intelligent Tapes" (AIT), whose current storage capacity is 25 GB and has a planned capacity of 100 GB.

Magnetic tapes have the disadvantage have the disadvantage, that only a sequential grip on the stored data is possible.

In order to read a specific data record all stored data must be read, sequentially, which leads to extended access times. For this reason tapes are primarily usually used as a backup medium, unintentional data deletion is unlikely and the data security is high (Lockup).

Analogue video cameras (VHS, Video8, Hi-8) store **analogue signals** onto a magnetic tape. Digital video cameras (Digital 8, DV) record **digital signals** onto magnetic tape.

The systems employ different tape cassettes. Basically the individual cassettes vary in the width of the magnetic tape, its length and external measurements. Four analogue systems (VHS-C, video 8, S-VHS-C, Hi-8) and two digital systems (DV, digital 8) are currently widespread:

VHS-C. This format uses cassettes, which are a mini edition of the recording procedure for home video equipment developed by JVC (Victor Company of Japan). VHS (1/2 inch tapes) became the world standard for private customers.

Video-8. An alternative to VHS from Sony. The procedure works with smaller video-cassettes (95 × 62,5 × 15 mm) and is therefore incompatible with video tape recorders (camcorder). Audio and video information are recorded by rotating video heads, independent of each other. This makes dubbing possible (synchronization). Additionally, a rotating erase head exists, with which two tracks are deleted and remagnetized when recording, thereby enabling an electronic cutting without interference. Through that an electronic cut without grasses becomes possible.

S-VHS-C. This is the compact form of S-VHS. With an adapter the cassettes can be also be played on a VHS video tape recorder.

Fig. 5.22 DV-Cassette

Hi-8. As a further development of Video-8, this was matched against the S-VHS standard.

DV. This Cassette has the size and form of a matchbox (Picture 5.22) and makes the compact video camera designs (Camcorder) possible.

Digital 8. Following up on the design of Video-8 and Hi-8, but with the digital recording format from DV it was planned to facilitate the change-over to Digital Video.

All CD Formates originate in CD-DA (Compact Disk Digital Audio), also called Music CD or just plain "CD"

5.2 CD-ROM

The CD-ROM (CD R) is an important storage medium everywhere, the three essential advantages are: large storage capacity (approximately 650 MB, 750 MB or 800 MB), wear-resistant and good data security.

A CD consists of a a reflective coating (usually aluminium) on a carrier shift (most often polycarbonate). This thin coating is the actual storage medium and is protected against mechanical harm by a protective coating.

On principle there are two possibilities to operate a CD :
1) **CAV** Constant Angular Velocity: the rotation speed of the CD always remains the same, the data rate is therefore different in the different sectors;
2) **CLV** Constant Linear Velocity: the track wraps itself *in a spiral* from the centre to the outside; the rotation rate of the CD must change in order to retain a constant linear rate.

The CD is an optical medium: A laser beam is carried through a dichroic (semipermeable) mirror and focusing onto the CD. It is reflected from the coating over the dichroic mirror on the photodiode. The data are in the form of lands („hills") and pits on the reflective coating. If the laser beam hits a pit, it can not be reflected any further. With the aid of the photodiode the „alternation" is optically measured between lands and pits and converted into corresponding electric signals.

CD-DA = Compact Disk Digital Audio (classical Music-CD with 74 Minutes)

CD-I = Compact Disk Interactive (MM-CD with possible interaction)

CD-R = Compact Disk Recordable (write-once-read-many-times disk)

CD-RW = Compact Disk Rewriteable (write-many-read-many-times disk).

CD-ROM = Compact Disk Read Only Memory (classical data CD).

Photo-CD = purpose made for storage of orthochromatic images (quality)

The smallest unit of information on a CD is the **Channel Bit.** A data byte consists of 8 data bits and is stored on the CD in 14 channel bits.

The transition from pit to land or land to pit stands for a logical „1". A „0" is the opposite, a stretch with no changes. No less than two, but no more than eleven Zeros may be written, before a „1". The "Eight to Fourteen Modulation Code" is used to convert 8 bit-data to 14 bit-data. Since this coding is still insufficient, three pack bits (merge channel bits) are added on. Thus, 8 data bits are expressed by 17 channel bits.

24 bytes are contained in a **frame.** Each frame ends with a check byte. This is followed by a further eight bytes for error correction. The error correction takes place in two layers.

Therefore, in order to put 24 bytes on a CD one needs:

(24 Bytes × 17 Channel Bits) + (1 Byte × 17 Channel Bits) + (8 Bytes × 17 Channel-Bits) + 27 Synchronisation C-Bits = 588 Channel Bits.

A **sector** contains 98 frames giving a total of 3234 bytes.

Re-writeable CDs (CD RW) are a little more complicated than the ordinary "once only writeable" CDs. They have three shifts instead of just one.

5.3 Video Storage Medium DVD

DVD Digital Versatile Disk, the future successor of the CD-ROM

CD-ROM, CD video 2.0 (playable with DVD Players) and DVDs are an ideal substitute for video cassettes (tapes). A VHS cassette is exposed to continuous mechanical pressure during playback. The result is that the picture quality diminishes very fast. A CD-ROM however, provides unchangeable quality.

The master tape (the initial source) can be, for example, S-VHS, Hi 8, DV or beta. The digitalization can be to a choice of formats, for example AVI (Indeo, Cinepak etc.), MPEG1, video CD, Quicktime (Indeo, Cinepak etc.) or RealMedia (see module 6). The conversion of one format into another is also possible (for example from AVI to MPEG-1).

The DVD was originally developed for the video market and should replace the VHS tape

The DVD is a medium of the future on which videos can be stored in high quality and interactively controlled. The DVD supports most audio formats such as, for example, Dolby Digital or MPEG-2. Up to 8 hours of film can be recorded on a DVD - with best quality in sound an picture (Surround-Sound, AC-3).

The size of a DVD is the same as that of a standard CD and consists of two sides, each with one OR two layers of information, giving a combination of four possible capacities:

- Single Sided & Single Layered (SL SS),
- Single Sided & Dual Layered (SS DL),
- Double Sided & Single Layered (DS SL) and
- Double Sided & Dual Layered (DS DL).

Diameter:	12 cm (4,68 inches)
Thickness:	2 x 0,6 mm (2 x 0,023")
Capacity SS SL:	4,7 GB
Capacity SS DL:	8,5 GB
Capacity DS SL:	9,4 GB
Capacity DS DL:	17 GB

Fig. 5.23 Capacity of different variantions of the DVD

In comparison to analog storage procedures (e.g. video-tape, VHS cassette) the DVD has several advantages, in addition to high storage capacity:

- cheaper production,
- higher quality,
- better copy protection possibilities (DIVX) and
- Deterioration free, something of particular interest for video-tape libraries).

DIVX = Digital Video Express, the encrypted contents is only viewable via „Pay per View"

DVD viewing equipment can be obtained separately, or as an installable disk drive. Both types of equipment should be downward compatible with all other CD standards. Audio-CD and CD-ROM compatibility is not really a problem except for the first generation CD-Rs which reflect insufficient light for the optical disk drive to read.

The main difference between CD and DVD is the recording density. Although a DVD looks the same as a CD, 7 to 26 times more data fits onto a DVD than a CD.

Practically, it means that the capacity is sufficient for at least 2 hours and 15 minutes playing time - enough for a full length film. In the higher capacity variations the DVD actually permits over 8 hours playing time. Mostly DVDs provide up to eight languages, 32 subtitles, 6 independent sound channels up to nine view angles and the possibility of interactivity.

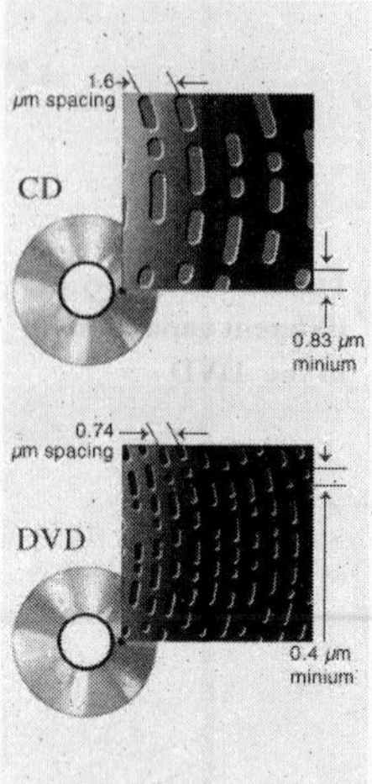

Fig. 5.24 Technological differences between CD and DVD

Technically the measurements of the individually **Pits** were reduced on the DVD as compared to the CD and the track pitch narrowed (fig 5.23). The wavelength of the laser was reduced from 780 nm to 650 nm.

Parallel to the DVD three more standards were developed:

- DVD-R (read - writeable once only - corresponds the CD-R),
- DVD RAM (random access memory - rewriteable- corresponds to CD RW) from a group of companies including Panasonic, Hitachi, Toshiba and Pioneer; and the also rewriteable:
- DVD+RW from a group of companies including Sony, Philips, Ricoh, Yamaha and Hewlett-Packard.

But this technology has already been surpassed in theory, since work is already being done on disk drives and mediums with 15 GByte capacity per layer. This should be is achieved with a blue laser with a wavelength of 415 nm.

5.4 FMD – Fluorescence Multilayer Disk

The demand for increasingly bigger memory storage increases continuously. The company Constellation 3D, Inc. (C3D), New York, has introduced a data medium that could be the answer to this. The technology was actually developed by JACOB MALKIN in 1995. The product itself was introduced as FMD with a 40 GB capacity in June 200 in Burbank (CA).

The size of the FMD corresponds exactly to that of a CD or DVD. The 40 GB are distributed on five layers of 8 GB each. The FMD technology employs several layers of "luminous paint" in pits similar to those on a CD. When the laser beam hits them, the layers light up differently.

According to C3D, only minimum changes in the hardware of existing DVD players is supposed to be necessary to be able to read FMDs. The next generation DVD Player could be constructed to remain downward compatible without problem and would be able to read DVD, CDs and CD-ROMs.

In future, it is expected that 30 or more data layers will be possible and something especially interesting, through different coatings some layers could be constructed as ROM (Read Only) and others as WORM (write once, read many).

6 Module Summary

The psychophysical qualities of our eyes also determine the limits or boundary conditions for our conception of „video": in this, our slow visual perception is useful. The lower limit for the appearance of movement to start lies between **16 and 24 frame changes per second.**

Analogue recording formats are mainly Betacam (SP), U-matic, S-VHS, Hi-8 and VHS. **Video signals** are differentiated according to quality, into **FBAS** (Composite), **separated video** (Y/C, S-video) and **component video** (Component).

Digital video (DV) has advantages (for example the quality is independent of the transmission channel, copyable, durable etc.) compared to analogue video, the usual methods include DV, DVCAM, DVPRO, Betacam-SX and digital Betacam. However, digital video also has enormous disadvantages: For instance, the bandwidth needed is 200-time higher than with analogue video signals.

The most common interface for transmitting digital video signals is **IEEE 1394** (Fire Wire, iLink) and the **USB-bus** is . Transfer standards (PAL, SECAM, NTSC) determine how a video signal is transmitted to a receiver.

It is necessary to differentiates between **architectures** (for example video for Windows, DirectMedia, real, Quicktime usw.), **codecs** (MPEG, Indeo, Cinepak usw.), **file formats** (MPEG-1, MHEG, AVI, usw.) and **streaming formates** (e.g. real, ASF, Quicktime).

Currently, MPEG-1 and MPEG-2 are mainly used for digital video in television quality. A **motion compensation** is the central component of the **MPEG** coding algorithm. An attempted is made to describe display sections only by the **difference in the frame content** to the previous coded frame. **MPEG-4** supplies a standard for a consistent description of interactive, object-oriented multimedia data. **MPEG-7** can be employed completely independently of the previous **MPEG** standards (1, 2, 4): This is *not* a procedure for the compression of audio-visual data, but is designed to be be a standardized description of different models of multimedia information and to enable efficient searching. For this reason the jump to the number 7 was made. There is no MPEG 3 (recalled) , MPEG-5 and MPEG-6 were never even planned.

Classical magnetic tapes will probably be replaced as a storage medium by the **DVD** (Digital Versatile Disk) with a storage capacity of up to 17 GB.

7 Module Supplement

7.1 Literature

7.1.1 Books in English

HEATH, STEVE (1999): *Multimedia and Communications Technology.* 2nd Ed. Oxford: Focal Press, Butterworth, Heinemann. 44-64 & 79-132.

HILLMAN, DAVID (1998): *Multimedia Technology and Applications.* Albany [et.al.]: Delmar. 123-148.

POYNTON, CHARLES (1996): *A Technical Introduction to Digital Video.* New York: John Wiley & Sons.

STERN, JUDY; LETTIERI, ROBERT (1998): *QuickTime and MoviePlayer Pro 3 for Windows and MacIntosh (Visual Quickstart Guide).* New York: Addison Wesley.

WU, CHWAN-HWA; IRWIN, DAVID J. (1999): *Emerging Multimedia Computer Communication Technologies.* Upper Saddle River (NJ): Prentice Hall. 23-70.

7.1.2 Articles in English

BATTISTA, STEFANO; CASALINO, FRANCO; LANDE, CLAUDIO (1999): MPEG-4: A Multimedia Standard for the Third Millennium. *IEEE MultiMedia,* October-December 99, 74-83.

CHIARIGLIONE, LEONARDO (1995): MPEG: A Technological Basis for Multimedia Applications. *IEEE MultiMedia,* Vol. 2, No. 1; Spring 1995, 85-89.

ECHIFFRE, MARICA; MARCHISIO, PIETRO (1999): A multimedia presentation system for MHEG-5 applications. *Computer Standards & Interfaces,* Vol. 20, Iss. 4-5, 375-387.

ECHIFFRE, MARICA; MARCHISIO, CLAUDIO; MARCHISIO, PIETRO; PANICCIARI, PAOLO; DEL ROSSI, SILVIA (1998): MHEG-5-Aims, Concepts, and Implementation Issues, *IEEE Multimedia,* January-March 98, 84-91.

MEYER-BOUDNIK, THOMAS.; EFFELSBERG, WOLFGANG (1995): MHEG Explained. *IEEE Multimedia,* Spring 95, 26-38.

PARKER, DANA J (1999): Defining DVD. *IEEE Multimedia,* Vol. 6, Iss. 1, January-March 99, 80-84.

7.1.3 Books in German

BIAESCH-WIEBKE, CLAUS (1991): *Videosysteme: Technik und Arbeitsweise von Videorecordern, Videokameras und Camcordern.* Würzburg: Vogel.

HOFMÜLLER, HELMUT; SEIWERT, MARTIN (1999): *Digital Audio/Video: Digitalisierung, Schnitt und Mastering unter Windows (Edition Screen Multimedia).* München: Addison-Wesley-Longman, 17-152.

GATES, BILL (1996): *Der Weg nach vorn: Die Zukunft der Informationsgesellschaft.* 3. Auflage. München: Heyne.

JARZ, EWALD M. (1997): *Entwicklung multimedialer Systeme: Planung von Lern- und Masseninformationssystemen.* Wiesbaden: Gabler. 238-252.

KRISCH, L. (1993): *Fernsehtechnik; Grundlagen – Verfahren – Systeme (Viewegs Fachbücher der Technik).* Stuttgart: Vieweg.

LIMANN, OTTO (1979): *Fernsehtechnik ohne Ballast.* 13. Auflage. München: Franzis.

LIMANN, OTTO; PELKA, HORST (1998): *Fernsehtechnik ohne Ballast.* 18. Auflage. München: Franzis.

MEYER-BOUDNIK, THOMAS (1995): *Interaktive Multimedia-Präsentationen in offenen Systemen.* VDI- Fortschrittsberichte, Band 10/365. Düsseldorf: VDI-Verlag.

OHM, JENS-RAINER (1995): *Digitale Bildcodierung.* Berlin: Springer.

REIMERS, ULRICH (1996): *Digitale Fernsehtechnik: Datenkompression und Übertragung für DVB.* 2. Auflage. Berlin: Springer.

SCHMIDT, U. (2000): *Professionelle Videotechnik: Grundlagen, Signalformen, Videoaufnahme, Wiedergabe, Speicherung, Signalverarbeitung, Studiotechnik.* Berlin: Springer.

SCHÖNFELDER, HELMUT (1995): *Fernsehtechnik im Wandel.* Berlin [et al.]: Springer.

STEINMETZ, RALF (1998): *Multimedia-Technologie: Grundlagen, Komponenten und Systeme.* 2. Auflage. Berlin [et al.]: Springer. 87-102.

WEBERS, JOHANNES (1998): *Handbuch der Film- und Videotechnik.* 5. Auflage. München: Franzis.

ZIEMER, ALBRECHT (1997): *Digitales Fernsehen: Eine neue Dimension der Medienvielfalt.* 2. Auflage. Heidelberg: Hüthig.

7.1.4 Articles in German

BÖGEHOLZ, HARALD (1999): Digitalstudios: Günstige Lösungen für DV-Videoschnitt. *c't: Magazin für Computer Technik,* 24/99, 158-162. Hannover: Heise.

LOVISCACH, JÖRN (1999): Vom Band auf die Platte: Videobearbeitung ohne Spezial-Hardware. *c't: Magazin für Computer Technik,* 24/99, 150-157. Hannover: Heise.

RAUTENBERG, MATHIAS (1999): MPEG-4: Ein neuer Standard für mehr Funktionalität in Multimedia-Anwendungen, *Informatik-Spektrum,* Volume 22, Issue 2, 82-87.

SIGMUND, ULRICH; UNGERER, THEO (2001): Die Multimediafähigkeit von mehrfädig superskalaren Prozessoren am Beispiel der MPEG-2-Decodierung. *Informatik Forschung und Entwicklung,* Volume 16, Issue 1, 14-22.

7.1.5 Journals

AV Video and Multimedia Producer (ISSN: 1090-7459) | Knowledge Ind. Pub. Inc.

DV – Digital Video (ISSN: 1075-251X) | Digital Video Magazine

IEEE MultiMedia Magazine (ISSN: 1070-986X) | IEEE Institute of Electrical and Electronics Engineers

Multimedia Information and Technology (ISSN: electronic:1466-9358) | World Wide Subscription Service Ltd.

Multimedia Systems (ISSN: 0942-4962; electronic: 1432-1882) | Springer Verlag KG

Multimedia Tools and Applications (ISSN: 1380-7501) | Kluwer

7.2 Internet Links

Up-to-date Internet Links for this module can be found on the homepage of this book **www.basiswissen-multimedia.at** (in English and German) under Volume 1: Technology - Module 5: Video available!

7.3 Examination Questions

Question-Type 1: Yes/No (Dichotomy):

01	The psychophysical boundaries of the human eye can be expanded today by technological possibilities.	❒ Yes ❒ No	
02	At a viewing distance of 2,5 m from the screen, a picture must be shown with at least 480 lines.	❒ Yes ❒ No	
03	Analogue video still has potential for improvement with regard to the quality.	❒ Yes ❒ No	
04	Using digital video requires a bandwidth, which is around 200 times higher than that of analogue video.	❒ Yes ❒ No	
05	Motion-JPEG is no more than JPEG-pictures presented sequentially.	❒ Yes ❒ No	
06	On a CD with a capacity of 650 MB there is space for 94 minutes MPEG video at 146 kbps.	❒ Yes ❒ No	
07	The MHEG provides very precise guidelines for the presentation of objects in the presentation program.	❒ Yes ❒ No	
08	The I in "Interleaved" of AVI means that audio and video are recorded on separate tracks.	❒ Yes ❒ No	
09	QuickTime is only a playback program not a method for the time-based compression of videos.	❒ Yes ❒ No	
10	Up to 8 hours of high quality video can be stored on a DVD.	❒ Yes ❒ No	

Question-Type 2: Multiple Choice :

01	For a traditional cinema film... ❒ a) ... relatively slow visual perception is used. ❒ b) ... the appearance of movement is achieved by a sequence of 6 frames/s. ❒ c) ... using 24 frames/s reduces flickering on the screen to zero. ❒ d) ... 48 or 72 light stimuli per second are displayed.	
02	For the representation of a television picture ... ❒ a) ... a bandwidth of 5 MHz is sufficient. ❒ b) ... line interlacing is used. ❒ c) ... the optical picture is broken down into a grid (raster). ❒ d) ... approximately 13 million image elements per second are needed.	
03	Codecs have various advantages and disadvantages ... ❒ a) ... Cinepak has good quality but a long calculation time. ❒ b) ... Indeo is good with low movement motifs. ❒ c) ... Video 1 has low quality but high data rates. ❒ d) ... MPEG-1 has high quality and low calculation time.	
04	For the physical size of video files one can say ... ❒ a) ... the smaller the size of the frames, the smaller the file itself. ❒ b) ... the more frames per second, the smaller the file. ❒ c) ... the size of the video file is independent of the soundtrack. ❒ d) ... the less colours used, the smaller the file actually is.	
05	MPEG ... ❒ a) ... uses the movement compensation as a coded algorithm. ❒ b) ... uses four frames (Picture types). ❒ c) ... allows 8 hours video to be compressed onto a CD-ROM. ❒ d) ... is very similar to the MHEG standard.	
06	MHEG ... ❒ a) ... describes multimedia presentations on an object level?. ❒ b) ... provides control mechanisms and determines structure information. ❒ c) ... is considered as a homogeneous transfer format. ❒ d) ... also allows the data exchange between heterogeneous platforms.	
07	AVI-files ... ❒ a) ... support solutions in full PAL format (768 × 576 pixels). ❒ b) ... have typical refresh rates of 15 frames per second (fps). ❒ c) ... consist of interleaved chunks. ❒ d) ... are not generally compressed.	
08	Quicktime ... ❒ a) ... is limited to use on Apple computers. ❒ b) ... uses the file extension .qui. ❒ c) ... needs an own player. ❒ d) ... can also play AVI files without any problems.	

7.4 Answers

Correct answers to Group „Question Type 1“:
01 No; 02 Yes; 03 No; 04 Yes; 05 Yes; 06 No; 07 No; 08 No; 09 No; 10 Yes;

Correct answers to Group „Question Type 2“:
01 a) d); 02 a) b) c) d); 03 a) b); 04 a) d); 05 a) 06 a) b) c) d); 07 a) c); 08 c) d)

7.5 Hands-On: Exercises

- You have raw material consisting of: 3 minutes of film, 30 minutes Audio, 4 sheets of text (letter or foolscap), 6 photos and 4 menu graphics: Which resolution may be used where and still fit onto a CD?
- Compare different video standards with regard to quality, space required and Handling ! Which format would you use for which purpose?
- Film a documentary video about "multimedia": It should show everywhere that multimedia technology is employed. The video should to be about 3 minutes long.

7.6 Themes for Debate

- Discuss the future of the MPEG-7 standards! Which problems are to be expected in future?
- Each person in the group selects a video format. Then everyone „defends“ „their“ standard by arguing „its“ advantages!
- Which new technologies are to be expected? Will television via mobile phone or wrist television ever become reality? Which problems could emerge?

7.7 Timeline: Video

1873 WILLOUGHBY SMITH (1828-1891) discovers that the resistance of selenium changes under influence of light.

1883/84: PAUL NIPKOW dismantles pictures into individual points with a rotating disk. With this principle he succeeds in the first electric picture transmission. Patent specification: "The apparatus to be described here has the purpose, of making an object at place A visible at an arbitrary place B."

1897: FERDINAND BRAUN develops the cathode-ray tube (Braunsche thermionic valve). With that the TV-Tube is developed - long before its application.

1906: DIECKMANN and GLAGE used the cathode-ray tube to display twenty-line black and white pictures.

1923: ZWORYKIN builds the first usable electronic image scanner, the "iconoscope thermionic valve" (Serial production from 1934).

1924: BAIRD transmits silhouettes with the „Nipkowschen Scheibe“ (NIPKOW-Disk) across a distance of three metres. He named his apparatus "television". There a similar experiments from him and DÉNES VON MIHÁLY in the following years.

1928: BAIRD stores video signals on a "record", first video disc.

1936: The electron-television-camera introduces the television age. The first electronic recording camera is used for the live transmission of the Olympic Games in Berlin. The Berliners can watch the games in television rooms.

1951: ALEXANDER M. PONIATOFF (Ampex Company) forms an investigation team for the evolution of video equipment (tape recorder). His team includes CHARLES P.

GINSBERG, CHARLES E. ANDERSON und RAY DOLBY.

1954: The NTSC-norm is introduced for colour television in America.

1955: Ampex introduces the first multimedia recording equipment (Ampex VR-1000).

1959: JVC builds the first Video recorder.

1963: BRUCH proposes the PAL-procedure for colour television in Germany.

1964: AT&T shows a „Picture phone" at the World Fair in New York.

1967: PAL is accepted by most west-European countries.

1972: Philips develops first video systems (VCR).

1975: Betamax is developed by Sony.

1982 Sony demonstrates the Betacam format as an analogue component (YUV), which becomes the worldwide broadcasting standard.

1989: Sony introduces 8-mm Video-tape.

1992: QuickTime released by Apple.

1994: Sony releases Digital Betacam on the Broadcasting market.

1995: „Toy Story", computer animated cinema film from Pixar.

1996: Digital TV.

1997: DVD.

1998: QuickTime 3.0 released.

1999: December: Microsofts' NetMeeting 3.01 released. MPEG-7 Video standard.

2001: SKY channel goes Digital and ceases analogue transmission completely

.2006: Probable end of analog television.

7.8 Glossary

AVI Audio/Video Interleaved. Alternation of signals to avoid flimmer.

BAS-Signal A video signal put together from picture signal, blanking signal and synchronizing signal; sendable, black and white television signal.

Betacam developed by Sony, records on 1/2 inch wipe tape and represented the first component technology in a portable camera/recorder in the middle of the 80s.

Betacam SP Component-Format from Sony, Standard for News Production in Europe.

Betacam SX Digital Component-Format from Sony with a sampling method of 4 : 2 : 2 and a compression ratio of 10 : 1.

Betacam, Digital digital component MAZ (german for **M**agnet **Auf**zeichnungssystem = magnetic recording system) from Sony with 1/2 inch MP (metal particle) tape.

A small compression instalment (2 : 1) allows high quality (4 : 2 : 2 at 10 bit). Cameras can record 4 : 3 and 16 : 9. On some equipment Betacam (SP) cassettes can also be played.

Betamax A magnetic recording system, developed by Sony, with 1/2 inch tapes. Particularly developed for the consumer market and fundamental for the professional Betacam-Format.

Chroma Abbreviation for Chrominance (Colour).

CVBS Composite Video Burst Syncron.

DIVX Digital Video Express; DVD copy protection.

DV Digital Video, a standard for Digitale Camcorder.

DVD Digital Versatile Disk, optical storage medium, successor of the CD.

DVD-Video is the usual name for Video films on DVD

DVD-ROM a disk drive for DVD and CD-ROMs. It is expected to replace CD-ROM drive. (eventually).

DVD-RW a rewriteable version the DVD.

FBAS-Signal **F**arb-**B**ild-**A**ustast-**S**ynchron-Signal (German CVBS).

FMD Fluorescent Multilayer Disc, possible successor of the DVD.

Hosiden 4 point round connection for the S-Video signal (component signal).

IEEE **I**nstitute of **E**lectrical and **E**lectronics **E**ngineers; world wide the largest proffesional society. (pronounced "I treble E").

IEEE-1394 Interface for the transfer of digital signals from a camcorder to a PCuter (Video cutting room); called **"Fire Wire"** by Apple and **"iLink"** by Sony.

JPEG Joint Photographic Experts Group.

Luma Luminanz, Black/White Signal, Brightness (Symbol: Y).

MPEG **M**oving **P**ictures **E**xpert **G**roup of the ISO (International Organization for Standardization), provides standards for motion picture data compression.

NTSC **N**ational **T**elevision **S**ystems **C**ommittee, Video standard in North Amerika und Japan, also humourously known as „**N**ever **T**he **S**ame **C**olour".

PAL Phase Alternation Line, Video standard in Europe.

SECAM Videostandard in France and some east Europian countries.

S-VHS Further development of VHS and downwards compatible. VHS recordings can be also be displayed on an S-VHS recorder.

VHS = **V**ideo-**H**ome-**S**ystem (most popular amateur video system).

Module 6: Multimedia via Internet

„The real Revolution in Computing within the last thirty years was not their further development, but their networking".

Hermann Maurer, TU Graz

Learning Objectives

In the last module we familiarized ourselves with some of the technological basics of the Internet and in particular with the World Wide Web (WWW) – which can undoubtedly be regarded as the most successful **Information System** in the history of mankind. In this module we will concentrate specifically on the transmission of Multimedia Files, examine the emerging **Bandwidth Problems** and get to know future **Broadband Technologies** as possible solutions. Multimedia Engineering, Programming Languages and Development Tools will be discussed in Volume 3.

Internet

WWW

Multimedia-Engineering in Volume 3

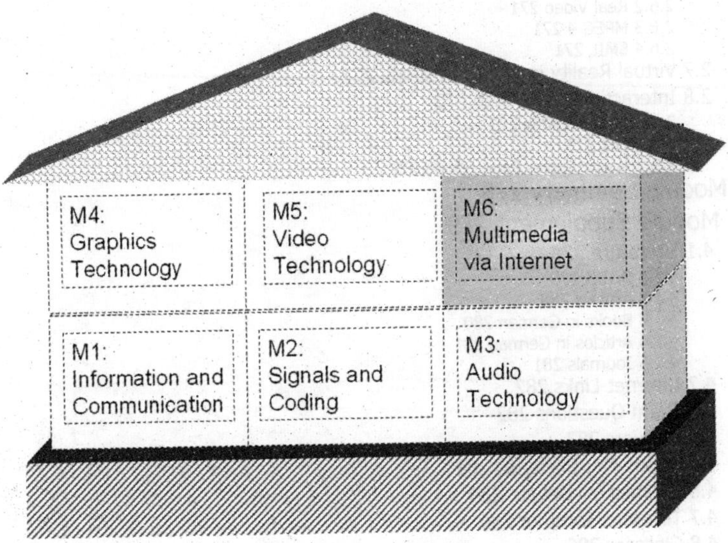

Considering the evolution of human information systems a little more closely several revolutionary milestones can be detected:

Language has always been the most important and – beside gestures – the oldest medium of human communication. Language represents knowledge in the form of sounds – formed to words. In this way humans can communicate knowledge to other humans. But language – as a fleeting medium – is still not suitable for the permanent collection and storage of large amounts of knowledge.

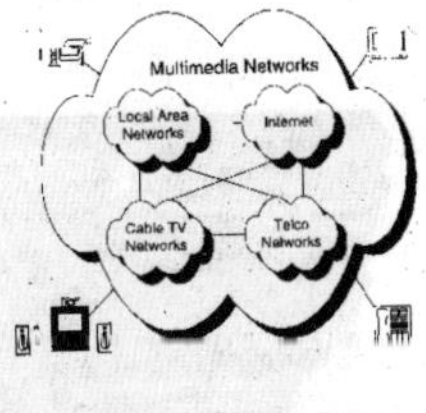

Fig. 6.1 Multimedia-Networks as integration of Internet, Local Area Networks, Telephone and Cable-TV; from: Wu & Irwin (98), 6

Writing allowed, for the first time, the storage of knowledge independently of any individual. With the spreading of the letterpress, written knowledge became public property. It could be arbitrarily reproduced and assimilated by everybody (at least those who were able to read). The book as a universal store of knowledge was devised.

Through the engagement of **radio broadcasting** and **television,** knowledge became even more widely accessible to the public; and finally through the enterprise of **telephone** and **telegraphy,** people were able to communicate worldwide effortlessly.

The **Internet** is probably humanities most successful information system. Since the introduction of the **WWW** it has spread rapidly throughout all parts of the world and in all sections of the population.

Fig. 6.2 The Internet – the most successful information system of mankind

---

The medium Internet integrates all – currently known – communication structures, and adds the fascinating possibility of **interactivity.**

---

1 Fundamentals of the Internet

Before we discuss Multimedia via Internet, we must begin by familiarizing ourselves with some of the elementary basics of networks.

1.1 Origin of the Internet and WWW

Fig. 6.3 The foundation was laid in the West of the United States – by connecting four university computers

The Internet has its origin in an investigation project in the sixties. It arose more or less from the DARPANET (Defence Advanced Research Projects Network Agency) and the ARPANET (the D for Defence has gone) in order to cross-link universities and military organizations.

The Internet is basically nothing other than an alliance of many worldwide **distributed local area networks** (LANs) through which computers – connected to that wide area network (WAN) – are able to communicate, with each other.

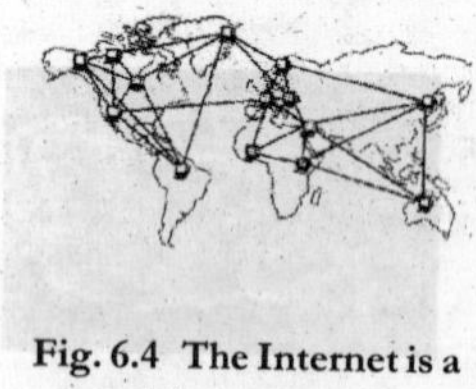

Fig. 6.4 The Internet is a connection of many distributed computer networks

So that different types of computers can be connected to this net, a special **Protocol,** a common language, was defined. At the Berkeley University of California further communication software components were developed. Today that is all summarized under the term **TCP/IP** (Transmission computer Protocol/Internet Protocol).

Every standard in the Internet is formed by a document that carries the title RFC (Request for Comments). RFCs exist since 1969 as working papers of the Internet investigation and developer groups. Usually, an RFC is the description of a protocol, a procedure or a service. To date more than 2000 published RFCs exist.

We distinguish between:

Internet = global network, connecting millions of computers

Intranet = local network within an organization

Extranet = between Intranet and Internet

- **Internet** is the worldwide, *decentralized* network technology on the basis of TCP/IP and offers *various* well known services (WWW, eMail, FTP etc.).
- **Intranet** is a *local (mostly private) network* within an organization , company, hospital, university etc. It is only accessible from *inside* the network.
- **Extranet** is a communication technology at the *interface* between Internet and Intranet (Keyword: Firewall). It also denotes a portion of an Intranet open to the public.

At the beginning *Internet* transmission was mainly data in character form. The Internet also allowed remote computing but only through a special service of the Internet has it became as well known to the public as it is today:

The **World Wide Web** (WWW) has its origin in CERN, the European research centre for particle physics in Geneva. At CERN, international teams of researchers cooperated over worldwide distances. The demand for efficient administration and the distribution of rapidly changing text and images was immense.

The proposition to implement a **„net of documents associated with each other“** (Hypertext) was made in March 1989 by TIM BERNERS-LEE.

The first (text based only) prototype was available 18 months later. In December 1991 this system was introduced at the „Hypertext '91“ conference in San Antonio (Texas).

Further development led, in February 1993, to the first version of a graphic WWW browser with the name „Mosaic“.

NCSA-Mosaic, the first browser with graphical surface which allowed the handling with hypermedia-data – surfing began ...

Mosaic became so popular that a year later its developer MARC ANDREESEN left his working place – the National Centre for Supercomputing Applications (NCSA) – in Chicago, and founded, with his partner, the Netscape Communication Corporation.

In 1994 CERN and MIT (Massachusetts Institute of Technology) signed a contract which established the **WWW Consortium (W3C).** This consortium has two very important objectives with respect to future developments of the WWW:

- the standardization of the protocols and
- the interoperability between different platforms.

The extent of information offered in the WWW increases rapidly .

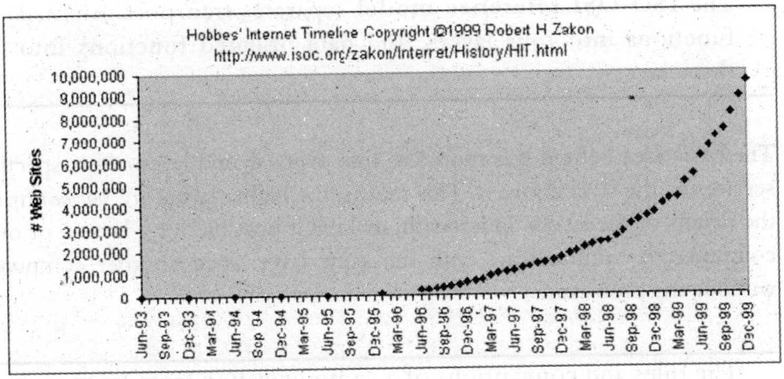

Fig. 6.5 The exponential growth of the information offered is amazing. A saturation is still not in sight (Robert H. Zakon)

The WWW is **one service** in the Internet. Today it allows not only the pure representation of text, but also the integration of Multimedia: Audio, pictures, video and *interactivity*.

Both, Internet and WWW, are based on the technological fundamentals of **computer networks** – which we will review subsequently.

1.2 Network Layer Model

Any communication between two partners is bound to extremely specific conditions. Hardware and data transmission facilities must have compatible **interfaces** and they have to follow **unambiguous declarations** (protocols) regarding the type and manner of the communication.

For the determination of interfaces and protocols there exist:

- a large number of different standards,
- both national and international norms and
- proprietary (vendor specific and system specific) company standards.

For every computer-computer communication are not only hardware elements and the architecture of the underlying nets important, but also records and software, which either determine the net or need the net.

In order to unite all these complex things under one "roof", the ISO (Internationally Standardization Organization, www.iso.ch) developed, in 1977, a reference model for OSI (Open System's Interconnection).

The **ISO-OSI reference model** separates transport oriented functions into four layers, and data oriented functions into three layers.

The basic idea behind this model is, that every shared layer offers specific services to the layer above it. This means, the higher layers are *shielded* from the details of the layers underneath, making it possible for a layer *n* of one computer to communicate with the same layer *n* of another computer without any problems.

The rules and conventions of a communication from layer *n* to layer *n* are called the **protocol of the layer** ***n***.

In reality the layers do not, of course, communicate directly with each other. Each layer passes his data and additional checking information on to the layer directly under it – until the deepest layer is reached. The physical medium in which the „genuine" signal communication takes place is under this layer.

Between the layers a defined **interface** exists. This interface determines the operations and services which the lower layer makes available.

Interface = specified connection between software, soft- and hardware and hardware to hardware for exchanging signals or data

---

A **network architecture** includes several layers and interfaces.

A list of protocols used by a specific system – one protocol per layer – is called a **Protocol Stack.** Generally, each protocol adds specific checking information (Header) to the data as they go through these layers from the top to the bottom. This additional information is intended for the layer's corresponding „counter-layer" on the receiver side and is removed again on the way to the uppermost layer.

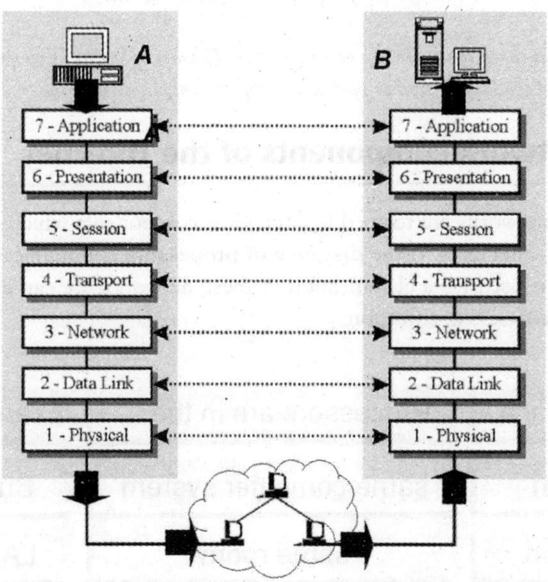

Fig. 6.6 The seven layers within the OSI-reference model are run through between two computers hierarchically

Physical Layer: Here the transfer of the bit-sequences along the physical medium (transmission channel), the physical connection, the signal coding and the setup and teardown of the connections take place.

Data Link Layer: The decomposition of the bit stream into individual packages (packets), the error detection and the time and sequence monitoring take place here.

Network Layer: Here the route is determined (routing) the load check and linking of partions is made and differences in the layers 1 and 2 are compensated.

Transport layer: The management of the transport connections and addresses as well as the direct communication of the terminal systems is effected.

Session layer: the scheduling, sequencing and the control of interactive applications (sessions) occurs, remote procedure calls RPC (Remote Procedure Call) and the file transfer.

Presentation layer: the different representation of the information occurs (for example ASCII EBCDIC, integer formats etc.) and the description of uniform data formats in the network, data compression and coding.

Application layer: In this, the final layer, the standard applications are provided (for example file transfer (FTP), eMail, etc.); also protocols and software interfaces for the development of applications.

QoS= quality of service

Every service is characterized in this case through the Quality of Service. This quality refers to the safety of the transfer and in part also to the efficiency concerning the transfer speed.

1.3 Network components of the Internet

Computer networks are formed by individual components which can have different architectures. If the **distance of processors** communicating with each other is used for a classification of these networks, we can determine following (coarse) classification:

Fig. 6.7 Classification of connected processors by distance. LANs can of course extend over several rooms or buildings; 1 meter (m) = 39,37 inches; 1 kilometre (km) = 1 650 miles

Distance	Processors are in the ...	Example
1 m	same computer system	Bus
10 m	same room	LAN
10 km	same area	MAN
100 km	same country	WAN
10.000 km	same planet	Internet

The „smallest network unit" of the Internet is a so called local area network (LAN). Such networks consist in a locally limited area (room, building, complex, campus) which is usually in the possession of an individual organization (enterprise, university, etc.).

The connection of several LAN segments occurs by using switching elements (Hubs, Switches, Bridges, router, etc.). Generally, LANs are classified by the following criteria:

- Network size,
- network topology and
- transfer technology.

The **network size** (distance) is determined by (the maximum allowed) delay times within the network. Typical delay times are approx. 10 microseconds.

In **network topology** we distinguish between star, ring, bus and mesh topology.

The **transfer technology** of a regular LAN consists mostly of copper wires (cables) which interlink the machines. Therefore either a data bus topology or a ring topology is favourable. A LAN in star topology requires a separate line for every connected processor and a central star distributor (Hub). Mesh topologies are the most complex – but also the most fail-safe.

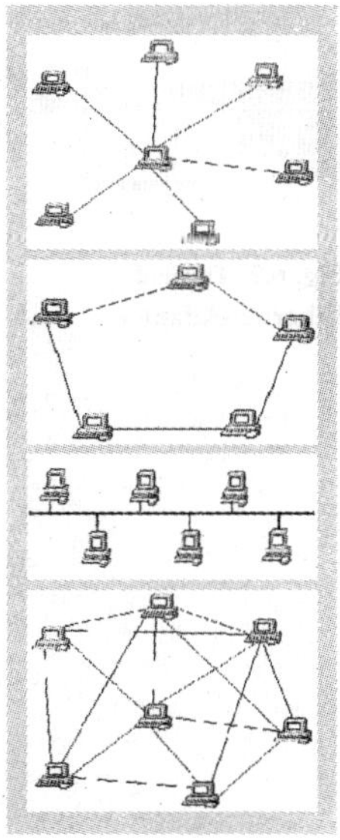

Fig. 6.8 From top to bottom: Star, Ring, Bus and Mesh topology

---

Different standards specify the network links (cable type), network topology and network access. The standard **„Ethernet"** plays a special role, particularly for Internet. .

The name Ethernet comes from Xerox and refers to the first mobile networks (ALOHA). It is supposed to remind us of the doctrine of wave propagation in the previous century by which a material carrier „Ether" was necessary in order to transfer signals. Ethernet is currently the most widespread standard for local area networks. The development originates from common specifications of Intel, DEC and Xerox. It was presented in the PARC (Palo Alto Research Centre) as early as 1973.

Ethernet can reach transfer rates of 10 Mbps, 100 Mbps and 1 Gbps. Every data processor can serve as master (i.e.: take control, contrast: slave) and send to the network any time. If there is a conflict (data collision) between two processors sending simultaneously , each data processor waits a specific time before attempting to send again.

Basis for Ethernet is the Network-protocol CSMA/CA (Carrier Sense Multiple Access/ Collision Avoidance)

The actual data transfer takes place using the CSMA/CD procedure.

Totally different protocols are executable on the Ethernet. For example TCP/IP, DECnet, IPX/SPX (Novell), etc.

Ethernet can consist physically of different types of 50-ohm coaxial cables, pairwise twisted lines (Twisted-pair), optical fibres or other media. The connection occurs over separate plug-in cards, so-called Ethernet adapters.

Fig. 6.9 Typical Ethernet-Adapter

Every **Ethernet adapter** can be unambiguously identified by its address anchored in the hardware.

This address consists of a 3-byte manufacturer specific code and one 3-Byte (24 bit) running serial number. In this way an unambiguous addressing is possible. The logical address must be changed into a hardware address by the network software. The specification of the address is usually in hexadecimal form, divided by „." (dot notation) or „:" (colon) for better legibility, for example 20:08:AA:10:00:CF.

In order to reach higher transfer rates in Ethernet, the Ethernet standard was expanded. The result was introduced officially in 1995 and is usually named **Fast Ethernet.**

The basic idea in this case is very simple: The old frame format, the interfaces and the procedural rules are maintained and only the bit-time is reduced from 10 ns to 100 ns.

10BASE-T: 10-Mbps, baseband medium; UTP (unshielded twisted pair) is the most common kind of copper telephone wiring

Furthermore the advantages of the **10Base-T** cabling (IEEE 802.3 physical layer specification for 10 Mbps Ethernet over two pairs of Category 3, 4, or 5 UTP wire) were used as a design basis.

Latest efforts increase in magnitude: **Gigabit-Ethernet** (1000Base-T Gigabit Ethernet specification for running over four-pair Category 5 UTP copper cabling for distances up to 100 meters, enabling networks with diameters of 200 meters). But to date the corresponding standard has not been finally determined.

The electric signals can run on physical lines only at limited distances – without losing power. In LANs different equipment is used, in order to regenerate the signals, or for the communication of wide area networks (WANs).

Repeaters overcome the attenuation caused cable loss

Repeaters repeat electric signals and „refresh" them, enabling the length restriction of an Ethernet segment to be bypassed. For example: an internal repeater interlinks two segments which would theoretically have a maximum functioning distance of 100 meters.

Bridges and Switches permit the connection of two LANs and also the combination of different cable types. **Bridges** interlink network segments with the same (compatible) protocols. **Switches** can interlink different network units with each other. Switches consist of a matrix of network segments (network in the box, figure 6.10). They guarantee the implementation of transitions. For example, Bridges and Switches divide two Ethernet LANs physically: Interferences (for example collisions and defective packages) are unable to pass through.

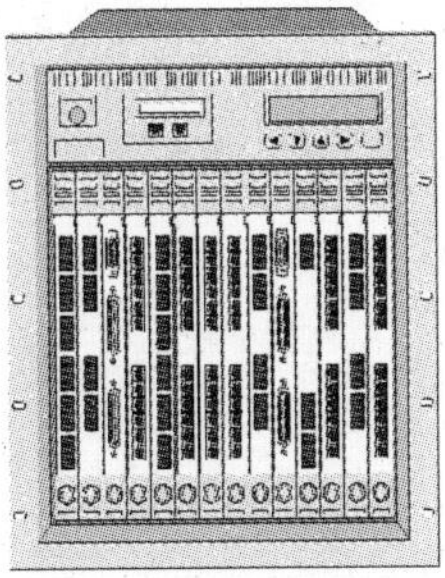

Figure 6.10 Switches are coupling elements between several segments: a network in the box; many switches have „built-in"-repeaters or plug-in repeater modules

Bridges are protocol transparent: for instance they transmit all protocols currently in use on the Ethernet. For a terminal the shared networks appear to be a single network. Bridges can also be used to overcome the length restrictions of the Ethernet.

Hubs work similarly to Bridges but were originally intended for star shaped network technologies (hub: pivot assembly).

Routers can cause *routing or rejection* according to the address of a data packet. This can help to reduce (redundant) network traffic drastically in LANs, since data packets are only let through if the destination address lies „beyond" the router. A router works on the network level (level 3 of the OSI model) and, as a rule, only transmits a protocol. It interlinks two or several networks which can be local or remote.

A router receives a data packet and routes to the to the desired recipient according to the addressing information it contains (for the network protocol intransparent). A router can also transmit data between different transmission media (for example from Ethernet to a serial connection).

Gateways can couple completely different (heterogeneous) networks to each other. They are a common (virtual) node which appertains to both networks and executes the multi-network data traffic. Gateways are used equally for the LAN-WAN linkage (or the LAN-WAN-LAN linkage) and for the transition between different services (for example the transmission of fax communications from a LAN).

A gateway is an active network node, that can be addressed from both sides. But not more than two networks can be coupled to each other. Gateways handle different protocols on both sides up to layer 7 in the OSI model.

In particular, an important task of the Gateways is the routing over network boundaries (correct addressing!). Basically two types are distinguishable:

- **medium converting gateways** (translators): establish the connection between different protocols of the lower two levels when the same method of transmission is used (different transport medium); and

- **protocol converting gateways:** execute and transfer the different protocols of levels 3 and 4 into each other.

The Gateway mainly supports two important services: the transmission of successive communications between source and objective as a independent unit and the establishing of a logical connection between source and target. In order to be able to deal with the different demands of the flow control of the two networks to be connected, the Gateway must be able to buffer data as necessary. If one of the shared networks is more efficient than the other one, the Gateway must recognize this and „decelerate" the „faster" network. If the networks work with different packet sizes, data packets must be „repacked". This can be done very simply through big packages being split into smaller packages and re-assembled at the target network.

Firewalls are computers which enable access from a public network into a LAN – but only at a defined location. All data traffic through the Firewall data processor is checked. This channelization increases the chances of identifying an „attempted burglary" by a malicious hacker by means of detailed log files since the intruder must pass first the Firewall.

For the software configuration of a Firewall two fundamental strategies exist:

- *„Everything is allowed, which is not explicitly prohibited"*: this strategy is user friendly since new services are allowed automatically, however, it is also critical, since the administrator must monitor the behaviour of the users continually and apply corrective action in time.
- *„All which is not allowed is prohibited"*: this strategy could be viewed as inconvenient by the users; applying for new services involves complicated formality. However it is also a protection against safety breaches in the operating service and in application programmes since it restricts access to unknown ports.

There are generally three types of Firewalls:

Package filters check the source and destination address (IP-address and TCP/UDP port) of a package and decide, whether it may pass through or not. The advantage lies in the transparency to the user. But this transparency is, however, at the same time disadvantageous: Package filters can not distinguish between users and their rights.

Package filters are generally located on routers and are now provided by most vendors as a supplement. In addition intelligent package filters analyse the content of the packages and also recognize the validity of connections which single package filters would not allow (e.g. data connection via FTP).

Circuit Level Gateways are comparable to package filters, work, however, on another level of the protocol stack. To a remote machine connections by this Gateway appear to exist within the Firewall host: Information about protected networks can be concealed.

Application Gateways, also called **„Proxy"** (substitute), demonstrate another Firewall design. Each Firewall-host has a gateway programme installed, for every permissible application. Frequently clients must authenticate themselves to the Proxy programme. The Proxy executes all actions as a „deputy" for the client in the LAN. This enables not only the creation of user specific access profiles (times, services, data processors) but also one can determine the permissible connections with according to the application. The resulting small separate control records are more manageable than the complex control record of a package filter.

By using the Proxy specific web addresses can be inhibited, or the data traffic can be filtered

---

Application Gateways are typical examples of the *„Everything is prohibited, which is not explicitly allowed" Strategy* and recognised as the most secure, but also the most complicated, solution.

Since with a Proxy all accesses outside is over a single channel/ authority, the Proxy can simultaneously be used as buffer memory (Cache). For example the Proxy buffers all stored WWW pages, so that the data is available without reconnecting outside and regardless which user originally requested it.

In order to enable the data traffic between firms, branches or universities within city limits, MANs were installed (Metropolitan Area Networks) as the extended version of LANs. Their most important representatives are IFDD (Interface Fibre Distributed Data) with a transfer performance of 100 Mbps and DQDB (Dual Distributed Queue data bus) with scalable transfer rates of 34, 45 or 140 Mbps. WANs spanning the globe (Wide Area computer communication Networks) are of the greatest importance to the Internet.

As a rule, they are based on the physical lines operated by the national telephone enterprises. One prominent – but for multimedia too inefficient – substitute for physical network technology is **ISDN** (Integrated digital service network, 64 kbps and 128 kbps to 2 Mbps, see chapter 2.1).

A more efficient WAN technology (also for LAN and MAN) is **ATM** (Asynchronous mode transfer): Data transfer rates of 155 Mbps allow the transfer of **time and synchronization critical** multimedia data types.

The topology of the underlying WANs can look very different. The possibilities extend from a star, ring, tree and coupled rings to complete pools (n-to-n) and irregular networks.

A topology becomes especially complex, when cable free network sections (Radio relay) and satellite communication are also included.

The connection of many WANs across gateways results in the **internetwork** or simpler: **Internet.**

1.4 Peer-to-Peer and Client-Server Architecture

In the last few years the network technologies for PCs and workstations have developed like the varying cultures in separate countries. Among the workstations so called „open" systems dominate, and standards become common property, while on the PCs companies such as Novell claim the standards for themselves. This market has finally been brought into motion again by the Workgroup initiative, which was started by Microsofts Windows for Workgroups.

Fundamentally one distinguishes between two architectures within a network domain: *Peer-to-Peer networks* and *client-server networks* (figure 6.12).

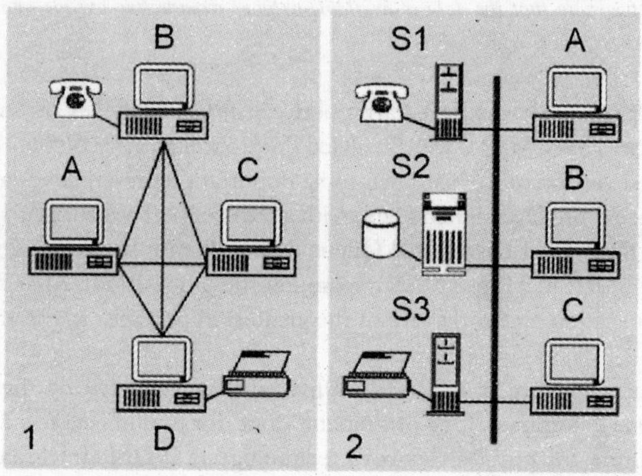

Fig. 6.11 (1): Peer-to-Peer Network, each of the computers A,B,C,D has access to the others. (2) Client-Server Network, each of the computers has access to every server S1, S2, S3 (The Web is a typical Client-Server Structure)

Peer-to-Peer Networks (1) implement point-to-point connections between computers. Parallel to its normal operation every computer can make in its resources available to the other computers in the network and in return has access to all the resources (files, catalogues, printers, fixed disks, compact disk drives, etc.) of the other data processors.

In a **client-server architecture** (2) the resource intensive tasks such as data management, printing, eMail Management or system administration remain limited to the server (job receiver). The clients (job initiator) only have direct connection to the server and serve as a communication unit. Thus, the network traffic is comparatively small compared to other architectures. However, the server requires a high processor performance, hard disk capacity, main memory capacity and data throughway. As a Rule the high demands on its response time for service requests precludes the server being used for other tasks.

Most of Internet multimedia applications are based on the client-server principle.

In the simplest case two computers communicate with each other, whereby the client process (with the subscriber interface) is running on one and the server process on the other. The client process is started only when required and attempts to establish contact with the server.

This presupposes that the server runs continually, the server behaves passively, and waits for the requests of a client. For use as a server, a high performance data processor is necessary, the client process on the other hand is often a simple programme which hardly makes demands on the data processor. A server can operate several client processes in parallel.

1.5 Services

Internet makes many different services available, for example:

- graphic (multimedial) user interface (WWW),
- electronic post (eMail),
- message groups (newsgroups),
- chatting in the Internet (Chat, IRC),
- file transfer (ftp),
- remote control of other computers (telnet).

All these services use individual protocols – based on IP – in order to provide these services.

1.6 The Domain Concept in the Internet

Every node in the Internet has a worldwide unambiguous address.

During communication, this address is used for the identification of the source and target of a data packet. The convention for the so-called **IP-**

addresses is based on a 32-bit value represented in decimal.

Each 8-bit decimal value (Octet) is separated from its neighbour by a dot (for example 143.50.35.6). This is referred to as *„Dotted Decimal Notation"*.

Programmes extremely seldom reference data processors and other resources by binary network addresses. Instead, ASCII character strings are more often used, as for example „kfunigraz.ac.at".

Nevertheless in general a network and specifically the Internet „understands" exclusively *binary addresses;* therefore mechanisms are needed for the conversion of one convention into the other one.

At the beginning of the DARPANET a simple ASCII file that listed all processor names and IP addresses was completely sufficient. At night all connected data processors fetched this file from the original source. This was suitable for a network with only a few hundred machines.

But as thousands of computers were interlinked in the Internet, this procedure no longer proved acceptable. In particular the increasing size of the files and the conflicting names associated with the linkage of new data processors required the development of a new concept – the **DNS** (Domain Name System). This is based on the introduction of a hierarchical, domain based name schemata and a distributed database system for the implementation of this name schemata. It is primarily used on IP-addresses for the representation (Mapping) of processor names.

Such a large and continually changing data base containing processor names is a non-trivial problem. As with a normal mail system the management of the names is regulated by the allocation of character strings for country, place, street and names.

The concept of the Internet is the division into many **top-level-domains**, each containing a large number of computers.

Each domain is divided into subdomains which in turn branch to (hierachically) lower subdomains. All these domains can be displayed in a **tree network.**

The leaves of these trees represent subdomains which do not contain any further subdomains. A leaf can be an individual computer – or can contain a whole university with thousands of autonomous computer systems.

Top Level Domains consists of two groups: generic and country specific. **Generic domains** are:

- com (Commercial),
- edu (Educational Institutions),
- gov (US Federal Government),
- int (specific international companies),
- mil (US Armed Forces),
- net (Network Providers) and
- org (Nonprofit Organizations).

The country specific domains, e.g.

- .in
- .uk
- .de
- .at
- .ch

contain an entry for every country as defined in **ISO 3166.**

Domain names are case independent, therefore edu and EDU are equivalent. Component names can be up to 63 letters long - the entire path up to 255 letters.

The highest committee in the Internet is the **IAB**. It approves decisions on standards and address assignment and publishes these decisions. Technical and operational problems are previously treated at the IETF (Engineering Internet task Force) meetings which are open to the public. Here standards are developed, documented and then set down in the RFCs (Request for Comments).

IAB Internet Architecture Board releases the Internet-Standards (www.iab.org)

So-called **NICs** work as executive institutions (Network Information Centres) with **NOCs** (Network Operation Centres), which exist on global, continental, national and regional level. The assignment and co-ordination of unambiguous addresses and names in Internet are the task of the NIC. For example the central **InterNIC** in the USA assigns whole address areas to the European NIC – the RIPE NCC (Europeans network Reseaux IP centre co consulting hour).

It is then possible for the German (DE-NIC) to assign addresses from this range ("pool") on a national level, for instance to an internal provider who, in turn, distributes addresses to end users.

The NOC attends to the operation of the network, as for example:

- Configuration of the network components (Router),
- the elimination of power failures and
- the consultation and co-ordination of the recipients.

1.7 Protocols

As mentioned before, while discussing the OSI model, we must distinguish between protocols (such as TCP/IP) and services (e.g. X.25, frame Relay, ATM or B-ISDN).

The entire communication in the Internet is based on the TCP/IP-protocol with bidirectional connection between two computers (socket arrangement). Under both UNIX and Windows (NT, 95, 98 and 2000) the TCP/IP functionality is already integrated in the operating system. For other operating systems there are corresponding protocol stacks.

Historically **TCP/IP** is the standard protocol for the linkage of all networks in the Internet as well as in Intranets.

When considering the Internet as a joint of subnets and autonomous computer systems, the IP (Internet Protocol) is the „glue" which holds everything together.

Datagram = data packet, also called PDU (protocol data unit)

During communication over the Internet the transmitter analyses the data streams in **datagrams** with a theoretical size of 64 KB (typically only about 1,5 KB). Every datagram is transferred over the Internet and possibly cut up into even smaller fragments. When these „fragments" have reached their final destination, they are re-assembled into the original datagrams and applied to the input data stream of the receiving process.

The **IP-datagram** consists of a header and a data section. The header subdivides into a 20 byte long static section and an optional section of changeable length.

The convention for the IP addresses is based on a 32-bit value, which determines the Network and the host number of the underlying address codes.

The networks are organised into different classes, which are determined by the corresponding subnet mask (for example 255.255.255.0). Each Subnet mask is used for identification of the Network and the host section of the address.

multi cast = communication between a single sender and multiple receivers

The addresses are separated by a worldwide legitimate schema into classes from A to G. Only the first three classes A to C are intended for subscribers. Class D addresses are allocated to multicasting purposes, and addresses of Class E addresses are used for test operations and future developments. The value 127 in the first of the Octets is allocated for a loopback, that is a feedback on themselves.

A network of class A has a subnet mask with a minimum length of bits. The subnet mask for a network of class B is at least 16 bits long, and the subnet mask for a network of class C at least 24 bits.

The protocols of the TCP/IP family were already developed in the seventies for data exchange in heterogeneous computer networks (computers of different manufacturers with different operating systems).

TCP stands for „Transmission Control Protocol" (Layer 4) and **IP** for „Internet Protocol" (Layer 3). The protocol specifications are published in RFC documents. Due to their enforcement they are quasi-standards.

Layers 5 to 7 of the OSI-standard are integrated in an application layer, because the application programmes all communicate directly with the transport layer.

In layer 4 – besides TCP, which enables secured data transfer (connection orientated, with flow control through windowing) – the **UDP** (User Datagram Protocol) is situated, in which connectionless and unsecured data transport is determined.

Both protocols enable several application programmes to simultaneously access one computer, through the introduction of so called **ports** .

Port = general logical or physical postal address of a data interchange point; in the Internet it denotes a "transport layer demultiplexing value", that is a 16-bit postal address that guarantees the data transfer between levels of equal rank. for example: http: 80; ftp:21; telnet:23;§ ftp: 21; telnet: 23;

In layer 3 the IP-addresses are determined. The routing also happens here, this means that the route control of a package from one network to another occurs. Also the ARP-Protocols (Address Resolution Protocol) are integrated into this layer, these are responsible for the decomposition (transformation) of a logical IP address into a physical (e.g. Ethernet) address.

For that purpose they use broadcasts (data packets through which all connected terminals are addressed). ICMP, a protocol which enables the exchange of control and error packages in the network, is also implemented in this layer.

The layers 1 and 2 are protocol transparent for layer 3. They can be implemented through so called standardized protocols, for example

- Ethernet (CSMA/CD),
- fiber distributed data interface (FDDI),
- SLIP (Serial IP Line),
- Point-to-Point Protocol (PPP) or
- other methods of transmission.

Several utilities of the higher OSI-layers appertain to the TCP/IP family:

Telnet (RFC 854): is a terminal protocol used to implement an interactive access to another system from a local computer system.

FTP (RFC 959): as a file transfer protocol, it permits the use of the file services of an external system interactively as well as to copy the files back and forth between both systems.

NFS (RFC 1094): The Network File System enables access to files at a remote system – as if they were on the users own system (transparent file access). NFS is based on the UDP (User datagram protocols, RFC 768, also layer 4), appertaining to the TCP/IP-family. Unlike TCP it does not establish any secured virtual connections between communicating hosts. Due to this feature it is intended for application in local area networks.

NNTP (RFC 977): The Network News Transfer Protocol specifies distribution, query, retrieval and the transmission of news items within a section or the entire Internet community. The items are held in regionally central data bases. To a subscriber it is possible to subscribe individual topics from the entire offered supply.

SMTP (RFC 821/822): The Simple Mail Transfer Protocol (RFC 821) is a mail protocol based on the IP-addressing as well as on the name structure determined by the RFC 822.

DNS (RFC 920): The Domain Name Service supports the allocation of network and host addresses to processor names. This service is for example necessary for the application from SMTP as well as in increasing extent of Telnet and FTP. From security reasons the other host turns to the DNS, in order to check the IP address of the data processor calling him, whether also a (domain) name can be assigned. If not, the connection setup is rejected.

With the TCP/IP protocol family a simple implementation of network pools is possible. Individual local area networks are interlinked about router or gateways. Individual hosts can communicate with each other, over several partial networks.

The lowest level is IP as a protocol of the level 3, the network layers being beneath that can be very different:

- LANs (Ethernet, token ring, etc.),
- WANs (X.25 etc.),
- point-to-point connections (SLIP, PPP).

It it is obvious that gateways have additional non trivial functions besides routing when they interact between differing partial networks (for example different protocols on level 2, different date packet size etc.).

Let us conclude: In the Internet three independent name and addressing levels exists:

- physical addresses (for example Ethernet address),
- Internet addresses (IP address) and
- domain names.

The conversion of the highest level (domain name) in IP addresses is effected by the DNS to which the utilities of the layers 5 to 7 have access.

The conversion of an IP address into a hardware address is effected with tables, and on the hardware level (for example Ethernet) automatically over the ARP (Adress Resolution Protocol).

Example: Computer A wants to send data to computer B having the Internet address I(B), whose physical address P(B) is not yet known. A sends an ARP-request (which contains its own physical address and the IP-address of B) to *all computers* in the network. All computers receive and check the ARP-request. The addressed computer B answers by sending an ARP-Reply (with the physical address of B) to computer A which stores the address in a table (Address Resolution Cache).

There is a also a standardized procedure for the reverse function; the RARP (Reverse ARP). Here computer A sends an RARP request specifying its physical address P(A). If a computer in the network is installed as an RARP server (a computer, that „knows" all allocations of P(x) ↔ I(x)) it sends a reply to the inquiring computer containing the address I(A). This function is important, for example for so-called „diskless workstations", which download their complete software from a server.

The Internet protocol (IP) is a connectionless service (unlike X.25) with an „Unreliable Datagram Service", which means neither the correctness of the data nor the compliance with sequence, integrity and uniqueness of the datagrams are checked on the IP-level. A reliable connection orientated service is implemented in the TCP-level above.

An IP datagram consists of a header and a subsequent data block which is then „packaged" in an Ethernet frame. The maximum data length is synchronized with the maximum frame length of the physical network. Since it is possible for a datagram to pass, on route, through a partial network with a shorter frame length, part datagrams must be created to ensure further transport.

To this end the header is substantially replicated and the data divided up into small transmission blocks. Every section datagram has therefore a header. This process is known as **fragmentation**. This is a purely network technical measure and the source and target node are not informed.

Naturally, there is an opposite function, **„Reassembly“** which packs the small datagrams back into a larger one. The entire datagram must be repeated if even a fragment disappears on the databus. It is recommended that datagrams of 576 Bytes and less be transmitted unfragmented.

HTTP (Hyper-Text Transfer Protocol) is very important for the multimedia area:

HTTP is a protocol of the application layer that offers all possibilities for the transfer of **Hypermedia.** HTTP is neither hardware nor operating system dependent.

HTTP has been in use since 1990 and is currently used most in the release version „HTTP/1.0“. Information systems naturally need more functions than just the simple transmission and receiving of communications. The development of HTTP/1.0 is not completed. It offers the possibility of further functionality development. The addressing of resources occurs in this case by means of URLs which can either be places (URL) or data names (URN). These simultaneously indicate the desired transfer arrangement. Communications are transmitted in the same format as used for normal mail transport.

MIME = Multipurpose Internet Mail Extensions, extended E-Mail Protocol (RFC 1341) for the sending of binary coded multimedia data

MIME is used often in this case. HTTP/1.0 is also suitable for access to a server with different protocols. This makes it possible for WWW Clients to communicate with servers and gateways by SMTP, NNTP, FTP, Gopher and WAIS.

The basic mode of operation of HTTP follows a question response procedure (query-answer). An asking programme (for example WWW browser) opens a connection to a programme waiting for questions (WWW server) and sends it a request.

The request contains the question method, the URL, the protocol release, information about the service and the actual content.

The server answers this question with a status message, followed by a MIME like communication that contains information about the server and possibly the requested document if already found.

Directly after the answer to this request is received the connection is broken to preserve line capacity. Currently, HTTP connections are mostly by TCP/IP. However, HTTP can also be set up on other network protocols. Both sides must be able to react correctly to a premature abnormal termination of the communication. Premature abnormal termination can be triggered by actions from end users, programme errors or exceeding the response time (time out). The entire communication process is interrupted by the abnormal termination of the connection.

Every communication between two WWW programmes consists of HTTP messages, which are exchanged in the form of requests and responses between client and server.

A HTTP message can either be a simple-request, a simple-response, a full-request or a full-response. The first two message types appertain to the HTTP/0.9 standard. The two last types already work with to the HTTP/1.0.

Each of the HTTP message-header fields displays the the same architecture. In RFC 822 was defined, that every array appears with a field name and the field contents. A colon must follow the array name. The array name can contain all characters except for a colon and escape sequences. General fields contain Information such as the date, the Message ID, the used MIME release and a „forwarded" field in order to ascertain whether the document comes from another address.

After this short introduction to the technique of networks, we now turn to the actual topic: Multimedia on the WWW.

2 Multimedia in the WWW

Multimedia features of Internet and Intranet applications are directly dependant on the possibilities of the WWW description language; the **Hypertext Markup Language (HTML).** Display formats which are not anchored there can only be realized by the use of supplementary Browser Plug-ins (small additional programs for browsers) or more complex languages, such as JAVA, JAVASCRIPT, FLASH or ACTIVE-X.

2.1 Bandwidth Problem

Multimedia applications stand and fall on the capacity of the data lines connecting the server (provider) to the client (user).

bps
bit per second

The bandwidth is the **maximum data set** which can be sent over a transmission path per unit of time, and is specified in bps, kbps (kBit/s) or Mbps (MBit/s).

Different media have very different file sizes: A text page with 3000 ASCII characters requires 3 KB. A colour picture with a 24 bit colour depth and a size of 640 × 480 pixels already has a file size of 75 to 900 KB, according to compression rate. For an one minute voice recording approximately 600 KB are required and for one minute of music in CD quality approximately 10 MB. However, for only one minute of video, according to size, compression rate and picture quality, between 15 to 400 MB are necessary! For example, an uncompressed AVI file of one minutes duration, with 320 × 240 pixels, 16 colour depth bit, a frame rate of 25 pictures per seconds, stereophonic sound in PCM-coding and 44,1 kHz, needs a storage space of 40 MB.

Fig. 6.12 Comparison of different media types and the corresponding file sizes

Media Type	File Size
1 page of text 3000 ASCII-characters	3 KB
1 color picture 640 × 480 px	75 to 900 KB
1 min. speech	600 KB
1 min. music (CD)	10 MB
1 min. video 320 × 240 px	15 to 400 MB

transfer rate

The following formula can be applied to calculate the transfer rate of different media over different transport paths:

$$t = \frac{f_s \cdot 1024 \cdot 8}{b}$$

t ... necessary transfer time in s (seconds)
f_s ... File size in MB
b ... Bandwidth of the used transmission channel in Kbps (Kbit/s)

Example: Standard-Modem (56,6 Kbps): One minute of Video has a transmission time of more than 2 hours

Using a standard modem with *an optimum (theoretical)* bandwidth of 56,6 Kbps and a practical average of 40 kbps the transfer of a one page text file takes less than one second.

For a colour picture with 300 KB approximately 60 seconds are needed.

A voice recording with a length of one minute requires approximately 2 minutes, and one minute of music in CD quality 30 minutes.

The enormous time of 2 hours, 16 minutes and 34 seconds is needed for one minute of video movie (our AVI file with 40 MB).

Even with the use of the famous ISDN (Integrated Service's Digital Network) with 64 kbps or even double ISDN with 128 kbps the transfer rates are not considerably shortened.

Emergency assistance has arrived in the form of the **Streaming** procedure, but multimedia can only actually be efficiently distributed through the use of broadband technologies.

Media Type	Transfer time using 28,8 kbps
1 page of text 3000 ASCII-characters	1 sec
1 color picture 640 × 480 px	20 to 91 sec
1 min. speech	166 sec (2,7 min)
1 min. music (CD)	3000 sec (50 min)
1 min. video 320 × 240 px	46 min bis 1,9 h

Fig. 6.13 Transmission times of various media using a MODEM with 28,8 kbps

In order to get a feeling for the current state of development, we will now take a more practical look at some of the currently available bandwidths:

Fig. 6.14 Current Internet connections and their transmission speeds

Internet connection	Data rate
MODEM	28,8 Kbps
ISDN	64 Kbps
ADSL	8 Mbps
Ethernet (im Internet)	10 Mbps
ATM	155 Mbps

2.2 Broadband technologies

2.2.1 xDSL – ADSL

xDSL is the generic term for:

- ADSL (Asymmetric Digital Subscriber Line),
- HDSL (High Data Rate Digital Subscriber Line),
- SDSL (Symmetric Digital Subscriber Line) and
- VDSL (Very high rate Digital Subscriber Line).

These are digital, broadband transmission technologies over (available) copper cables within a local telephone network area. ADSL in particular is meant to replace the ISDN in order to make (real) multimedia and VoD (Video-On-Demand) possible.

ADSL is a broadband (about 1 MHz) data transfer technology over normal *twisted-pair copper lines* of the telephone network by means of a substantially higher frequency spectrum than ISDN, whereby normal telephone transmission is not impaired. While with the (older) HDSL which was developed as a cost effective alternative to T1-lines, broadband full duplex connections are being possible, ADSL is designed to be unsymmetrical.

T1 (Transmission Link 1), The Bell Company's Data Transmission Standard with 1,5 Mbit/s

ADSL is unsymmetrical: a maximum of 768 kbps upstream (from user to network) and a maximum of 6,144 Mbps downstream (from the network to the user) are obtainable.

Unlike traditional modems, only a few kilometres can be bridged with ADSL, (a maximum of 5 km). This should (hopefully) be sufficient to reach the switching centre of the network, which must then arrange a connection with the Internet. ADSL uses DMT (Discrete Multi Tone) as modulation technique. Like ISDN, it has a control channel with a capacity of 16 or 64 kbps designed for the connection between user and network node. The user is connected to the system through an ADSL adapter.

Slightly more than 53 seconds are needed for the download of our one minute testvideo.

ADSL: 53 seconds for 40 MB download

2.2.2 Cable TV

television cable modems are basically indistinguishable from conventional modems. However, since these are interlinked with the (broadband) coaxial cable of the television network, they naturally offer considerably higher data signalling rates. A cable modem is permanently online.

The PC can be connected to the cable modem with an „Ethernet" card or with the use of a **Settop Box** it is possible for a television set to become a multimedia Internet computer.

But a conventional telephone line is still necessary in order to send requests to the Internet. In theory up to 30 Mbps are possible. In various field tests they currently worked at around 14 Mbps.

Cable-TV: 23 seconds for 40 MB download

Our „test video" (1 minute, 40 MB) is transmitted in 23 secs.

2.2.3 Powerline

There has been speculation for some time as to how the low tension network of the utility companies, which is available practically everywhere, could be used for communication services.

One problem is the immanent interferences on electric lines. A transfer technology using this power supply network must guarantee an EMC (Electro-Magnetic Compatibility) with existing applications and, for commercial use, be able to achieve an attractive transfer distance.

With a data signalling rate of about 1 Mbps the **DPL** (Digital PowerLine) should not only be used for Internet services but also for many other control and communication tasks.

In spring 1999 the company Ascom [W11] presented, in a common project with the RWE (Rheinisch Westfaelische Utility Companies), a PLC (Powerline Communications) Demonstrator for broadband access. This Demonstrator was installed on an exist-

ing low tension power line of the RWE in Leichlingen (Duesseldorf) and operated over a period of 6 months without faults. This Demonstrator not only bridges the „last mile" of the low tension transformer to the telephone receiver, but it also uses the building's internal electrical cabling for the further primary distribution of the broadband signal. This means that virtually every socket is turned into a broadband communication interface to the public network. The Demonstrator achieved a data rate of about 1,3 Mbps in the first release and enabled an extended radius (outside the buildings) of approximately 300 metres. The Ascom PLC system supports standardized communications interfaces and offers a transparent platform for the protocol layer TCP/UDP/IP on the application side. [W11].

PowerLine: about 4 Minutes for 40 MB download

2.2.4 ATM

ATM (Asynchronous Transfer Mode) presents completely new approaches for the implementation of universal broadband networks. ATM is intended as a technology for extended, connection orientated LANs and WANs enabling high-speed connections for a (theoretically) unlimited number of users. The greatest advantages of ATM lies in a service independent uniform network structure, which is characterized by:

- Decoupling of the channel types for network and services: The network does not make any service specific channels available;
- Decoupling of the clock pulses for network and services: Service specific clock pulses do not have to be derived of a nut clock pulse of the network;
- Decoupling of network and service specific information: The network does not have any knowledge of syntax or semantics of the data of the service.

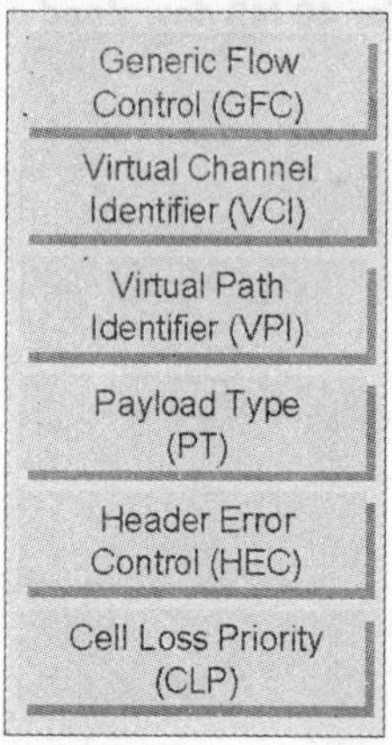

Fig. 6.15 The Header contains the virtual channnel identification (VCI) and determines by CLP the cell-priority

The ATM principle is based on **packet switching:** The information is exchanged in the form of length determined packages. The smallest unit is the cell.

The cells do not have any fixed position in a time slot, but are created in asynchronous mode from the sources. The services are not assigned any specific bandwidths, but the sources load a certain number of cells in a specific time slot. The resultant bandwidth must be requested during the connection setup in order to prevent an overload of the network and in order to guarantee that the cells are accepted by the recipient.

A cell contains information and a header which identifies the cells (Figure 6.17), which belong to the same **virtual channel.** The cells are created on demand by the sources. If there is no demand to transmit information, empty cells are created. This causes a **continuous cell current** .

The CCITT recommendations to ATM were first published in 1990 and re-released in 1992 in a revised version. In them the ATM cell is determined.

The ATM technique proposed by CCIT transmits cells of **constant length.** Therefore no supplementary flags („setable bits") for the cell limitation are necessary.

The cells of different connections can be transmitted also in the multiplex mode (nested within a given time). Communication sources of higher (non-constant) bit rates reserve in this case several cells. But also services with continuous data rates can be transmitted (Video Conferences, speech transmission). In case of the use of STS-3 (Synchronous Transport Signal) it works with a bandwidth of 155,52 Mbps, which is in fact sufficient for multimedia data transfers .

Our Test Video will transmit in approximately 2 s.

ATM: 2 seconds for 40 MB download

2.2.5 Terrestrial Microwave Links

This technology presupposes that a radio link is installed and the users are equipped with conforming hardware and antennae. The costs are correspondingly high. The data are then transmitted over specific open radio frequencies. This enables the users to connect to an Internet Provider locally, independent of location and telephone adapter socket.

For example the company Mediascape [W12] offers an Internet access in Hamburg over radio relay in four different bandwidths (2 Mbps, 10 Mbps, 34 Mbps, 155 Mbps). These services are available in **full-duplex,** so that no compromises in the downstream or upstream have to be made.

2.2.6 Mobile Radio

The new Internet protocol **WAP** (Wireless Application Protocol) was specially developed for mobile phones („Handies"). WAP is comparable to the HTTP protocol – short texts are transmitted with a bandwidth only of 9,6 Kbps.

Consequently a new page description language was developed for the read out: **WML** (Wireless Markup Language) which is based on XML (Extensible Markup Language).

XML is a manufacturer independent and program independent format for every type of document, in addition to complex layouts (including data records from data bases).

XML, see Volume 3, module 1

UMTS as a further development of GSM-technology (module 3, chapter

In order to make Multimedia acceptable on mobile phones work is being done on the **UMTS** (Universal Mobile Telecommunication System) – with a bandwidth of 2 Mbps. Which, according to a decision of the European Unions Standardization Commission, is to be officially introduced in 2002.

2.2.7 Satellite Links

Satellite communications systems display some advantages over terrestrial transmission equipment:

- distributing capability (broadcast),
- simple and rapid extension of network and
- flexibility and mobility.

Due to the expansion of the Internet the importance of communications satellites will increase considerably. Particularly multimedia data can be transported efficiently via satellite to the end user. Data rates in the region of several Mbps are supported, which is higher than with many terrestrial solutions. The propagation time is determinated (through the constant distance between satellite and user) and less problematic than with congested terrestrial connections.

Through the use of the distribution capability of satellites an efficient and cost-effective usage of the attainable bandwidth is guaranteed. Satellite transmission is very suitable for the implementation of new Internet protocols and the superimposed applications.

Over satellite the user can be offered access to the Internet with high velocity and stability. The DVB (Digital Video Broadcast) Norm not only provides the high quality digital transfer of television, but is also a cost-effective solution for multimedia services via satellite.

Applications of satellite supported multimedia services lie in the fields of business (for example LAN networking, video conferences), tele-medicine and tele-education and in the entertainment sector.

Tele-Education, see Volume 2

One technology is **Sky DSL,** which is similar to the transmission of television channels via satellite. The PC is connected to a parabolic antenna. The receipt of the signals is adjusted at the monitor. The bit rate is changeable.

However, the conventional Internet access via the telephone line is still necessary.

2.3 Text in the Web

Originally, neither the Internet nor the Web were primarily „multimedial", but were organized for the transfer of plain text using the Hyper Text Markup Language (HTML).

HTML documents are pure text files which contain specific control commands and formatting specifications (Tags).

A HTML Tag consists of a name and (optional) parameters. It is enclosedbetween angled brackets (< and >). All Tags that are not empty, e.g. contain text, need a final tag, that of </ and > is enclosed. Upper and lower case Tags are equivalent.

A HTML document is opened by <HTML> and closed by </HTML>. Within the document there is the header, limited by <HEAD> and </ HEAD> which only contains selected, administrative data and metadata, and the main part, limited by <BODY> and </BODY>. Within the main part (the body) all information and mark-ups that structure the document are contained.

In the meantime there are different standards (e.g. HTML 4.0), for precise information see reference and Internet addresses.

ISO Latin-1 (ISO 8859-1) is the font, valid for HTML. On data processing systems which are only able to display 7-bit characters, the characters above can be formed by 127 specific „character entities". These begin always with one ampersand(&), followed by the character name and concluded by a semicolon. In this way all additional characters can be displayed even if they are unavailable on the data processor or the keyboard of the document author.

In addition the allocated characters must always be copied to the HTML Tags. These are: &='&', "=' " ', <='<' and >='>'. The German „ae" becomes for example &auml(a-umlaut); an „AE" is represented by &Auml (A-umlaut) and a "ß" is ß.

Vannevar Bush and Hypertext, see Volume 2, Module 4, chapter 1.5

The concept of the HTML is **Hypertext** whose roots go back to VANNEVAR BUSH in the year 1945.

Branch destinations can be specified within hypertext documents. The links are accomplished by URLs.

An **URL (Uniform Resource Locator)** is a reference to a file or other resource. This reference is needed to specify links located in the current document, or locations in other documents on the current server or documents on other servers. In addition, an Internet Service can be specified with an URL. URLs are also used to include graphics or other multimedia entities.

The setup schema of an URLs is

Service://Host.Domain:Port/Path/Filename

When the port specification is left out, the **standard port** for the specified service is inserted as the **default port** (email, newsgroups, FTP etc.). In the same way host and domain are unnecessary when the address lies on the local server and the path can be left out if the file being searched for is within the current catalogue.

2.4 Audio in the Web

A first step to making a web page „multimedial" is the linkage of audio contents. But not even simple music files are so effortlessly transmitted:

Audio, see Module 3; compression concepts, see Module 4, chapter 4

Audio files make considerably higher demands on the network than text files. For CD quality (44,1 kHz, 16 bit, Stereo) we need a bandwidth of approximately 1,5 Mbps. This confirms the importance of a compression concept (see module 4).

For example the same audio file compressed with MUSICAM only requires a bandwidth of approximately 190 kbps (from 1500 kbps).

MUSICAM is a technique for data reduction which uses the psycho acoustic effect of sound masking: Sounds in specific heights and sound intensity are heterodyned by other masks. These are redundant for the human ear (because outside of the audible range) and therefore this sound information is extracted by MUSICAM before the transfer.

The most important web file formats are WAV, AIFF (Apple), AU and MIDI (refer to module 3).

Concerning the Web, two methods of transmitting audio files exist:

- Downloading the whole audio file or
- Streaming Audio.

An audio file is embedded in HTML as shown in figure 6.18:

```
<embed src="../sounds/orinocl.mid" autostart="true" loop="1"
width="144" height="15" mastersound controls="smallconsole">
```

Bild 1.16 An Example for an Audio console

Through the attribute STARTUP = „true“ the file is played immediately the downloading is completed (at „false“ the file is not played until the user activates the start key on the console). The **console** indicated in Netscape Navigator shows figure 6.18. The console can also be concealed by the attribute HIDDEN = „true“ .

2.4.1 Real Audio

Bild 1.17 The Real Player from Real Networks [W3]

Another possibility is Streaming, for example with Real Audio from Real Networks [W3]. One needs the Real Player software (figure 6.19). on the client. This is a Plug-in which permits one to play an audio file in Real Player time over the Web.

In order to play sound files on the client, *another* “Plug-in” is required for the browser.

The solution of the US company Real Networks consists basically of three components:

- Real Player (Plug-in embedded in the browser),
- Real Producer (Encoder for conversion into the Real format),
- Real Server (allocation of the Real data over the Web).

2.4.2 MP 3

MPEG layer 3 (designated short as MP 3) is a format that enables a high compression of audio data with a relatively small loss of quality.

The whole frequency range and the audio frequency signal-to-noise ratio are very nearly maintained. Possible losses are not audible even on „good“ HiFi equipment (only, of course, if the source files are good quality recordings).

With the MP 3-compression redundant audio information is simply left out. A further advantage of the MP 3-format is that it is a header-less file format. MP 3-Files does have a „header“, however the MP3s can still be played without it.

This makes it possible to play a section cut out of the middle of a file. This is what makes Streaming possible. A prerequisite is that the bit rate does not become larger than the bandwidth of the Internet connection. The limit is currently 128 kbps, this means, it would take two ISDN lines and a rapid Provider to listen to MP 3 files directly (without Streaming).

A disadvantage of MP-3 is the necessary CPU performance (software frequency analysis).

2.5 Graphics in the Web

The two predominant graphic file formats in the Web are GIF and JPEG. The simplest and frequently quoted rule reads:

Graphics in Module 4

JPEG for photographic pictures, where it depends on precise colour rendering. GIF for graphics which manage with little colour. PNG is treated as GIF's successor.

Pictures can be embedded in HTML documents in two ways :

- with hyperlinks (the picture is not loaded until "clicked" on) or
- as an „inline image" (the picture is bound between the print lines).

The instruction for the embedding of pictures reads:

<IMG SRC = "Picture-URL" ALIGN = "Text extension" ALT=" alternative representation" WIDTH = „www" HEIGHT = „hhh" BORDER = „marginal width">

Graphic URL: This is an URL *pointing* to the graphics, in the simplest case this can be a local file, however it can also be a link to a graphics file on a remote computer.

Text extension: This value specifies where the print lines, subsequent to the <IMG>, are supposed to begin – at the top, in the centre or the trailing edge of the picture. Possible values are LEFT, RIGHT, TOP, MIDDLE or BOTTOM. This specification is optional, the preset value is BOTTOM.

Alternative representation: This specifies what is shown, in place of the graphics, on non-graphical browsers or when the graphic mode is turned off. With newer browser releases a text is displayed when the mouse cursor is moved across the picture. This should declared in a few words what the picture actually represents. This specification is also optional, the IMAGE word is preset, if no entry is desired one writes ALT = " " .

Using WIDTH and HEIGHT the screen size can be optionally specified in pixels. This facilitates the calculation of the page partitioning for the browser since the browser already „knows" the screen size before loading the picture. Most browsers can also extend or reduce the picture according to the given specifications.

Lastly, if the picture serves as a link, the parameter BORDER specifies the width of the coloured margin. For no margin one specifies 0.

The reduced pictures can also be made into hyperlinks, which first show the full size picture when the preview image („Thumbnail") is "clicked". The size of the original should be added to this Thumbnail (for example „Original 800 × 600 pixels, 154 KB").

Thumbnail, small preview image - e.g. format: 128 × 192 Pixel

Of course Graphics can be used within links. A mouse-click on the graphic leads to a new document:

<A HREF = „targettext.html"><IMG SRC = „picturegif"> Click!</A>

Here both the word „Click!" and the graphics is activated. In the above example the graphics receive a coloured frame in the colour used to denote links (usually blue). If this is not desired, the option BORDER = 0 can be appended to the IMG tag.

Pictures should be optimized on the communication lines of the target group. Lengthy loading times reduce motivation.

Association between loading time and Motivation, see Volume 3, Module 5

Many browsers also give the subscriber the possibility to deactivate the automatic loading of embedded graphics and to load and display these when requested.

The GIF format supports – from the release 89 onward – the possibility of combining several graphics in the same graphics file. The individual graphics of the file are displayed one after the other.

In this case it is also possible to store control instructions, such as delay times between the individual pictures, at the same time. This feature offers two interesting possible applications:

- Slide show-effect and
- simple video animation.

In order to construct animated graphics, the individual images must first be created or selected using a suitable graphics programme. All pictures must be copied into the new graphics file with uniform width, height and colour palette and then saved as GIF.

In practice numbered file names have proved to be the best, as for example „pic1.gif", „pic2.gif", in the order in which the pictures are saved in the animated graphics.

After these preparations have been made, the animation software can be started with the following possibilities:

- **Loop** determines how often the entire picture sequence is repeated;
- **Control elements** control the operational sequence between two individual images (for example the time delay until the read-out of the next individual image);
- **Text** (plain text) can complement the execution of the animated graphics.

2.6 Video in the Web

Streaming Video is frequently used for video signal transmissions in the Web. The most frequently used video formats are VDO-Live, Real Video, MPEG 4 (similar to MPEG 1 but with Streaming capability) and ASF which supports numerous different codecs similar to AVI (among others; Real Video and VDO-live).

2.6.1 Streaming Video

With the method of **„Streaming"** the video files are not completely loaded, but are imparted successively in small data packets while the playback begins instantly.

For this purpose the corresponding software at the „sending" server and the corresponding „plug-in" at the receiving client must be installed.

Fig. 6.18 Different media distributors and some pros and cons

Media	pros	cons
SAT-TV	low cost, HQ	Dependent on Programmes
VCR	HQ	Transport
Download Video	On-Demand	LQ + delay
Streaming Video	no waiting	LQ

2.6.2 Real Video

The market leader in Streaming is the Real Player [W03] with the formats Real Audio and Real Video.

The implementation of the US company's Real Network consists basically of three components (ref 2.4.1: Real Audio):

- Real Player (Plug-in for the browser),
- Real Producer (Encoder to the transport into the Real format) and
- Real Server (Allocation of the real dates about the Web).

The original signal (of an available video file or the live signal of a video camera or webcam) is converted through a special „codec" into the streamable compressed Real format (encoded).

Since the introduction of the **G2 system** it is also possible to stream pictures – for example as a slide show or animation. A further improvement is the „sure stream" feature: The data signalling rate of the retrieved contents is automatically adapted to the end user's bandwidth. It also supports SMIL (ref: 2.6.4).

2.6.3 MPEG-4

First experiences with MPEG-4 show that a video with a resolution of 240 × 160 and 15 pictures per second can be compressed, with an acceptable quality, to about 15 KByte per second. Sufficient for a problem-free transmission over ISDN. For comparison: In this quality almost 12 hours of video fit onto a CD-ROM.

MPEG see Module 5, chapter 2

2.6.4 SMIL

SMIL stands for **Synchronized Multimedia Integration Language**.

A team from the World-Wide-Web Consortium (W3C) is working on the specifications of the transfer standard SMIL which is expected to process web contents to the pattern of interactive television telecasts.

SMIL – a HTML comparable language – is used to optimize the chronological co-ordination of audio and video files.

The specification of the SMIL language can be found on the home page of the W3C [W5].

2.7 Virtual Reality in the Web: VRML

One example of three dimensional graphic notation is the description language VRML **(Virtual Reality Modelling Language).** Only statements about *how* the three dimensional animation is to look are sent. The animation is then created on the local computer.

Raytracing = Calculation method for 3D Objects (rendering)

Each **Raytracing Programme** works with this kind of three dimensional language. The software computes the respective scenery by means of the description and displays it graphically on the screen.

VRML is currently being specially adapted for the needs of the WWW and Internet and therefore possesses specific capabilities, e.g. the linkage of HTML documents in three dimensional scenes. The development of VRML began in the spring of 1994. The name was coined at the time but in its original form: „Virtual Reality Markup Language".

In order not to begin at zero and instead to use a suitable, already available three dimensional technology, the choice of the developers fell on „Open Inventor" from SGI (Silicon Graphics). Open Inventor supports three dimensional scenarios with polygon entities, different illumination possibilities, materials or textures. Furthermore SGI made one of the first VRML Parser Libraries available which served as a basis for the implementation of three dimensional viewers.

In the meantime the development had progressed further. VRML sceneries are stored in separate files, which are pointed to – as with normal HTML files – by means of links in URLs. When subscribers click on this type of links in WWW browsers, the software recognizes the three dimensional file and starts a **VRML viewer** that takes over the further representation.

VRML neither replaces HTML nor does it represent an extension of HTML.

Both are separate languages, supplement each other however in the respect that hypertext links from HTML to three dimensional data are possible, and vice versa.

The basics of VRML are quite simple. Each scene is assembled from different entities, the **Nodes**. A node can be a geometrical configuration, such as a ball or a cone.

In addition nodes exist, which determine a specific material and features (gloss, reflection, colour), with which all subsequent nodes are constructed. Some nodes determine the position of other nodes in VRML's three dimensional coordination system. Specific nodes serve as parent entities for other nodes, so that a tree structure of Parent-Child Nodes is possible. Furthermore, VRML allows an outline of the description with data transmission blocks, similar to the {}blocks in the programming language C. In this way all entities of a scene can be clearly determined.

Further information on VRML under: [W6, W7, W8, W9] and in Volume 3.

2.8 Interaction in the Web

In principle, everything which it is possible to achieve on paper can also be done on the Web. (Forms, purchase orders, information requests, visitor book etc.).

2.8.1 HTML FORMs

For this purpose HTML has so-called FORMs. Input fields, selection menus, tick-boxes, and so forth. HTML forms designed this way can be analysed on a WWW server with specifically designed programmes. Also data base queries are implemented in this manner, from which the result is returned directly. One possibility for this form of interaction is a CGI programme:

2.8.2 CGI

CGI
Common Gateway Interface

A **CGI** programme runs directly on a WWW server and sends the output to the Client. As a rule this output consists of an HTML Document. Unlike HTML Files, which have a fixed content, information can be generated dynamically. For example information which changes constantly or which is dependent on user inputs can be transmitted.

A **CGI script** is a programme that can read from STDIN, the standard input and can write to STDOUT, the standard output, whereby it is irrelevant whether it is an Unix-Shell-Script, a C program, a pearl script or anything else.

CGI is a protocol which is used for the communication between HTML Forms and a programme. A CGI script can be in any written language – as long as reading from STDIN and writing to STDOUT is possible and it can read Environment Variables regardless of the environment.

A CGI script executes the following typical steps:

- Read the data created by the Client (from the parameter line or STDIN),
- process the data,
- write a response in HTML to STDOUT.

When the user sends his data **(Submit button),** the script receives all created data as a record of **name-value pairs**:

- The **name** is, in each case, the one determined by the INPUT Tag, SELECT Tag or TEXT AREA Tag.
- The **value** (content value) is that which the users have entered or selected.

This record of name-value pairs is sent in a long string which the programme must decipher.

The call of a CGI programme occurs in a hypertext link or a form with an URL in the format:

- http://host.domain/cgi-directory/filename, or
- http://host.domain/cgi-directory/filename/parameter-list

Example: A simple UNIX-Shell-Script, which displays date and time:

```
#!/bin/sh
echo "Content-Type: text/html"
echo ""
echo "<html><head><title>Datum</title></head>"
echo "<body><p>Today is "
date
echo "</body></html>"
```

CGI procedures can be written in most languages (for example shell scripts, Pearl scripts, C) – depending on the WWW Server used.

Do not confuse PERL with PEARL!

PERL (Practical Extraction and Reporting Language), a script language used particularly on UNIX servers, should not be confused with PEARL (Application Process and Experimental Realtime Language) a programming language for automation and robot control.

Script languages are also designated as macro languages and are formalized languages for the execution of functions within a program. The commands are entered directly into the user data (Tags).

Example of a FORM:

```
<!DOCTYPE HTML PUBLIC "-//W3C//DTD HTML 4.0//EN">
<!--Created from Andreas Holzinger-->
<html>

<head>
<meta name="Author"
content="Dr.Andreas Holzinger, andreas.holzinger@kfunigraz.ac.at,
www-ang.kfunigraz.ac.at/~holzinge">
<title>Formular: Interesse an Multimedia</title>
</head>

<body>

<form METHOD="GET" ACTION="http://www-ang.kfunigraz.ac.at/~holzinge/cgi-bin/test">
  <p>Interesse an Multimedia </p>
  <p><input TYPE="radio" NAME="kommt" VALUE="ja" CHECKED> Ja, ich bin an Multimedia
  interessiert.<br>
  <input TYPE="radio" NAME="kommt" VALUE="nein"> Nein, ich bin nicht an Multimedia
  interessiert.</p>
  <p>Mein Name: <input NAME="Name" SIZE="40" MAX-LENGTH="60"><br>
  Meine Telefonnummer: <input NAME="tel" SIZE="20" MAX-LENGTH="20"> </p>
  <p><input TYPE="submit" VALUE="Absenden"> </p>
</form>
</body>
</html>
```

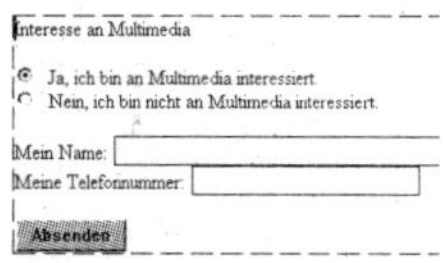

Fig. 6.19 The source shown on the left produces the above form on the screen

Explanation (Picture 6.21): The logon procedure stores the acceptance or refusal with name and telephone number in a data base and sends a confirmation to the Client.

The transmission of such a response is always necessary, so that the subscribers can see that the clicking of the Submit Button has functioned.

In the simplest case a short message is sufficient, that the input is being processed, and a note informing the user that with the keyboard backspace or the browser previous page button he can return the previous information and continue working.

GET or POST can be used as a method for the acceptance of the input data:

- GET couples the input data to the URL (Length restriction - only practical with few inputs),
- POST creates an own data stream.

CGI programmes must be written so that their execution can not involve any safety hazard for the server, independent of possible user input.

---

see Server Administration Strategies

Forms are delimited by the Tags <FORM> ... </FORM> while the attributes METHOD and ACTION specify the type of processing and the processing program on the server:

<FORM METHOD=POST ACTION = „URL of the programme">. Within a form three Input-Tags, INPUT, SELECT and TEXT AREA can be used. The INPUT-Widget <INPUT ... attributes ... > is the most frequently used and has numerous attributes:

- TYPE=" .... " Type of the Widgets. When type denoters are possible: CHECK MAILBOX, HIDDEN, PASSWORD, RADIO, RESET, SUBMIT, TEXT, IMAGE.
- NAME=" .... " Name of the input field. This name is given back in the data stream.
- VALUE=" .... " Default value (TEXT, HIDDEN), value of the menu item (CHECK MAILBOX, RADIO), label of the array (RESET, SUBMIT).
- SRC=" .... " Source file for an image button.
- Default setting CHECKED near CHECK MAILBOX and RADIO.
- SIZE=" .... " Array size (Character number) at the TEXT-Widget.
- MAXLENGTH=" .... " Maximum length of the input at the TEXT-Widget.
- ALIGN=" .... " Position of the text next to a picture at the image day.

With radio buttons one value can be selected from the choices offered, with a CHECK MAILBOX several may be selected.

Image-Maps allow branching to specific information through selection ("clicking") from specific places within a picture. For this there are two different techniques:

- In HTML 2 *only* server Image-Maps (ISMAP) are provided with and processed by a CGI programme at the server.
- Since HTML 3.2 client Image-Maps (<MAP> and USEMAP) that can be specified directly in the HTML file and processed from a WEB browser are also provided.

In HTML 4 it is recommended to only use Image Maps on clients and not to install any ISMAPs in the HTML files.

With server Image Maps the processing is done by a CGI program on the server. In the HTML file a combination of a <A HREF> command for the CGI programme and a <IMG>-Tag for the picture with the specification "ISMAP" has to be specified:

<a href="http://host.domain/cgi-bin/mapper"> <img src="image.gif" ismap></a>

On client Image-Maps the processing is done through the browser in the

HTML file. No CGI is necessary. This has been possible since HTML 3.2 and is supported by all newer WEB browsers. Which parts of the picture contain which hyperlink address is determined with the aid of <MAP> either in the same HTML file as the picture definition or in a separate file that is stored together with the picture. In the <IMG> Tag or <OBJECT> Tag of the picture this Map specification is referred to with „USEMAP".

Since not all subscribers activate the representation of pictures option and since some WEB browsers and many search machines do not process such Image-Maps correctly, an additional „normal" link must be specified, in text form, which leads to a list of hypertext links. This guarantees that all subscribers and search aids obtain the relevant information.

Active Server Pages are an alternative to CGI, particularly for those wanting to use a Microsoft Web Server but unable to use PERL

2.8.3 Active Server Pages (ASP)

Attention: do not confuse with ASP: Application Service Providing

ASP was developed by Microsoft and introduced together with Internet Server Information (IIS) 3.0. Scripts for the server can be written in virtually any language, but generally VBScript or JavaScript are used.

The official comment from the Microsoft site:

„Active Server Pages is an open, compile-free application environment in which you can combine HTML, scripts, and reusable ActiveX server components to create dynamic and powerful Web-based business solutions. Active Server Pages enables server-side scripting for IIS with native support for both VBScript and Jscript".

Some advantages of ASP:

- already integrated into Microsoft Web Server,
- good integration of the structures existing in the Web,
- database assistance

Some disadvantages of ASP:

- data protection problems,
- synchronization problems with local programs,
- runtime problems with graphic applications.

3 Module Summary

The Internet is a amalgamation of **world-wide LANs.** The computers communicate with each other by using **protocols** (e.g. TCP/IP). The **WWW** (Web) is *one specific* Internet Service which makes the inclusion of Multimedia data (via HTTP) possible.

The **OSI Layered Model** is extremely helpful in understanding the communication between individual computers: **seven layers** are "stacked" hierarchically: the physical layer (lowest level), data link control layer, network layer, transport layer, session layer, presentation layer, application layer (highest level). HTTP is an application layer protocol, which forms all the possibilities for the transfer of hypertext forms (for example about HTML).

Cables, network topologies (such as star, ring, bus, mesh), network adapters, repeater, bridges, switches, hubs, router, gateways, firewalls are used to connect the computers to **Networks**. The WWW frequently works with a **Client-Server architecture.** The Internet also offers other services e.g. eMail, newsgroups, IRC (chat) and telnet. Every **node** in the Internet has an internationally unique **address.**

Multimedia applications stand and fall with the **bandwidth.** One minute of an AVI file requires 40 MB, which takes approx. 2 hours to transmit by MODEM.

The solution may be found in technologies such as ASDL (8 Mbps), Cable TV, Powerline, ATM (155 Mbps), terrestrial microwave links, mobile communications (UMTS) and satellite communications.

HTML documents are the basis of the Web. **Audio files** (see Module 3) can either be „downloaded" or „streamed" (Real Audio, MPEG 3). The dominant (main) **picture formats** in the Web are **GIF** and **JPEG** (see: module 4). **Video files** can also be „downloaded" or „streamed" (Real Video, MPEG 4, see Module 5). There are also special transmission standards such as **SMIL** for multimedia and **VRML** for virtual reality.

Interaction, see Volume 3

Interaction in the Web often takes place using **CGI Programs**, however, these must be written to ensure that no safety risk is caused for the server (independent of possible input from the user). Active Server Pages are an alternative to CGI, particularly for those wanting to use a Microsoft Web Server but unable to use PERL.

4 Module Supplement

4.1 Literature

4.1.1 Books

ALVEAR, JOSE (1998): *Web Developer.Com Guide to Streaming Multimedia.* New York: John Wiley & Sons.

BOTTO, FRANCIS (1999): *Dictionary of multimedia and internet applications: a guide for developers and users.* Chichester et.al.: Wiley.

COMER, DOUGLAS E.: DROMS, RALPH E. (1999): *Computer Networks and Internets.* Second Edition. New York: Pearson.

DAVIE, BRUCE S.; PETERSON, LARRY L.; CLARK, DAVID (1999): *Computer Networks: A Systems Approach.* San Francisco (CA): Morgan Kaufman.

FOSTER, IAN; KESSELMAN, CARL, ED. (1999): *The Grid: Blueprint for a New Computing Infrastructure.* San Francisco (CA): Morgan Kaufman.

FURHT, BORIVOJE, ED. (2000): *Handbook of internet and multimedia: Systems and applications.* Boca Raton (FL): CRC Press.

GATES, BILL (1996): *The Road Ahead.* London: Penguin.

GUELICH, SCOTT; GUNDAVARAM, SHISHIR; BIRZNIEKS, GUNTHER; MUI, LINDA (2000): *CGI Programming with Perl.* Cambridge (MA): O'Reilly.

HEATH STEVE (1999): *Multimedia and Communications Technology.* 2nd Ed. Oxford: Focal Press, Butterworth, Heinemann. 148-281.

HILLMAN, DAVID (1998): *Multimedia: Technology and Applications.* Albany [et. al.]: Delmar. 193-213.

KENNEDY, ANGUS (2001): *The Rough Guide to the Internet.* 7th Edition. Rough Guides.

LEVINE, JOHN R.; BAROUDI, CAROL; YOUNG LEVINE, MARGARET (2000): *The Internet For Dummies.* 7th Edition. Hungry Minds, Inc.

PAYNE, CHRIS; MITCHELL, SCOTT (2001): *Sams Teach Yourself ASP.NET in 21 Days.* Indianapolis (IN): Sams.

SPURGEON, CHARLES E. (1998): *Ethernet: The Definitive Guide.* Cambridge (MA): O'Reilly and Associates.

STEIN, LINCOLN (1998): *The Official Guide to Programming With Cgi.Pm.* New York: John Wiley & Sons.

TANENBAUM, ANDREW S. (1996): *Computer Networks.* Third Edition. London: Prentice Hall.

THAKKAR, SHREEKANT S. (2000): *Programmer's Guide for Internet Streaming SIMD Extensions.* New York: John Wiley & Sons.

WELLING, LUKE; THOMSON, LAURA (2001): *PHP and MySQL Web Development.* Indianapolis (IN): Sams.

WU, CHWAN-HWA; IRWIN, DAVID J. (1998): *Emerging Multimedia Computer Communication Technologies.* Upper Saddle River (NJ): Prentice Hall. 127-334.

4.1.2 Articles

FEUSTEL, BJÖRN; SCHMIDT, THOMAS C. (2001): Media objects in time: a multimedia streaming system - work in progress paper v 1.5. *Computer Networks,* Volume 37, Issue 6, December 2001, Pages 729-737.

GUNASEKARAN, A.; LOVE, P. E. D. (1999): Current and future directions of multimedia technology in business. *International Journal of Information Management,* Vol. 19, Iss. 2, April 99, 105-120.

JAYANT, NIKIL; JOHNSTON, JAMES; SAFRANEK, ROBERT (1993): Signal Compression Based on Models of Human Perception. *Proceedings of the IEEE, October 1993,* IEEE, Volume 81, Number 10. 1385-1421.

PRAKASH, CHITRE; FERIT, YEGENOGLU (1999): Next generation satellite networks: Architectures and implementations, *IEEE Communications Magazine,* Vol.37, Iss. 3, March 99, 30-36.

RADHA, HAYDER; YINGWEI, CHEN; PARTHASARATHY, KAVITHA; COHEN, ROBERT (1999): Scalable Internet video using MPEG-4. *Signal Processing: Image Communication,* Vol. 15, Iss. 1-2, September 99, 95-126.

REID, MARK (1999): Multimedia conferencing over ISDN and IP networks using ITU-T H-series recommendations: architecture, control and coordination. *Computer Networks,* Vol. 31, Iss. 3, February 99, 225-235.

TUNG, BUI (2000): Building agent based corporate information systems: An application to telemedicine. *European Journal of Operational Research,* Vol. 122, Iss. 2, April 2000, 242-257.

4.1.3 Books in German

BALZERT, HELMUT (1999): *Lehrbuch Grundlagen der Informatik: Konzepte, Notationen im UML, Java, C++, Algorithmik und Software Technik (Lehrbücher der Informatik.* Heidelberg; Berlin: Spektrum.

GATES, BILL (1996): *Der Weg nach vorn: Die Zukunft der Informationsgesellschaft.* 3. Auflage. München: Heyne.

HOFMÜLLER, HELMUT; SEIWERT, MARTIN (1999): *Digital Audio/Video: Digitalisierung, Schnitt und Mastering unter Windows (Edition Screen Multimedia).* München: Addison-Wesley-Longman. 367-375.

LINDEMANN, CHRISTIAN; IMMLER, CHRISTIAN; HARMS, FLORIAN; KÜRTEN, OLIVER; HACKL, YAN; BARG, MICHAEL (1999): *Internet intern.* Düsseldorf: Data Becker.

SIEGMUND, GERD (1994): *ATM – Die Technik des Breitband-ISDN.* 2. Auflage. Hannover: Decker.

STEINMETZ, RALF (1998): *Multimedia Technologie: Grundlagen, Komponenten und Systeme.* 2. Auflage. Berlin [et.al.]: Springer. 23-46.

4.1.4 Articles in German

CARSTENS, MATTHIAS (1999): Musik kompakt: Audio-Kompression mit MPEG Layer-3. *c't, Magazin für Computer Technik,* 21/99, 242-250. Hannover: Heise.

OBERDÖRSTER, ALEXANDER; CARSTENS, MATTHIAS (1999): Frontalangriff: Internet-Audio und -Video: Microsoft contra Apple und MP3. *c't: Magazin für Computer Technik,* 10/99, 52-250. Hannover: Heise.

STEINBRINK, BERND (1999): Die Zukunft der Audio-CD: Formatvielfalt oder Standardscheibe ? *c't: Magazin für Computer Technik,* 21/99, 252-253. Hannover: Heise.

4.1.5 Journals

IEEE ACM Transactions on Networking (ISSN: 1063-6692; electronic: 1063-6692; combined: 1063-6692) | IEEE Institute of Electrical and Electronics Engineering

IEEE Internet Computing (ISSN: 1089-7801) | IEEE Institute of Electrical and Electronics Engineers

IEEE MultiMedia Magazine (ISSN: 1070-986X) | IEEE Institute of Electrical and Electronics Engineers

Inside the Internet (ISSN: 1075-7902) | Ziff Davis Journals

Internet and Higher Education (ISSN: 1096-7516) | Elsevier

Internet Gaming International (ISSN: 1097-4466; electronic:1097-4466; combined: 1097-4466) | Mary Ann Liebert

Internet Magazine (ISSN: 1355-6428) | Tower Publishing Services Ltd.

Internet Magazine – Net (ISSN: 1355-7602) | Future Publishing Ltd.

Internet Research - Electronic Networking Applications and Policy (ISSN: 1066-2243 | MCB University Press Ltd.

Internet Today (ISSN: 1355-5219) | Paragon Publishing Ltd.

Medical Informatics and the Internet in Medicine (ISSN: 1463-9238; electronic: 1464-5238) | Taylor & Francis Ltd.

Multimedia Systems (ISSN: 0942-4962; electronic: 1432-1882) | Springer Verlag KG

Multimedia Tools and Applications (ISSN: 1380-7501) | Kluwer Academic Publishers Group

Theory and Event - Internet (ISSN: 1092-311X; electronic:1092-311X) | Johns Hopkins University Press

4.2 Internet-Links

Up-to-date Internet Links for this module can be found on the homepage of this book **www.basiswissen-multimedia.at** (in English and German) under Volume 1: Technology, Module 6: Internet Supplement.

4.3 Exam Questions

Question Type 1: Dichotomy Yes/No Decisions:

01	The Internet integrates all known forms of communication (Writing, Speech, Pictures, Movies).	☐ Ja ☐ Nein	
02	The quantity of information offered in the WWW increases linearly.	☐ Ja ☐ Nein	
03	The LAN is determined by the Network size, Network elements and the Protocol.	☐ Ja ☐ Nein	
04	Knowledge of the local Firewall Policy is important to Multimedia designers.	☐ Ja ☐ Nein	
05	The majority of Multimedia applications are based on the Peer-to-Peer principle.	☐ Ja ☐ Nein	
06	1 minute of uncompressed Video is uses approximatly 15 MB storage.	☐ Ja ☐ Nein	
07	Due to the use of ISDN, the transmission of multimedial data is not a problem.	☐ Ja ☐ Nein	
08	With Streaming, the file replay can be started during the downloading.	☐ Ja ☐ Nein	
09	SMIL is a transmission standard which follows is similar to VRML.	☐ Ja ☐ Nein	
10	Every form in paper format can also be made interactively available in the WEB.	☐ Ja ☐ Nein	

Question Type 2: Multiple Choice:

01	The Internet ... ❒ a) ... is a world-wide amalgamation of computer networks. ❒ b) ... based on the WWW. ❒ c) ... offers various services. ❒ d) ... is a centralized network based in the USA.	
02	Computer Networks can contain ... ❒ a) ... Repeaters to „Refresh“ the sygnal. ❒ b) ... Routers to forward the data packets to another address. ❒ c) ... Gateways to connect heterogeneous networks ❒ d) ... Firewalls to control data accessability.	
03	With an Internet connection via ... ❒ a) ... MODEM a data transmission rate of more than 56,6 kBit/s is possible. ❒ b) ... ISDN Multimedia transmissions are no longer a problem. ❒ c) ... ADSL Bandwidths of up to 8 Mbit/s are attained. ❒ d) ... ATM theoretically a Bandwidth of 155 Mbit/s can be attained.	
04	The memory storage required by ... ❒ a) ... Multimedia applications is always dependant on the compression. ❒ b) ...one page of text is approximately 75 KB. ❒ c) ... one minute of Video can be as high as 400 MB. ❒ d) ... a music transmission is independant of the quality.	
05	Audio transmissions on the WEB ... ❒ a) ... are mainly in the formats WAV, AIFF, AU as well as MIDI and MP3. ❒ b) ... are dependant on the volume used. ❒ c) ... can be made user-friendly with Streaming. ❒ d) ... are comparable to the transmission of ASCII characters.	
06	Pictures in the Web ... ❒ a) ... are mainly offered in TIFF format. ❒ b) ... should have a resolution of more than 150 dpi if possible. ❒ c) ... should be small, to speed up loading. ❒ d) ... a „colour depth“ of 8 Bit is amply sufficient.	
07	Video transmissions on the WEB ... ❒ a) ... are frequently „streamed“. ❒ b) ... have a quality equivalent to satellite television. ❒ c) ... make the highest demands of the Bandwidth. ❒ d) ... can be optimised by using SMIL	
08	VRML ... ❒ a) ... requires high Bandwidth because animated pictures are being transmitted. ❒ b) ... requires a VRML Viewer. ❒ c) ... assembles each scene from nodes. ❒ d) ... is a description language.	

4.4 Answers

Answers to Question Type 1:

01 Yes; 02 No; 03 No; 04 Yes; 05 No; 06 No; 07 No; 08 Yes; 09 No; 10 Yes;

Answers to Question Type 2:

01 a) c); 02 a) b) c) d); 03 b) c) d); 04 a) c); 05 a) c) 06 c) d); 07 a) b) c) d); 08 b) c) d)

4.5 Hands-On: Exercises

- Design and create a simple web pages. Use a text editor and then a web editor, for example GoLive, Front Page or similar.
- Test different search machines with the same word and compare the results.
- Do the online quiz games [W18], [W19] and [W20]. Compare the different forms of interactivity and make a Pros and Cons List.

4.6 Themes for Debate

- Discuss the advantages and disadvantages of using normal text editors and web pages editors. (GoLive, Frontpage etc.)!
- Discuss the reasons why there is such a widespread misunderstanding about World Wide Web (WWW) and the Internet and whether they are synonymous.
- Speculate about the future of the internet. How will it look in three, in five and in ten years? Which new technologies are to be expected? What changes will mobile Computing cause?

4.7 Timeline: Internet

1945: VANNEVAR BUSH published his article „As We May Think" in the Atlantic Monthly with his (proposed) MEMEX (memory expander).

1965: TED NELSON coined the term Hypertext.

1972: First international conference about communication between computers (Washington, DC); RFC 318: Telnet Specification.

1974: BOB KAHN und VINTON CERF published „A Protocol for Packet Network Internet working", with presented the Transmission Control Protocol (TCP) for the first time. Probably the first use of the term Internet.

1983: TCP/IP replaces NCP an "defines" the „Internet".

1984: WILLIAM GIBSON coins the word Cyberspace in his Science-Fiction story "Neuromancer".

1988: JARKKO OIKARINEN develops the Internet Relay Chat (IRC).

1990: TIM BERNERS-LEE begins work on a WWW Browser and Editor (for NeXT).

1991: WWW released on the central computers of CERN.

1992: First draft of HTML.

1993, February: NCSA releases the first version of Alpha for Mosaic for X.

1993, July: First Internet draft für HTTP.

1993, October: Number of Internet hosts: 2,056,000.

1993, September: NCSA delivers Browser for X11, PCs and MACs.

1994, March: MARC ANDRESSEN and JIM CLARK found the Mosaic Communications Corporation (later renamed Netscape Communications).

1994, 12. April: The lawyers CANTER und SIEGEL are the first to send E-Mails on a massive scale (Spam) causing a storm of protest.

1994, 25. to 27. May: First WWW Conference (Geneva/Switzerland).

1994, 1. October: Founding of the World Wide Web Consortium (W3C) in the Computer Science Laboratory of MIT.

1994, 5. December: Netscape Navigator 1.0 released.

1994, 14. December 1994: First meeting of the World Wide Web Consortium (W3C) in MIT.

1994, December: Number of Web Hosts: 10,022.

1995, February: VocalTec presents the first Internet Telephone Software.

1995, June: Number of Web Hosts: 23,500.

1995,Summer : Internet Explorer 1.0 glimpses the virtual light..

1995, December: Blue Ribbon Campaign started as part of the Digital Be-In in San Francisco.

1996, January: Microsoft releases Internet Explorer 2.0.

1996, 9. February: JOHN PERRY BARLOW publishes „A Cyberspace Independence Declaration".

1996, 29. May: Sun announces JavaOS und RMI (Remote Method Invocation) as part of /during JavaOne (convention?)

1996, July: Number of Internet Hosts: 12,881,000.

1996, 9. September: Keio University (Tokio) becomes the third leg of the W3C, after MIT and INRIA.

1997, 8. July: Sun and Netscape deliver JFC (Java Foundation Classes).

1998, 19. February: W3C open offices by GMD in Germany.

1998, 29. June: IEEE acclaims Gigabit-Ethernet.

1998: The well-known Hobbes' Internet Timeline is published as RFC 2235 & FYI 32 (http://info.isoc.org/guest/zakon/Internet/History/HIT.html).

1998, July: Number of Internet Hosts: 367,390,000.

1998, November: Microsoft Internet Explorer 5.0.

1998: Technologies of the Year: E-Commerce, E-Auctions, Portals.

1999: RFC 2626: Internet and the „Millennium"-Problem (Y2K).

1999, 22. February: The „First Internet Bank of Indiana", which can only be reached via the Internet, is opened.

2000 Technologies of the Year : E-Trade, Online Banking, MP3.

2000 10.-11. April: In Lisbon the „eEurope – a Web of Knowledge" takes place. Unanimous opinion: Multimedia and Internet is becoming more and more important (eLearning, eScience) and must be included into the basic education of the European youth.

2003 UMTS should become the standard in the mobile communication system technology making Multimedia possible on Handies (Mobile phones)

4.8 Glossary

@ „at" element of every eMail-Adress for the purpose of separation of name and servername, e.g. andreas.holzinger@uni-graz.at

ADSL Asymmetric Digital Subscriber Line, transmission procedure, with 8 Mbps downstream and 768 kbps upstream over normal analogue telephone wires (POTS).

ARP Address Resolution Protocol is a protocol for mapping an Internet Protocol address (IP address) to a physical machine address that is recognized in the local network.

ASP Active Server Page (http://www.activeserverpages.com). Microsofts Concept for Web-Server-side Scripting, simple embedding of own Server-Applications including data bases. Confer with CGI.

ATM Asynchronous Transfer Mode. The prespecified bit rates are either 155 Mbps or 622 Mbps. Speeds on ATM networks can reach up to 10 Gbps. Along with Synchronous Optical Network (SONET) and several other technologies, ATM is a key component of broadband ISDN (BISDN).

Avatar virtual figure (digital characters), e.g. used in VRML coded 3D-Chat.

Backbone generally is a larger transmission line that carries data gathered from smaller lines that interconnect with it. On the Internet, a backbone is a set of paths that local or regional networks connect to for long-distance interconnection. The connection points are called network nodes (data switching exchanges (DSE).

BNC **B**ritish **N**aval **C**onnector or **B**ayonet **N**ut **C**onnection. Used for Coax, e.g. with 10Base2.

CAT 1 ... 7 Category. UTP-cables are arranged in categories. UTP CAT 3 and UTP CAT 5 are the most important. UTP CAT 5 is specified up to 100 MHz and also suitable for 100BaseTX and ATM.

CDMA Code Division Multiple Access.

CGI Common Gateway Interface. Programming-Interface to Web-Servers.

CORBA Common Object Request Broker Architecture, OO-Programming Standard from OMG, which handles the communication between distributed software objects via ORB (Object Request Broker).

CSMA/CD Carrier Sense Multiple Access with Collision Detection. With collision detection in Ethernet-Networks.

CSS Cascading Style Sheets, see http://www.w3.org/Style. It is an extension to HTML to allow styles, e.g. colour, font, size to be specified for certain elements of a hypertext document.

DHCP Dynamic Host Configuration Protocol. Provides a means to dynamically allocate IP addresses to computers on a LAN. The system administrator assigns a range of IP addresses to DHCP and each client computer on the LAN has its TCP/IP software configured to request an IP address from the DHCP server.

DIGI Deutsche Interessengemeinschaft Internet e.V. (http://www.digi.de). German Interest Community Internet.

DMAP DECT Multimedia Access Profile. Extends DECT up to 550 kbps.

Ebone European Backbone.

ECMA European Computer Manufacturers Association (http://www.ecma.ch). Standardising committee.

Ethernet first described by Xerox PARC in 1976. Specified by DEC, Intel and XEROX (DIX) as IEEE 802.3 and now recognised as the industry standard. Data is broken into packets which are transmitted using the CSMA/CD algorithm until they arrive at the destination without colliding with any other. The first contention slot after a transmission is reserved for an acknowledge packet. A node is either transmitting or receiving at any instant. The bandwidth is about 10 Mbit/s. It works on 10Base2- or 10BaseT-cables.

ETSI European Telecommunications Standards Institute (www.etsi.org).

Extranet allows only selected users to access private data and applications.

Fast-Ethernet version of the Ethernet which can carry 100 Mbps compared with standard Ethernet's 10 Mbps. It requires upgraded network cards and hubs and 100 Mbps, 100BaseTX- or 100BaseFX-cables, star topology.

FDDI Fiber Distributed Data Interface. Network technology (ANSI X3T9.5) in token ring topology (100 Mbit/s architecture). The medium is optical fibre (though it can be copper cable, in which case it may be called CDDI). FDDI rings are normally constructed in the form of a "dual ring of trees". Not as common than Fast Ethernet.

Fibre optical cable in form of glass fibre (fibre optics, FO, US "fiber", light pipe). Consists of plastic or glass (silicon dioxide) fibre no thicker than a human hair used to transmit information using infra-red or visible light. Optical fibre is less susceptible to external noise than other transmission media, is cheaper than copper wire, but it is much more difficult to connect. It is to distinguish between multimode and monomode. Common plugs are MT-RJ, VF-45 Volition, SC and ST.

Firewall is a dedicated computer which works as gateway machine with security precautions, used to service outside network, especially Internet, connections and dial-in lines. The idea is to protect a cluster of more loosely administered machines hidden behind it from „hackers“.

FTP-Protocol File Transfer Protocol (RFC 959, 765). It is the most important client-server protocol which allows a user on one computer to transfer files to and from another computer over a TCP/IP network.

Gigabit-Ethernet 1000-Mbps standard, similar to Ethernet with CSMA/CD and 1000Base...-cables.

Hub generally a device that serves as the centre of a star-topology network. Hubs can be active (where they repeat signals sent through them) or passive (where they do not repeat, but merely split, signals sent through them).

IANA Internet Assigned Numbers Authority (http://www.iana.org). Internet-Organisation, provides IP-numbers.

ICANN Internet Corporation for Assigned Numbers and Names (http://www.icann.org). See also IANA.

IEEE Institute of Electrical and Electronics Engineers. Defines Networking standards.

ISOC Internet Society (www.isoc.org).

ISP Internet Service Provider.

MAC Media Access Control, lower of the two sub-layers of the data link layer defined by the IEEE. The MAC sub-layer handles access to shared media, such as whether token passing or contention will be used (standards.ieee.org/regauth/oui).

MIME Multipurpose Interchange Mail Extensions (RFC 2045, 2049). Standard for transmitting non-text data (or data that cannot be represented in plain ASCII code) in Internet mail, such as binary, foreign language text (e. g. Chinese), audio, or video data.

NetBEUI NetBIOS Extended User Interface. Enhanced version of the NetBIOS protocol used by network operating systems, such as LAN Manager, LAN Server, Windows for Workgroups, and Windows NT. NetBEUI formalizes the transport frame and adds additional functions.

Netiquette Network Etiquette. Rules for correct behaviour within the Internet.

OSI Open Systems Interconnection of the ISO 7498.

Port is generally an interface on an internetworking device. In IP terminology, an upper-layer process that receives information from lower layers. Ports are numbered, and each numbered port is associated with a specific process. For example, 80 for HTTP, 20 und 21 for FTP, 25 for SMTP, 110 for POP3 and 119 for NNTP.

POTS Plain Old Telephone Service.

RFC Request for Comment, Internet-Standards (www.ietf.org).

RJ 45 Western-Plug. Standard for connections in LAN and ISDN.

SGML Standard Generalized Markup Language. ISO 8879. Meta language, subsets are HTML and XML.

SMIL Synchronized Multimedia Integration Language. XML-based language.

SSL Secure Sockets Layer. Encryption technology first used by Netscape used to provide secure transactions, such as the transmission of credit card numbers for e-commerce. Relies on RSA. The Web-Browser shows during use of SSL HTTPS (instead of HTTP)!

T1, T3 Trunk Line. Digital WAN carrier facility. T1 transmits DS-1-formatted data at 1.544 Mbps through the telephone-switching network. T1 to T3 corresponds to the European classes E0 to E4. T3 contains 28 T1 connections with 45 Mbps.

TCP/IP Transmission Control Protocol / Internet Protocol (RFC 793). Common name for the suite of protocols developed by the U.S. DoD in the 1970s to support the construction of WANs. TCP and IP are the two best-known protocols for the Internet as well as for Intranets and LANs. Transport protocol TCP is in OSI layer 4 and network protocol IP in layer 3.

TDMA Time Division Multiple Access. In rivalry to CDMA.

T-DSL ADSL-Variant of the German Telekom. 768 kbps Downstream and 128 kbps Upstream (T-ISDN dsl) and up to 6 Mbps Downstream and 576 kbps Upstream (T-Interconnect Classic T-DSL).

Telnet is a standard terminal emulation protocol in the TCP/IP protocol stack. Telnet is used for remote terminal connection, enabling users to log in to remote systems and use resources as if they were connected to a local system (RFC 854).

TEN-155 Trans European Network, 155 Mbps.

Terminal is a simple device at which data can be entered or retrieved from a network. Generally, terminals have a monitor and a keyboard (e.g. VT 100), but no processor or local disk drive. Often used with main frame computers.

Terminal Emulation Programme e.g. for PCs, that emulates („imitates“) a terminal. e.g. to connect to a host or mainframe.

Thin Client Network-Computer (NC). A simple client program or hardware device (with low resources) which relies on most of the function of the system being in the server.

Three-Tier-Architecture Three-layer-model. Separation of the three tasks: client-server/presentation, application-server and database-server.

Token Ring Token-passing LAN developed and supported by IBM. Token Ring runs at 4 or 16 Mbps UTP cables over a logical ring topology (IEEE 802.5). Layer 2 in OSI. Not as common than Ethernet.

Twisted Pair low-speed transmission medium consisting of two insulated wires arranged in a regular spiral pattern. The wires can be shielded (STP) or unshielded (UTP). Twisted pair is common in telephony applications and is increasingly common in data networks.

UMTS Universal Mobile Telecommunications System (http://umts-forum.org). ETSI-suggestion for an international Standardization as successor for GSM. Data transmission mobile up to 114 kbps and stationary up to 2 Mbps.

URL Uniform Resource Locator, unique identification of a resource (e.g. a Web-page) through access mechanisms (e.g. HTTP or FTP) and the location (server). The most common appearance is: Protocol://Rechner.Domain/path/file.

URN Uniform Resource Name. Independent of location.

UTP Unshielded Twisted Pair, not shielded cable for LANs. They are arranged in categories: CAT 1 ... 5. As connection usually the eight pin RJ-45-Western-Plug is used; competes with Coax and fiber.

W3C World Wide Web Consortium (www.w3.org).

WAP Wireless Application Protocol (http://www.wapforum.org). Interface for Internet-Applications for GSM-Handys (mobile phones).

Index

A

A

B

B

C

C

D

D

E

E

F

F

G

G

H

H

I

J

J

K

K

L

L

M

M

N

O

O

P

P

Q

Q

R

R

S

T

U

V

W

W

X

X

Y

Y